A Critical Guide to *Leaves of Grass*

A Critical Guide to

Leaves of Grass

By James E. Miller, Jr.

"... I delight to make a poem where I feel clear that not a word but is indispensable part thereof & of my meaning."

—WALT WHITMAN

Phoenix Books

THE UNIVERSITY OF CHICAGO PRESS

CHICAGO AND LONDON

This book is also available in a clothbound edition from

THE UNIVERSITY OF CHICAGO PRESS

SBN: 226-52608-9 (clothbound); 226-52609-7 (paperbound)

THE UNIVERSITY OF CHICAGO PRESS, CHICAGO 60637

The University of Chicago Press, Ltd., London

To
CHARLOTTE *and* JIMMY
And especially to
BARBARA

Preface

     When I decided to write a book on Walt
Whitman, I first determined what I would *not* do. I would not
read *Leaves of Grass* as biography or use the poetry as a basis for
speculation about the life. I would not examine the *Leaves* as a
neurosis, nor would I place book or poet on the psychoanalyst's
couch. I would not search the economic, social, or political milieu
for the causes of the volume of poetry. I would not attempt to make
Whitman the poet of some particular cause—science, democracy,
sex, or religion. I would not even search in the earlier editions and
the manuscripts for the primary evidence for criticism. In spite of
their attractions and their own special validity, I have avoided as
far as I could all these approaches to Whitman.

  Instead, I resolved to focus attention from first to last on the book
Whitman left to the world. I decided, above all else, to be persistently critical and analytical and, under all circumstances, to examine
Leaves of Grass as what it purports to be and is—poetry. The first
part of my book consists of a series of structural analyses of some of
Whitman's finest poems. The last part proposes a comprehensive
structure for the whole of *Leaves of Grass*. The element focused
upon throughout is *structure*—structure of the whole work and
structure of individual poems. It is my hope to help dispel the common notion that Whitman was a formless, even a chaotic, poet. He
wished, as he said in the quotation on the title page of this book
(from a letter to William Douglas O'Connor dated January 6, 1865),
to have every word "indispensable" to his meaning.

  In writing this book, I have sought neither to worship nor to ridi-
cule Walt Whitman. Both his friends and his enemies have done him
harm by their exaggerations, the first by their comparisons with
Christ perhaps even more than the second by their "exposé" of the

poses. But I must confess that my admiration for the art of Walt Whitman, poet, has increased immensely as a result of my labors. *Leaves of Grass* is proving more durable as poetry than either friend or foe dreamed, and probably because those furious battles over Whitman were fought for all the wrong reasons.

Acknowledgment

No student of Whitman can finish his studies without an immense, though largely unstated, debt to a number of distinguished Whitman scholars, among them Emory Holloway, Clifton Joseph Furness, Sculley Bradley, Harold Blodgett, Floyd Stovall, and the current dean of Whitman studies, Gay Wilson Allen, author of the invaluable *Walt Whitman Handbook* and the definitive biography, *The Solitary Singer*. I owe much to a number of other scholars: to Walter Blair for what he taught me about the study of literature; and especially to Napier Wilt, whose graduate class in Whitman at the University of Chicago some years ago contributed more to this book than either teacher or student can tell. I learned a great deal about Whitman in informal discussions with many people, including my wife Barbara, whose sympathetic judgment and encouragement I found in abundance when I needed them most.

I am grateful to the Research Council of the University of Nebraska for financial assistance granted for the preparation of the manuscript for the press.

The chapters of this book on "Song of Myself" and "Calamus" originally appeared in *PMLA*. I appreciate the kindness of the editors in granting permission to include the essays in this volume.

Although I must credit others with the virtues of this book, for its faults I can blame nobody but myself.

Contents

Part One
Close-Ups: The Dramatic Structure

Introduction

From the time Whitman began his career as the New World poet, critics have decried the formlessness of his work. His detractors have suggested that he did not write verse at all, but a chaotic prose. His defenders have sought diligently for an order—any order—in his poetry; some have proclaimed their discoveries of obscure or hidden formal elements, others have asserted that genius has the privilege of anarchy.

In spite of the vast number of revisions and rearrangements through the successive editions of *Leaves of Grass,* both friend and foe have assumed that Whitman was the finest example of the romantic writer, composing "automatically" with a wild and savage frenzy. It is to Whitman's artistic credit that he has "taken in" almost all his readers. Seldom, even in prose, did he show his hand. The most revealing instance occurs in an 1865 letter to William Douglas O'Connor. In explaining why he believed *Drum-Taps* better than *Leaves of Grass* (the 1860 edition), he asserted that it was "certainly more perfect as a work of art, being adjusted in all its proportions, & its passion having the indispensable merit that though to the ordinary reader, let loose with wildest abandon, the true artist can see it is yet under control."[1] Underlying this remark is an unmistakable and profound sense of the dramatic, an acute awareness of the wide gap in art separating the manner of achievement by the artist and the final effect on the reader.

Whatever his readers believed, Whitman knew that the "frenzied fit" never resulted in poetry. He once musingly commented on the poetic process: "The play of Imagination, with the sensuous objects of Nature for symbols and Faith—with Love and Pride as the un-

1. Emory Holloway (ed.), *Walt Whitman: Complete Poetry and Selected Prose and Letters* (London: Nonesuch Press, 1938), p. 949.

seen impetus and moving-power of all, make up the curious chess-game of a poem" (V, 40).[2] No romantic who genuinely believed in the prevailing "automatic"-writing theories would ever have conceived the process of writing a poem as the strategy of a game of chess.

But Whitman lived in a day when a poet was a poet both in and out of his work. He affected poses and played a part in his poems and in his life. He had a highly developed dramatic sense, and he could play a role to the hilt—so well, in fact, that he frequently persuaded his friends and his readers that a particular poetic pose was the real thing. For the people who believed, there was bound to be disillusionment; and in our own time there are those who, because they have discovered the poses, assume that they have exposed a fraud who could not be a genuine poet.

They forget that every man who lifts pen to write is assuming a poetic pose. In a sense, all poets are frauds in that they diligently attempt to palm off an imaginative as an "actual" experience. The most "fraudulent" poets are the most successful in persuading the reader to "believe."

In Whitman's successive "poses" may be found the secret not of his failure but of his immense success. His poems are plays; he is the protagonist. These "plays," like those of the stage, have as their parts a number of "acts" created out of an unfolding action complete with beginning, middle, and end. The stages of this "action," rather than divisions of subject matter or variations on a theme, inform Whitman's poems structurally. Too frequently, Whitman's readers, disappointed in their search for some kind of philosophical progression and conclusion, have been blinded to the basic dramatic nature of his poems. Whitman was not stating philosophical truths so much as he was dramatizing himself and his life of the imagination.

The following chapters are a series of analyses of the dramatic structure of some of the finest and most appealing poems and sections in *Leaves of Grass*. The comprehensive intention is to demon-

2. Whitman quotations are, where possible, identified in the text by volume and page number of *The Complete Writings of Walt Whitman,* ed. Richard M. Bucke *et al.* (New York: G. P. Putnam's Sons, 1902).

strate that Whitman's poetry was not formless but sensitively ordered and that the nature of the form originated not from fraudulent pose but from genuine drama. The pervading intention is to illuminate the poems wherever and whenever possible. The constant intention is to lure the reader back to *Leaves of Grass* with fuller understanding and richer appreciation.

CHAPTER ONE

"Song of Myself"
as Inverted Mystical Experience

"Song of Myself" has long been considered a loosely organized, perhaps even chaotic, poem held together, if at all, by the robust personality of Walt Whitman. Whitman himself may have contributed to this concept of the poem. Untitled when it appeared in the first edition of *Leaves of Grass* in 1855, it was called "Poem of Walt Whitman, an American" in the 1856 edition, "Walt Whitman" in the 1860 edition, and was given its present title in the 1881 edition. This frequent change of title, together with the many revisions made in the numbering of the sections and in the text itself, suggests two possibilities: either Whitman was uncertain, perhaps confused, as to the basic nature of what he was writing; or he was struggling to perfect a work of art the execution of which had fallen short of the conception. Too frequently the critics have assumed as self-evident the first of these possibilities.[1] Inability to find a structure in "Song of Myself" has resulted from a failure to find a center of relevancy, an "informing idea," to which the parts of the poem may be related.

"Song of Myself" is the dramatic representation of a mystical experience. The term "dramatic representation" indicates an important distinction: the poem is not necessarily a transcript of an actual mystical experience but rather a work of art in which such an

---

1. A notable exception is Carl F. Strauch, "The Structure of Walt Whitman's 'Song of Myself,'" *English Journal*, XXVII (September, 1938), 597–607. Mr. Strauch's analysis of the poem, in which he combines sections 1–18, 19–25, 26–38, 39–41, and 42–52, has been widely quoted. Although my analysis differs considerably from his, I agree thoroughly with his basic thesis that the poem has a structure and that "Whitman was in command of his materials." Gay Wilson Allen's valuable *Walt Whitman Handbook* also contains an illuminating discussion of "Song of Myself" (pp. 114–21).

experience, conceived in the imagination, is represented dramatically, with the author assuming the main role. The mystical experience
is dramatically represented in the sense that the poet portrays his
preparation for and his entry into a state of mystical consciousness
(sections 1–5), his progressively significant and meaningful experience while in this state (sections 6–49), and finally his emergence
from the mystical state (sections 50–52).

The central portion of the poem, sections 6–49, may be related,
step by step, to the "Mystic Way," as described by Evelyn Underhill
in her valuable study *Mysticism*.[2] In what she herself labels an "arbitrary classification," she analyzes five "phases of the mystical life":
(1) the awakening of self; (2) the purification of self; (3) illumination; (4) the dark night of the soul; (5) union. These phases, Miss
Underhill insists, answer only "loosely and generally to experiences
which seldom present themselves in so rigid and unmixed a form."[3]
"Song of Myself" conforms in framework remarkably well to these
five stages, but with some significant differences from the traditional
mystical concepts or attitudes. These differences, central to the
poet's meaning and intention, represent an inversion of some of the
steps in the mystic way or a reversal of values held by the traditional mystic.

"Song of Myself," considered as the dramatic representation of
an inverted mystical experience, may be analyzed as follows:

    I. SECTIONS 1–5: Entry into the mystical state
    II. SECS. 6–16: Awakening of self
    III. SECS. 17–32: Purification of self
    IV. SECS. 33–37: Illumination and the dark night of the soul
    V. SECS. 38–43: Union (faith and love)
    VI. SECS. 44–49: Union (perception)
    VII. SECS. 50–52: Emergence from the mystical state

The third and fourth stages in the mystic way (illumination and the
dark night of the soul) have been combined in sections 33–37; Miss
Underhill indicates that, in reality, the fourth phase sometimes accompanies, intermittently, the third and that her separation of the
two is somewhat arbitrary. Each of the two parts of "Song of Myself" devoted to the fifth stage of the mystic way is concerned with

2. Evelyn Underhill, *Mysticism: A Study in the Nature and Development of
Man's Spiritual Consciousness* (11th ed.; London: Methuen & Co., Ltd., 1926).
3. *Ibid.*, p. 205.

separate, distinct characteristics of union as described by Miss Underhill.

Portrayal of the entry into and emergence from the mystical state of consciousness in sections 1–5 and 50–52 conforms to the popular concept of the behavior of the mystic, his "going into" and "coming out of" the mystic trance. This portrayal represents what William James called the "sporadic type" of mystical experience in which the individual gains sudden, fleeting insight or transcendent knowledge.[4] But, between the beginning and the end of this trancelike state, the poet portrays the laborious steps of the traditional mystic in his efforts to achieve union with the Transcendent. The poet not only fuses the two kinds of mystical experience into one but also, for poetic economy and dramatic intensity, portrays the five stages of the mystic way as following one another immediately in time, whereas in reality the mystic might take years to reach his goal of union. Justification for this departure from reality may be found in the requirements of a work of art: "Song of Myself" is a poem, not a historical, philosophical, or religious document.

I. Sections 1–5: Entry into the Mystical State

In the opening section of "Song of Myself" the poet, while in the passive and receptive state of "leaning" and "loafing," "observing a spear of summer grass," sends forth what is to prove a significant invitation: "I loafe and invite my soul."[5] In section 5 the soul not only accepts the invitation but also consummates a union with the poet. The intervening sections of the poem portray the poet's mental and physical preparation for this union. "Creeds and schools," secondhand knowledge, are to be held in "abeyance," and the poet will "permit to speak at every hazard, / Nature without check with original energy." Surroundings congenial to the experience must be found: "I will go to the bank by the wood and become undis-

4. William James, *Varieties of Religious Experience* (New York: Longmans, Green & Co., 1920), pp. 395–96. James cites section 5 of "Song of Myself" as an expression of the "sporadic type" of mystical experience.

5. All quotations from "Song of Myself" may be easily located in any edition by the references to the sections of the poem. I have used here as elsewhere the "deathbed" edition of *Leaves of Grass,* the last edition Whitman saw through the press, as it appears in *The Complete Writings of Walt Whitman,* ed. Richard M. Bucke *et al.* (New York: G. P. Putnam's Sons, 1902).

guised and naked." In order for nature to speak "with original energy," all man-made objects—houses, rooms, clothes—must be, at least for the moment, forsaken. The importance of the senses to the anticipated experience is suggested in the catalogue in the middle of section 2, in which the poet expresses delight in and implies unqualified acceptance of each of the senses: of taste ("the smoke of my own breath"); of sound ("echoes, ripples, buzz'd whispers"); of odor ("the sniff of green leaves and dry leaves"); of touch ("a few light kisses, a few embraces"); of sight ("the play of shine and shade on the trees").

The nature of the knowledge to be gained through the experience is indicated when the poet invites the reader to "stop this day and night" with him and discover "the origin of all poems," "the good of the earth and sun." There are further hints in sections 3 and 4 of the kind of knowledge nature will bestow. The "talkers" of section 3 and the "trippers and askers" of section 4, with their doubt and their skepticism and debate about a "beginning" and an "end," are too much involved in the minutiae of daily living and too readily accept inherited beliefs to experience the "felt" order in the apparent chaos of existence: "Out of the dimness opposite equals advance, always substance and increase, always sex." The knowledge to be gained is to reconcile "opposite" yet "equals," the "distinction" and "breed" yet "knit of identity": "To elaborate is no avail, learn'd and unlearn'd feel that it is so." The pastime of the age, "showing the best and dividing it from the worst," is futile and misleading. The poet will not engage in the talk about the beginning and end, nor will he, with the age, make judgments about the best and the worst, nor will he surrender himself to the trippers and askers: "Apart from the pulling and hauling stands what I am." At the close of section 4, the poet, "both in and out of the game and watching and wondering at it," portrays himself as withdrawn, withholding comment and judgment—prepared for the imminent union with his soul: "I witness and wait."

In section 5, while the poet is in this state of bemused detachment, the soul materializes and is invited to loaf on the grass, to loose the "stop" from his throat, to "lull" and "hum" with his "valvéd voice." The poet then portrays his entry into the mystical state of consciousness:

I mind how once we lay such a transparent summer morning,
How you settled your head athwart my hips and gently turn'd over
   upon me,
And parted the shirt from my bosom-bone, and plunged your tongue to my
   bare-stript heart,
And reach'd till you felt my beard, and reach'd till you held my feet.

The sexual connotations are unmistakable: implicit in the imagery
is the consummated marriage of body and soul. The preceding sections of the poem have given ample preparation for such a symbolic
marriage: "Clear and sweet is my soul, and clear and sweet is all
that is not my soul." Throughout sections 1–5 of the poem, the
senses have been defiantly accepted and even celebrated, with the
suggestion that they are to have a significant part in the approaching union with the soul. This attitude toward the senses constitutes
the basic paradox in the poem. Whereas normally the mystical state
is achieved only through a mortification of, or escape from, the
senses, the poet of "Song of Myself" asserts that it is *through* the
transfigured senses that he reaches mystical consciousness.

   In "Song of Myself" the self is not, as in the traditional mystical
experience, submerged or annihilated, but rather celebrated; the
senses are not humbled but glorified. When the soul plunges his
tongue to the "bare-stript heart" of the poet, the physical becomes
transfigured into the spiritual, the body from beard to feet is held
in the grip of the soul, and body and soul become one: "Lack one
lacks both." The imagery of the tongue and heart is ingenious: the
spiritual tongue informs; the physical heart receives. Such imagery
suggests that it is only through the intimate fusion of the physical
and spiritual, the ennobling of the physical through the spiritual,
that one can come to know transcendent reality. The poet's mystical
state of consciousness results in immediate "knowledge":

Swiftly arose and spread around me the peace and knowledge that pass
   all the argument of the earth,
And I know that the hand of God is the promise of my own,
And I know that the spirit of God is the brother of my own,
And that all the men ever born are also my brothers, and the women my
   sisters and lovers,
And that a kelson of the creation is love.

This knowledge would confound the trippers, askers, and talkers:
it is not rational knowledge at all, but the "peace and knowledge,"

or love, that the tongue of the soul imparts to the heart of the body. It is, in short, the beginning of the spiritual awakening of the physical self.

II. *Sections 6–16: Awakening of Self*

The poet's sudden certitude that the "hand of God" is the "promise" of his own and that the "spirit of God" is the "brother" of his own is the mystic's awakening to "consciousness of Divine Reality."[6] The poet's intense vision brings an intuitive awareness of the relationship of self to God, to other men and women, and to nature, and the sum of the knowledge is "A kelson of the creation is love." The awakening of self begins, as with the mystic, in "a disturbance of the equilibrium of the self, which results in the shifting of the field of consciousness from lower to higher levels, with a consequent removal of the centre of interest from the subject to an object now brought into view."[7] The nature imagery at the end of section 5 trails off with "elder, mullein, poke-weed," which leads naturally to the question posed in section 6, "What is the grass?"

The grass becomes, in this important section, a key to the ultimate enigma of Divine Reality. The poet, now become intensely aware and perceptive, searches out the grass's significance in relation to self (the "flag of my disposition"), to God (the "handkerchief of the Lord"), to life ("a uniform hieroglyphic . . . Sprouting alike in broad zones and narrow zones"), and to death ("the beautiful uncut hair of graves"). These large subjects (self, God, life, death) introduce the areas into which insight is to be sought and perhaps gained through the mystic way. The poet seems most fascinated by the puzzle of death, and he attempts to "translate the hints" given by the grass of the fate of the dead:

The smallest sprout shows there is really no death,
And if ever there was it led forward life, and does not wait at the end to
  arrest it,
And ceas'd the moment life appear'd.

All goes onward and outward, nothing collapses,
And to die is different from what any one supposed, and luckier.

6. Underhill, *op. cit.*, p. 205.
7. *Ibid.*, p. 213.

The imagery is complex, suggesting a threefold view of death. The "smallest sprout" of grass offered as proof that there is no death suggests pantheism. But the lines that follow suggest that faith is placed in evolution: death is the void that existed on earth before life existed; the "moment life appear'd" death ceased, and now all "goes onward and outward"—the race has eternal life though the individual dies. But implicit in "And if ever there was it [death] led forward life, and does not wait at the end to arrest it" is the suggestion of the eternal life of the individual; death is the nonentity of the individual before birth rather than after death. Once the individual achieves existence, eternal life is bestowed; there is change ("onward and outward"—material and spiritual) but not disintegration ("collapse").

But all these thoughts to which contemplation of the grass has given rise are merely hints, a groping about for insight by the newly awakened self. They indicate to the reader the nature of the journey on which the poet is embarking, the kind of knowledge after which he is striving. In section 7 there is a return to the probing of self, an attempt to express what the self really is. The poet is "not contain'd between [his] hat and boots," nor is he "an earth nor an adjunct of an earth." This indication of what the self is *not* launches the poet into an expanding vision of what the self *is,* a vision that begins in section 7 and runs through to a climax in section 16. These sections represent a gradual intensification of the poet's awakening of self, and, as in the traditional mystical experience, the awakening tends not inward but outward; the "object now brought into [the poet's] view" is other life of all kinds, in all emotional states, in all conditions and situations.

Section 8 introduces the poet observing the cycle of life—birth ("The little one sleeps in its cradle"), love ("the youngster and the red-faced girl turn aside up the bushy hill"), and death ("The suicide sprawls on the bloody floor"). This cycle fades into the montage of city-street life, beginning with "the blab of pave" and concluding with the poet's observation, "I mind them or the show or resonance of them—I come and I depart." In section 9 the scene changes from city to country, with a full picture of a farm; the poet is there: "I help, I came stretch'd atop of the load [of the wagon]." In section 10 there is a series of pictures in which the poet sees himself or observes others in activities that isolate the individual: he hunts "alone far in the wilds," and he sails on the Yankee clipper; he observes the "marriage of the trapper in the open air in the far west," and he plays generous and tender host to the runaway slave. The observation of the lonely and isolated reaches a climax in section 11, which is devoted in its entirety to the vivid picture of the young woman, whose life has been "all so lonesome," secretly observing, longing for, and imagining herself joining the twenty-eight young swimmers, whose "bellies bulge to the sun." In section 12 the poet shifts his observation to the lowly, as he loiters and enjoys the "repartee" of the butcher boy and follows the movements of the blacksmith. Section 13 continues with the life of the humble in the full portrait of the Negro holding "firmly the reins of his four horses."

This portrait brings into focus another element of life that, after a brief reference to the role of self, causes another shift in the poet's vision:

I behold the picturesque giant and love him, and I do not stop there,
I go with the team also.
In me the caresser of life wherever moving, backward as well as forward sluing,
To niches aside and junior bending, not a person or object missing.
Absorbing all to myself and for this song.

"Caresser of life" suggests the role of the poet throughout this first phase of his mystical experience. The love that the soul has bestowed in the heart has awakened the poet to a sympathetic awareness of life outside self—to all life, "backward" or "forward." The "niches" is a vivid image connoting all the lonely, the isolated, whom others, but not the poet, pass by. And the poet's love is extended to life other than human. With "I go with the team also," the poet begins a series of pictures of such life, from the oxen, wood-drake, wood-duck, tortoise, jay, and bay mare of the latter part of section 13, through the gander, moose, cat, chickadee, prairie-dog, sow, and turkey hen of the first half of section 14. All this life, like the wild gander, finds "its purpose and place" and, like the tortoise, is not "unworthy because [it] is not something else." Through this animal life, the poet awakens further to self: "I see in them and myself the same old law." The poet is "enamour'd of growing out-doors," where such self-awareness or self-knowledge is granted so freely and easily. Section

14 closes with the first clear indication that the poet identifies himself with those whom he observes—the "commonest, cheapest, nearest, easiest." In going in for his chances, "spending for vast returns,"
the poet is asserting that he will have ample reward for the love and
affection he seems to be bestowing so indiscriminately—the reward of
an awakened self and the resulting insight into the riddle of existence.

Good will is indeed scattered freely in section 15, a long catalogue of rapid one-line pictures, ranging from contralto to lunatic,
from opium-eater and prostitute to flatboatmen and coon-seekers,
ending:

> And these tend inward to me, and I tend outward to them,
> And such as it is to be of these more or less I am,
> And of these one and all I weave the song of myself.

The awakening of self has been an awakening to the realization of
the potentiality in the self to be all these, to have all their varied
emotions, to engage in all their sundry activities. The awakening has
caused the eyes to turn not inward but outward and has resulted in
not contraction but expansion of self, excluding none, including all.

The poet insists on even greater diversity of self in section 16: "I
am of old and young, of the foolish as much as the wise." Emphasis
in this section, in contrast with the preceding, is placed on the merging of sectional or geographical differences. The poet is "one of the
Nation of many nations," a Southerner, a Northerner, a Yankee, a
Kentuckian, a Louisianian, a Californian, and many more: "Of every
hue and caste am I, of every rank and religion." What had started,
in section 8, as observation, coming and departing, has become by
now complete identification—the poet no longer watches, or is "of"
what he sees, but actually *is* all he observes. Self has been expanded
to include the whole of America, high and low, far and near, divine
and degraded. And accompanying this vision of the diversity of self
is the sense of the fitness of things as they are. Section 16 closes with
the poet asserting,

[I] am not stuck up, and am in my place.

(The moth and the fish-eggs are in their place,
The bright suns I see and the dark suns I cannot see are in their place,
The palpable is in its place and the impalpable is in its place.)

In the first phase of the mystical experience, the poet has achieved
an acute awareness of an expanded self and a supreme confidence

in the fitness of that self in its place. Implied in this sense of "place," not only for the self but for all else, is the sense of design or plan transcending the self and all things, animate and inanimate, seen and unseen. Awakening of self has bestowed an intuitive glimpse of this design—the Divine Reality.

III. *Sections 17–32: Purification of Self*

In section 17 of "Song of Myself" there is a pause in the long catalogues, and the poet appears to assess the value of what he has so far learned:

These are really the thoughts of all men in all ages and lands, they are not original with me,
If they are not yours as much as mine they are nothing, or next to nothing.

The poet's thoughts on himself are, in reality, thoughts on selfhood and belong not to just one but to all. And these thoughts are the "riddle and the untying of the riddle." The awakening of self, the realization of the otherness or diversity of self, is a riddle, but in the awakening lies the clue to the solution of the riddle. As the first lines of section 17 comment on the foregoing experiences, so the last lines introduce, metaphorically, a change in the direction of the mystical journey:

This is the grass that grows wherever the land is and the water is,
This is the common air that bathes the globe.

As contemplation of the meaning of the grass launched the first phase of the mystical experience, so one particular symbolic quality of it is used to begin the second phase. The image of the grass is joined with the image of the air to suggest, particularly through the word "common," the equality of all. Although the subject matter ranges widely in sections 17–32, the theme of equality is constant. It is through this insistent theme that the poet achieves purification of self.

As it has been through acceptance of the body, not through mortification of it as something evil, that the mystical experience has been launched in "Song of Myself," it should not be surprising that in the "purification" phase the traditional values of the mystic are inverted. Purification is achieved, not through "purgation," not through "discipline and mortification,"[8] but by an ennobling and an

8. *Ibid.*, p. 205.

accepting of what has been mistakenly reviled and degraded. Whitman's reversal of the traditional mystic values, values not necessarily peculiar to the mystic, is the heart of his meaning: man's sense of sin is his greatest sin, his greatest delusion; in order to purify himself, he must purge this false sense.

Throughout sections 18–32, the degraded and rejected are ennobled and accepted through a reconciliation of opposites usually considered irreconcilable: in section 18, the vanquished and victor; in section 19, the wicked and righteous; in section 20, the self and others; in section 21, the body and soul, and woman and man; in section 22, vice and virtue; in section 23, the present and past, and science and spirit (or reality and spirituality); in section 24, the self and others, and body and soul (or the lusts of the body and the desires of the soul); in section 25, the unseen and the seen, or the felt and the provable; in section 26, the inflow and the outflow, or the heard and the spoken; in sections 27 through 30 (the well-known sections on the poet's sensitivity to touch), the body and soul, or the physical and spiritual; in section 31, the common and the miraculous, or the known and the unknown, or the familiar and the unfamiliar; in section 32, the animal and man.

The dropping and subsequent return to a particular subject, what has frequently been called the "symphonic treatment" of theme, may be justified on the basis of the dramatic situation of the poet: in the emotional state imposed by the mystical experience, something approaching ecstatic frenzy, it is natural that the poet's thought should lack logical continuity. But the disunity is more apparent than real: when a subject is reintroduced, it is treated in a new light, from a different point of view; such periodic and gradual treatment builds up to a climax. The most notable example is the celebration of the body, begun in section 21, returned to in section 24, and become an ecstatic eulogy in sections 27–30.

The act of purification begins in section 18 with "conquer'd and slain persons," as the poet imagines himself a band, with cornets and drums, beating and pounding "for the dead": ". . . it is good to fall, battles are lost in the same spirit in which they are won." In section 19 the poet elevates the wicked alongside the righteous. His "meal [is] equally set" for the kept woman, sponger, thief, slave, "venere-

alee": "There shall be no difference between them and the rest." And
to those who question his motive, the poet answers:

Do you guess I have some intricate purpose?
Well I have, for the Fourth-month showers have, and the mica on the side
   of a rock has.

His motive is no different from Nature's; in him exist the same "ele-
mentary laws." In section 20 there is an almost arrogant egotism
which has frequently been found objectionable: "I wear my hat as
I please indoors or out." But, as the poet insists, this seeming arro-
gance is not meant to be an expression of superiority: "In all people
I see myself, none more and not one a barley-corn less." The source
of the poet's strong feeling of equality is his knowledge that he is
"deathless," but his immortality is no more than any other man's:

> My foothold is tenon'd and mortis'd in granite,
> I laugh at what you call dissolution,
> And I know the amplitude of time.

The only superiority he has is his intuitive knowledge of immortality—he knows that man is deathless; others do not.

   The first lines of section 21 announce the theme crucial to the
purification of self:

I am the poet of the Body and I am the poet of the Soul,
The pleasures of heaven are with me and the pains of hell are with me,
The first I graft and increase upon myself, the latter I translate into a new
   tongue.

As the poet will, through self, "increase" the "pleasures of heaven"
(the spiritual), so he will "translate into a new tongue"—transfigure,
purify—the "pains of hell" (the physical). Although the poet mo-
mentarily passes on to other aspects of his central theme of equality
("I am the poet of the woman the same as the man"; "I show that
size is only development"), he returns to the body-soul theme in
the celebrated passage, extending into section 22, which delicately
fuses imagery of night, earth, and sea with sexual imagery:

> I am he that walks with the tender and growing night,
> I call to the earth and sea half-held by the night.

The night is masculine, "bare-bosom'd night," "mad naked summer
night," while the earth is feminine, "voluptuous cool-breath'd earth!"
"earth of the mountains misty-topt!" Whereas the earth's lover is the

descending night, the poet himself is beckoned by the "crooked inviting fingers" of the sea and hurries to it, undresses, and is dashed by "amorous wet." This delicate portrayal of sexual feeling in nature imagery is the "translation into a new tongue" promised by the poet. The gross language in which such feelings are usually embodied, with its connotations of sin and evil, is abandoned, and the sensitive, delicate imagery of nature transfigures the emotions and ennobles them. When, later in section 22, the poet exclaims, "I am not the poet of goodness only, I do not decline to be the poet of wickedness also," "wickedness" must be interpreted in the context of what has preceded: inasmuch as the word has been associated with the body, the physical, the sexual impulse and fulfilment, then the poet does not decline to be the "poet of wickedness." The physical may be reconciled with the spiritual: "I find one side a balance and the antipodal side a balance."

The theme of equality of the present is introduced in the latter part of section 22 ("This minute that comes to me over the past decillions, / There is no better than it and now") and is carried over into the first part of section 23 ("Endless unfolding of words of ages! / And mine a word of the modern, the word En-masse"). The poet accepts "Time absolutely" and accepts "Reality and dare[s] not question it." Reality is "materialism," symbolized by "positive science," which the poet enthusiastically accepts but by no means considers final:

> Gentlemen, to you the first honors always!
> Your facts are useful, and yet they are not my dwelling,
> I but enter by them to an area of my dwelling.

Acceptance of the body would necessarily entail the acceptance of the physical world, or materialism; but just as the body offered the way into the mystical state, so positive science offers the way to something other than itself, to "life untold."

Section 24 reintroduces the egotistic tone of section 20, but again emphasis is placed on equality, not superiority. The poet is "no stander above men and women or apart from them":

I speak the pass-word primeval, I give the sign of democracy,
By God! I will accept nothing which all cannot have their counterpart of
on the same terms.

Following this passionate outburst asserting equality, championing the "rights of them the others are down upon," there is a return to the body-soul theme:

> Through me forbidden voices,
> Voices of sexes and lusts, voices veil'd and I remove the veil,
> Voices indecent by me clarified and transfigur'd.

The aim of the poet is, clearly, transfiguration, purification, spiritualization of the physical self. The senses, "seeing, hearing, feeling, are miracles" as much as are faculties of the soul. But the transfiguration is not to be accomplished through mere assertion only; it is to be accomplished poetically through association of the physical with the innocence, beauty, and divine mystery of nature. The poet sees the innocence of the sensual and sexual in the primitive, natural, eternal world about him, in such symbolic products of nature as "Root of wash'd sweet-flag! timorous pond-snipe! nest of guarded duplicate eggs!"

Sections 25 and 26 of "Song of Myself" complement each other; in the first the poet conceives of himself as imparting, in the latter as receiving. When, in section 25, he says, "My voice goes after what my eyes cannot reach," he is asserting the importance of the unseen alongside the seen. But when, farther on, he says, "you conceive too much of articulation," he is asserting the importance of the felt or inexpressible alongside the provable, the demonstrable. The desire to impart of section 25 becomes a desire to receive in section 26:

> Now I will do nothing but listen,
> To accrue what I hear into this song, to let sounds contribute toward it.

Underlying these two sections is the theme of the equal validity of the outflow and the inflow, the imparted and the received. The sounds accrued range from the sounds of the city to the sounds of the country, from the sounds of the day to the sounds of the night, and they conclude with an orchestra which "wrenches such ardors" from the poet that he reacts with emotional violence:

> . . . I lose my breath,
> Steep'd amid honey'd morphine, my windpipe throttled in fakes of death,
> At length let up again to feel the puzzle of puzzles,
> And that we call Being.

Sections 27 through 30 are an exploration of this puzzle of "Being": "To be in any form, what is that?" Is "Being" the body or the soul, or the one transfigured by the other into a new self infinitely more significant than either alone? The answer lies only in the self: "I merely stir, press, feel with my fingers, and am happy." The body cannot be denied; the instinctive reaction to touch confirms it as a basic truth, not a lie; as good, not evil. Through touch the poet is quivered "to a new identity"—the purified self. The remarkable imagery, in which the poet's other senses, bribed by touch, "go and graze at the edges" of him, suggests sexual ecstasy and fulfilment, reaching a climax as the poet cries out, "Unclench your floodgates, you are too much for me." Section 29 portrays the poet, after the departure of "blind loving wrestling . . . sheath'd hooded sharp-tooth'd touch," emotionally fulfilled but exhausted, and section 30 shows him reflecting on the significance of his ecstatic encounter with touch: "All truths wait in all things . . . (what is less or more than a touch?)." As touch, in spite of "logic and sermons," "proves itself" to the poet, the body is accepted. The self, through instinctive insight, has been purified by a purgation not of the senses but of the illusion of the senses as vile.

The grass imagery, which has appeared previously at key points in the poem, is reintroduced in section 31: "I believe a leaf of grass is no less than the journey-work of the stars." The leaf of grass here becomes a symbol of the insignificant that is "as big" to the poet "as any." The miraculous may be found in the smallest or the most commonplace object. In the latter part of section 31, the poet shows an awareness of self as the product of a long, evolutionary development. When he says, "[I] have distanced what is behind me for good reasons," he suggests that he too, like the leaf of grass, the pismire, the grain of sand, and the rest, is "miracle enough to stagger sextillions of infidels."

Section 32, which closes the second phase of the mystical experience, celebrates the primitive life of the animals. When the poet exclaims, "I think I could turn and live with animals," he is acknowledging that he has achieved purification of self, a purification that the animals do not need to struggle to attain, inasmuch as they are born with an innate primitive purity:

> They do not sweat and whine about their condition,
> They do not lie awake in the dark and weep for their sins,
> They do not make me sick discussing their duty to God,

Not one is dissatisfied, not one is demented with the mania of owning
  things,
Not one kneels to another, nor to his kind that lived thousands of years ago,
Not one is respectable or unhappy over the whole earth.

In the animals exist all the traits the poet has attempted, in sections
17–32, to ennoble and celebrate, traits frequently considered evil.[9]
It is this sense of evil that the poet has purged in the purification
of self. These traits are now so much the poet's own that he wonders
where the animals got them: "Did I pass that way huge times ago
and negligently drop them?" Man, in the primitive state of his evolution, had such traits but, in the development of his civilization,
lost them to the animals. The section closes with the vivid picture
of the poet riding the "gigantic beauty of a stallion," whose "well-
built limbs tremble with pleasure"; the stallion is symbolic of all
the primitive innocence that the poet admires and has achieved. But
the poet says,

> I but use you a minute, then I resign you, stallion,
> Why do I need your paces when I myself out-gallop them?
> Even as I stand or sit passing faster than you.

The poet realizes that the animal, with all his innocence and purity,
cannot achieve what a man of similar nature can achieve—what the
poet is to achieve in the next stage of his mystical experience.

IV. *Sections 33–37: Illumination and the Dark Night of the Soul*

Illumination, when it comes to the purified self, is swift; the poet
at the opening of section 33 bursts forth with the "knowledge of
Reality"[10] that is suddenly his:

Space and Time! now I see it is true, what I guess'd at,
What I guess'd when I loaf'd on the grass,
What I guess'd while I lay alone in my bed,
And again as I walk'd the beach under the paling stars of the morning.

My ties and ballasts leave me, my elbows rest in sea-gaps,
I skirt sierras, my palms cover continents,
I am afoot with my vision.

9. Among these traits, the only one that resembles the ideal of the mystic is
the indifference to "owning things." In the purification of self, the traditional
mystic cultivates poverty, chastity, and obedience, all resulting in the desired
humility (*ibid.,* pp. 247–48).
10. *Ibid.,* p. 205.

It is as though the poet, after the struggles of awakening and purification of the previous two phases of the experience, has finally
achieved existence outside space and time and has sudden insight,
like the mystic's, into the "secret of the world."[11] What had only
been felt before, or "guess'd," receives confirmation through intuitive
but certain knowledge. The emotional feeling accompanying the insight is evoked in the image of the balloon, its ties and ballasts cast
off, ascending above the world. But this image merges immediately
with that of a giant self, whose "elbows rest in sea-gaps" and whose
"palms cover continents." The one image suggests upward movement
or flight, while the other suggests immense power; together the
images imply greater physical sight, symbolic of the greater spiritual insight that has been attained. The poet is "afoot" with his
vision at last; the self, awakened and purified, apprehends directly
Divine Reality.

The increase in energy of the "intuitional or transcendental self"[12]
is manifested in the poet's sense of ubiquity or all-inclusiveness. The
first half of section 33, the longest section in the poem, consists of
the long catalogue in which the poet imagines himself "by the city's
quadrangular houses," "where the panther walks," "scaling mountains," "where the human heart beats with terrible throes under its
ribs," "under Niagara," and elsewhere, near and distant, placid and
dangerous. This catalogue has, however, a significant difference
from those found in the sections describing the poet's awakening of
self (particularly in sections 8, 15, and 16). For the first time the
poet imagines himself out of time, "Walking the old hills of Judaea
with the beautiful gentle God by my side," and not confined to this
world or hampered by space: "Speeding through space, speeding
through heaven and the stars." A sense of existing outside both
space and time is conveyed in:

> I visit the orchard of spheres and look at the product,
> And look at quintillions ripen'd and look at quintillions green.

All this imagery of movement up and down, over, through, in, and
out, flung out in an almost frenzied state though it may seem, evokes

---

11. *Ibid.,* p. 289. One of the characteristics of the stage of illumination is that
the "self perceives an added significance and reality in all natural things: is often
convinced that it knows the 'secret of the world.' "
12. *Ibid.* Another characteristic of illumination.

the feeling of ecstatic insight appropriate to the emotional state of the poet. He is flying the flight of a "fluid and swallowing soul," and his course runs "below the soundings of plummets."

In the latter part of section 33 the imagery becomes gradually morbid: the man's body, fetched up "dripping and drown'd"; the "wreck of the steamship, and Death chasing it up and down the storm"; the "old-faced infants and the lifted sick"; the "mother of old, condemn'd for a witch"; and the "hounded slave." The poet not only observes but becomes what he observes: "I am the man, I suffer'd, I was there"; "Hell and despair are upon me, crack and again crack the marksmen." After reaching the emotional heights of the ecstasy of illumination, the poet seems suddenly plunged into the depths of "hell and despair":

Agonies are one of my changes of garments,
I do not ask the wounded person how he feels, I myself become the
    wounded person,
My hurts turn livid upon me as I lean on a cane and observe.

In the experience of the traditional mystics the dark night of the soul (also "mystic pain" and "mystic death") sometimes accompanied the preceding stage, illumination. In this fourth phase of the experience, the "consciousness which had, in Illumination, sunned itself in the sense of the Divine Presence, now suffers under an equally intense sense of the Divine Absence. . . ."[13] There is a feeling of "great desolation in which the soul seems abandoned by the Divine."[14]

The dark night into which the poet's soul is plunged brings an acute consciousness of identity with the sinful, the suffering, the downtrodden, the injured, the sick, the wounded. The poet assumes the agony and despair of the world. The imagery of war, of fighting, of battles, of violence, introduced in the latter part of section 33, continues through section 36. Section 34 is the narrative of the "murder in cold blood of four hundred and twelve young men." The most ghastly aspects of the massacre are dwelt upon, from the "maim'd and mangled" digging in the dirt to the "burning of the bodies." This narrative is a story of tragedy in defeat, as the sea fight in sections 35 and 36 is a story of tragedy in victory. Again, the details

13. *Ibid.*, p. 206.
14. *Ibid.*

emphasized point up the terrible human woe resulting from the battle. The triumphant captain's "countenance [is] white as a sheet," as near him lies the "corpse of the child that serv'd in the cabin." On deck are "formless stacks of bodies and bodies by themselves," and nearby is heard

> The hiss of the surgeon's knife, the gnawing teeth of his saw,
> Wheeze, cluck, swash of falling blood, short wild scream
>   and long, dull tapering groan,
> These so, these irretrievable.

Although the land battle and the sea battle exhibit man courageous in the face of defeat and victory, such courage becomes meaningless in the face of the resulting misery and suffering and death, in the face of the "irretrievable."

In section 37 the poet reaches the climax in his dark night of the soul. First he imagines himself imprisoned:

> . . . I am possess'd!
> Embody all presences outlaw'd or suffering,
> See myself in prison shaped like another man,
> And feel the dull unintermitted pain.

In quick succession the poet becomes a convict, a mutineer, a "youngster" taken for larceny, a cholera patient. And it is not with courage and optimism that the poet assumes these roles; he feels and shows suffering and despair when he is the "hand cuff'd" mutineer or the cholera patient with "ash-color'd" face. Certain it is that he no longer feels a sense of the Divine Presence, nor does he any longer feel the exultation of sudden insight felt when he was "afoot" with his vision. At the end of this section, the poet identifies himself with the beggar:

> Askers embody themselves in me and I am embodied in them,
> I project my hat, sit shame-faced, and beg.

Here the poet reaches the nadir in degradation, particularly in the emotion of shame, an emotion foreign to his mystical experience up to this point. It is with this emotion that his dark night of the soul draws to a close.

V. Sections 38–43: Union (Faith and Love)

In sections 38 through 43 of "Song of Myself," the poet seems filled with "peaceful joy" and "intense certitude" and seems granted "enhanced powers."[15] He is intoxicated with a "consciousness of sharing" the strength of the "Infinite," of "acting by Its authority."[16] Section 38 opens with strong repudiation of the attitudes and emotions expressed in the preceding section, the emotions of the dark night of the soul:

Enough! enough! enough!
Somehow I have been stunn'd. Stand back!
Give me a little time beyond my cuff'd head, slumbers, dreams, gaping,
I discover myself on the verge of a usual mistake.

The "usual mistake" is the exclusion of the Divine, the Infinite. What seems lost is not, as the poet had thought, "irretrievable." The hell, the despair, the shame are illusion, false reality; genuine reality may be perceived by union with the Transcendent, out of time, out of space. Such union results not in identification with the lowly, the degraded, the sinful and suffering, and acceptance of them on their own terms, but in infinite sympathy and tenderness and granted power for them.

The poet suggests his union with the Transcendent through imagery of the Crucifixion of Christ:

That I could forget the mockers and insults!
That I could forget the trickling tears and the blows of
the bludgeons and hammers!
That I could look with separate look on my own
crucifixion and bloody crowning!

I remember now,
I resume the overstaid fraction.

The insight of the illumination ("I see it is true, what I guess'd at"), though intense, had not been complete; a "fraction" had been "overstaid," a fraction large enough to plunge the poet into the dark night of the soul. Now, however, the "overstaid fraction" is "resumed"; the poet achieves the complete insight brought by union with the Transcendent. Whereas in illumination the poet's apprehension of Divine Reality was symbolized by his "walking the old hills of Judaea" with Christ, in union the poet's merging with the Transcendent is symbolized by outright identification of self with Christ. As the Crucifixion of Christ resulted not in death, meaningless suffering,

15. *Ibid.*, p. 207. These are characteristics of union.
16. *Ibid.*, p. 497.

or shame but in eternal life and joy, so the poet's dark night results in renewed vigor and life ("Corpses rise, gashes heal, fastenings roll from me") and in supreme power. Through union, the poet is suddenly changed from the passive sufferer into the powerful healer, issuing "swift ordinances . . . over the whole earth." the "bloody crowning" is transfigured into the "blossoms we wear in our hats."

The Christ figure merges with the "friendly and flowing savage" in section 39. Like Christ, wherever the savage goes, men and women "desire he should like them, touch them, speak to them, stay with them." The savage, like Christ, is God become man: his behavior is "lawless as snow-flakes" and his words "simple as grass." He does not conform to man's law but to divine or Nature's law; his teachings are simple, cast in the common language and the homely figure all can understand. In him the "common features" and "common modes . . . descend in new forms from the tips of his fingers" and "fly out of the glance of his eyes." Through him the common is transfigured into the divine. In this description, the poet, Christ, and the savage merge into one. The savage, man in his primitive original state, becomes the symbol of the divinity that civilized man has lost. The poet has had to strip away the errors and delusions of civilization in order to achieve his union.

Throughout the remainder of the sections (40–43) devoted to this phase of the mystical experience, the "I" is the poet as Christ-savage. The supreme power resulting from union enables the poet, like the mystic, to become "an actual parent of spiritual vitality in other men."[17] He will not give "lectures or a little charity" when he gives but will give himself. He has "stores plenty and to spare" and will never "deny" the lowliest "cotton-field" drudge. He takes the place of the physician and the priest at the bedside of the dying, and he calls to the "descending" man, "here is my neck . . . hang your whole weight upon me." His power is sufficient for all, as he exclaims, "I dilate you with tremendous breath, I buoy you up."

But the poet in his new-found power is not concerned solely with the downtrodden and the suffering: ". . . for strong upright men I bring yet more needed help." This "help" is a supreme faith in the order and harmony of the universe. The poet has heard "what was said of the universe" but finds these theories—these religions—insuffi-

17. *Ibid.*, pp. 497–98.

cient, incomplete. He does not reject them. He takes them all—
Jehovah, Kronos, Zeus, Brahma, Buddha, and the rest—"for what
they are worth" but fills out the "rough deific sketches" in himself,
in the "framer framing a house," in the "mechanic's wife with her
babe," in common people and in the commonplace. The poet's divinity is derived from and freely dispensed to all.

In section 42 the poet imagines himself an orator, perhaps like
Christ delivering his Sermon on the Mount, bringing his message to
the multitude. A feeling of flux, of eternal change, movement, recurrence, is evoked by the seven-line stanza in which each line
begins with "Ever" ("ever the upward and downward sun, ever the
air and the ceaseless tides"), followed by the five-line stanza, each
line ending with the gerundive form. The latter stanza is suggestive
of a biblical parable:

Here and there with dimes on the eyes walking,
To feed the greed of the belly the brains liberally spooning,
Tickets buying, taking, selling, but in to the feast never once going,
Many sweating, ploughing, thrashing, and then the chaff for payment re-
    ceiving,
A few idly owning, and they the wheat continually claiming.

The selfish rich are the spiritually dead ("with dimes on the eyes
walking") who devote their minds "to feed the greed of the belly,"
who take the wheat and leave the chaff to the laborers, but who in
reality never go in to the significant feast, where spiritual sustenance
may be gained—perhaps the "feast" of labor itself, with its inter-
course with other human beings.[18] The latter part of section 42
places, as did the previous section, the ultimate value on man as
against the material or "things":

    Not words of routine this song of mine,
    But abruptly to question, to leap beyond yet nearer bring.

The intent is to "leap beyond" the object or image and bring nearer
the human behind it: the printer beyond the book, the wife or friend
beyond the photograph, the "captain and engineers" beyond the

18. There are echoes in this stanza of several biblical passages. The references
to the spiritually dead ("dimes on the eyes walking") is similar to Christ's in his
advice to let the dead bury their own dead (Luke 9:60). The rich who are so
busy buying and selling that they never once go "in to the feast" are similar to
those who refused the invitation in Christ's parable of the great supper (Luke
14:16–24).

"black ship mail'd with iron," and, finally, the "fathomless human brain" beyond the "sermons, creeds, theology."

The poet, in section 43, envisions himself as "enclosing worship ancient and modern and all between ancient and modern." As in section 41 the poet accepted religions of all kinds and varieties, so in section 43 he accepts religions of all ages, from the earliest which made "a fetich of the first rock or stump," to the latest of the "winders of the circuit of circuits" (the itinerant evangelists). Nor are the "down-hearted doubters," lost in a "sea of torment, doubt, despair and unbelief," to be excluded. The poet's supreme power, his "spiritual vitality," is sufficient for all:

I do not know what is untried and afterward,
But I know it will in its turn prove sufficient, and cannot fail.

Each who passes is consider'd, each who stops is consider'd, not a single
   one can it fail.

"What is untried and afterward" is the Absolute, the Divine, the Transcendent, which the poet has come to know intuitively through union; he speaks with the supreme faith of his "intense certitude." "What is untried and afterward" will not fail those who have died, the "old man who has lived without purpose," "him in the poor house tubercled by rum," the "numberless slaughter'd and wreck'd." No longer does the poet, as in his dark night of the soul, accept the suffering and despair of the outcast, injured, and dying as his own; instead, he gives hope to all from his abundant faith and love derived from his union. It remains for him to convey to the reader what he can of his transcendent mystical knowledge.

VI. *Sections 44–49: Union (Perception)*

The final stage of the mystical experience is announced abruptly in the opening line of section 44: "It is time to explain myself—let us stand up." And the intent of conveying hints of the "supreme perception"[19] granted in union is made immediately clear:

What is known I strip away,
I launch all men and women forward with me into the Unknown.

19. Underhill, *op. cit.*, p. 100: "True mystical experience is the most complete and most difficult expression of life which is as yet possible to man. It is at once an act of love, an act of union, and an act of supreme perception: a trinity of experiences which meets and satisfies the three activities of self."

"What is known" is that which is usually considered reality but which, by the mystic, is designated "illusion": it is the world familiar to man through his senses. The "Unknown" is that which is not perceived by the senses, known only to the mystic, and designated by him the "transcendent reality." At the beginning of the illumination stage, the stage of intuitive insight, the poet exclaimed, "Space and Time! now I see it is true"; through the supreme perception of union, the poet becomes intensely aware of the relation of self to time (section 44) and to space (section 45).

When, in section 44, the poet asks, "The clock indicates the moment—but what does eternity indicate?" he is suggesting that man's relation to the moment is trivial compared to his relation to eternity, that eternity is the transcendent reality; the moment, illusion. The remainder of section 44 is filled with imagery which evokes a vision of eternity and the self's relation to it:

> We have thus far exhausted trillions of winters and summers,
> There are trillions ahead, and trillions ahead of them.

It is through time, through the symbolic "trillions" suggesting infinity, that eternity is to be conceived: eternity is endless time before and after "now." The self, at a point in time, is intimately related to before and after: "I am an acme of things accomplish'd, and I an encloser of things to be." Eternity has its only existence in self, flows with self from the before to the after. There are no "before" and "after" to the self:

> My feet strike an apex of the apices of the stairs,
> On every step bunches of ages, and larger bunches between the steps,
> All below duly travel'd, and still I mount and mount.

In this striking imagery, the self is conceived as coeval with eternity, mounting the stairway of time. There was never a period when the self did not exist: "Afar down I see the huge first Nothing, I know I was even there." Using the imagery of physics and evolution,[20] the poet says that he "slept through the lethargic mist" and took "no hurt from the fetid carbon," that for him the "stars kept aside in their own rings," that for his embryo the "nebula cohered to an orb" and that "monstrous sauroids transported it [his embryo] in their mouths

20. Joseph Beaver's *Walt Whitman—Poet of Science* (New York: King's Crown Press, 1951) contains many excellent interpretations of the passages in "Song of Myself" containing scientific imagery.

and deposited it with care." The cumulative effect of this startling imagery is to convey the impression of form and plan in the flow of time, the impression of the oneness of self and eternity.

In the closing line of section 44, the poet exults, "Now on this spot I stand with my robust soul." The opening lines of section 45 express the self's ecstatic joy in the "now," from youth through manhood to old age, and its faith in the future: "And the dark hush promulges as much as any." But after this outburst of joy in existence, the poet opens his "scuttle" and looks at the "far-sprinkled systems." Using the imagery of astronomy, he evokes the endlessness of space:

> My sun has his sun and round him obediently wheels,
> He joins with his partners a group of superior circuit,
> And greater sets follow, making specks of the greatest inside them.

Time, "a few quadrillions of eras," cannot "hazard the span," cannot affect space. "Limitless space" and "limitless time" and the form and plan implicit in their infinity, instead of shrinking the self into insignificance, give certain assurance of the "rendezvous" with the "great Camerado," assurance of the ultimate union with the Transcendent—union after death similar to the union in life of the mystic. The poet's description of the "great Camerado" as "the lover true for whom I pine" is suggestive of the symbolism of the "Mystical Marriage"[21] with which, as Evelyn Underhill has noted, many mystics describe their union with the Absolute.

When the poet states, at the opening of section 46, "I know I have the best of time and space, and was never measured and never will be measured," he is presenting the essence of his transcendent knowledge or "supreme perception." It is not a static knowledge that can be codified for church or philosophy, expressed in a book, or conveyed through logic. Rather it is a dynamic, intuitive insight that each man must gain for himself. The poet can only point the way. Travel imagery dominates the section, beginning with the poet's "I tramp a perpetual journey" and extending through his direct address to the reader:

> Not I, not any one else can travel that road for you,
> You must travel it for yourself.

21. Underhill, *op. cit.*, p. 207.

The poet's exhortation to the reader to begin the journey ("Shoulder your duds dear son"), to rely on self, continues into section 47: "The boy I love, the same becomes a man not through derived power, but in his own right." As the poet achieved his "supreme perception" through the contemplation of a spear of summer grass, so others may discover his meaning in observation of the most commonplace objects: "The nearest gnat is an explanation, and a drop or motion of the waves a key." In the latter part of section 47, the poet identifies both self and meaning with a series of familiar objects with which people are intimately associated: the poet and his "meaning" exist in the ax and jug that the woodman takes to his work and in the blanket that rubs the hunter's face when he sleeps at night. For each individual there lies near at hand the poet's meaning to decipher; in each individual lies the potentiality of discovering for himself the transcendent Reality.

As the vision began in section 6 with "guesses" about the significance of the grass in relation to self, God, life, and death, so the mystical experience draws to a close in sections 48 and 49 with observations on these same subjects, but now the poet speaks with the authority given him by his union with the Transcendent. Assured that he has "the best of time and space," he can speak with conviction on these great and eternal questions. Self is both body and soul, the one not more than the other, and "nothing, not God, is greater to one than one's self is." As the poet has discovered, it is only through the united self that God may be apprehended; self, then, cannot be abased or considered subordinate. The poet admonishes, "Let your soul stand cool and composed before a million universes. . . . Be not curious about God." With the proper perspective on the relation of self to infinity, one is not curious but is "at peace about God." No one can "understand" God, but one can see him "each hour of the twenty-four," "in the faces of men and women," in "letters . . . dropt in the street." God may be apprehended, "known," anywhere, any time, for he is in "limitless space" and in "limitless time."

Death, the "bitter hug of mortality," cannot "alarm" the poet: he marks the "outlet" and marks the "relief and escape." Death is not an end of the self, but an outlet for it into the Transcendent, a relief from life, an escape into permanent union with the Absolute. The corpse, the body deprived of the soul, becomes "good manure" and

has its eternity in the life it gives to the white roses and the melons
—and to succeeding generations. Thus life is the "leavings of many
deaths." This pantheistic belief is not necessarily in conflict with
the belief in God as the great Camerado. The eternity of the soul
exists in God, in the transcendent Reality, outside time and space;
the eternity of the body exists in life, in the material world, inside
time and space; the latter serves as a symbol (a letter "from God")
for the former. Such a reconciliation of the two points of view is
suggested in the "whispering" that the poet hears from the "stars of
heaven" and from "the grass of graves": "O perpetual transfers and
promotions." The whispering of the "grass of graves" gives insight
into the "perpetual" *transfer* of life from the dead to the living; the
whispering of the "stars of heaven" gives insight into the "perpetual"
promotion of souls to the Transcendent. Eternal life is granted to
both body and soul, both the material and the spiritual.

The mystical experience ends in a series of vivid images connota-
tive of death. The "turbid pool that lies in the autumn forest," reflecting the twilight moon, is surrounded by "black stems that decay
in the muck," and above all is heard the "moaning gibberish of the
dry limbs." But the poet perceives the illusion in this scene of desolation, decay, and death:

I ascend from the moon, I ascend from the night,
I perceive that the ghastly glimmer is noonday sunbeams reflected,
And debouch to the steady and central from the offspring great or small.

Paradoxical, but surely intentional, is the use of the scientific to symbolize the spiritual truth. The "ghastly glimmer" of the moon is but
"sunbeams reflected." The moon and night, suggestive of death, are
but the "offspring" of the "steady and central" sun. The figure is
apt: death is an "offspring" of God, a birth into the "steady and
central" transcendent Reality. The poet sees in death the ultimate
permanent union he has fleetingly achieved in his mystical experience.

VII. *Sections 50–52: Emergence from the Mystical State*

The lucidity with which the poet spoke during his mystical experience disappears when he emerges from the mystical state in
section 50:

There is that in me—I do not know what it is—but I know it is in me.

Wrench'd and sweaty—calm and cool then my body becomes,
I sleep—I sleep long.

I do not know it—it is without name—it is a word unsaid,
It is not in any dictionary, utterance, symbol.

Two aspects of the typical mystical experience are described. First, the physical condition of the poet, upon emergence from the mystic state, is one of exhaustion. There has been nervous excitement and tension that, when it releases the poet, leaves him "wrench'd and sweaty," and sleep is needed as a restorative. Second, it becomes extremely difficult for the poet, after the mystical state of consciousness has passed, to formulate its significance in words. The poet is portrayed as groping about for what is "without name," for the word that "is not in any dictionary." He can only hint at the significance of the knowledge his mystical experience has bestowed:

Something it swings on more than the earth I swing on,
To it the creation is the friend whose embracing awakes me.

"It" is not tied to the earth as is the poet; it is outside time and space. To it the creation of the universe is no greater miracle than the love of a friend for the poet.

But the desire to sum up the knowledge of the experience in an inadequate word is compulsive; the poet continues to grope:

Perhaps I might tell more. Outlines! I plead for my brothers and sisters.

Do you see O my brothers and sisters?
It is not chaos or death—it is form, union, plan—it is eternal life—it is Happiness.

The searching about for the precise word is almost frenzied; the motive is love, love for those "brothers and sisters" intuitively discovered after entry into the mystical state in section 5 ("And that all the men ever born are also my brothers, and the women my sisters and lovers"). Outside space, outside time, from the point of view of the Transcendent, life is not "chaos or death"; there are "form, union, plan" and there is "eternal life." And the key to human existence is not rejection, not the "beginning" and "end" of the talkers, or the division of the best from the worst but simply—"Happiness." As "form, union, plan" refer to the not-self, so "Happiness" points to the self and indicates the proper or ideal relationship of man to the universe.

Happiness is the ultimate state of that self assured that "chaos and death" are illusion, that "form, union, plan" and "eternal life" are reality. Such a self, firmly rooted in supreme faith, may indeed sing. Each individual may, like the poet, go forth on his journey singing the "Song of Myself." As Whitman's dramatization of the entry into the mystical state is inverted, so also is the hint at the meaning of self and existence grasped from the quickly receding mystical consciousness. At some stage in the traditional mystical experience, "the human instinct for personal happiness must be killed."[22] Whitman has used the mystical experience as a framework within which to deny some of its basic traditions. The form of the experience is adhered to, but its substance is transfigured.

The last two sections of "Song of Myself" show the poet, the agony and the ecstasy of the mystical experience now behind him, pleading for a response from the reader. There is, as the poet holds back the evening ("snuff[s] the sidle"), an acute sense of urgency in the plea: "Will you speak before I am gone? will you prove already too late?" The emotional tone suggests here and elsewhere the religious fervor of the will to convert: the poet urgently feels the need for acceptance of his startling new insight; when he exclaims

> Do I contradict myself?
> Very well then I contradict myself,
> (I am large, I contain multitudes.)

he is asserting the importance of reliance on self that is, in reality, obedience to the Transcendent in self. Consistency in transient ideas is irrelevant; consistency in faith to self is supreme.

The last section of the poem introduces a series of images of swift movement and departure. The poet is like the spotted hawk, swooping over the roof tops sounding his "barbaric yawp," or he is like a meteor, shaking his "white locks at the runaway sun." Each of these images has connotations which relate to the mystical experience from which the poet has just emerged: the yawp of the hawk is "barbaric," like the "Nature" which has been permitted to

22. *Ibid.*, p. 206.

speak "without check with original energy"; the meteor, i
ing, effusing, drifting, suggests the intensity, in both
height, of the experience, as well as its defiant exulta¹
Like the hawk, the poet is "untranslatable," incomprehensible except in his own language, upon his own terms. When he bequeaths
himself "to the dirt to grow from the grass" he loves, and confides
to the reader, "If you want me again look for me under your boot-
soles," he returns to the central symbol of the poem, the grass, the
contemplation of which at the opening of the poem launched him
on his journey into the Unknown. More important than the pantheism on the surface of the line is the suggestion that every man has
easily within his grasp, his for the taking, the means for his own
mystical journey. The poet is under the "boot-soles" only in the
sense that the clue to what he has hinted at is there for each man
to discover for himself. The poet is one with the riddle whose un-
raveling each man, each self, must undertake on his own.

CHAPTER TWO

Informing Myth
in "Children of Adam"

"Children of Adam" was originally called "Enfans d'Adam" upon its first appearance in *Leaves of Grass* in 1860. Three of the poems had appeared in earlier editions: "I Sing the Body Electric" in 1855, untitled; "A Woman Waits for Me" in 1856, entitled "Poem of Procreation"; and "Spontaneous Me" in 1856, entitled "Bunch Poem." Two poems that appeared in *Drum-Taps* in 1865 were later transferred to "Children of Adam": "Out of the Rolling Ocean the Crowd" and "I Heard You Solemn-Sweet Pipes of the Organ." After the first appearance in the 1860 edition, "Children of Adam" did not pass through any major revisions. The structure of the 1860 version is essentially that of the poet's final edition.

The sixteen poems of the "Children of Adam" section of *Leaves of Grass* are bound together and "ordered," not by the logical development of a philosophical position, but by the myth, or allegory, introduced in the title. The first, eighth, and last of the sixteen poems are given over entirely to this myth, and it permeates and gives heightened significance to all the other poems. One of Whitman's manuscript notes, which appears to be jottings in preparation for the composition of the "Children of Adam" poems, confirms the central relevance of the myth in Whitman's conception of the section:

Theory of a Cluster of Poems the same *to the passion of Woman-love* as the *Calamus-Leaves* are to adhesiveness, manly love.
Full of animal-fire, tender, burning,—the tremulous ache, delicious, yet such a torment.
The swelling elate and vehement, that will not be denied.
Adam, as a central figure and type [IX, 150].[1]

1. Whitman quotations are where possible identified in the text by volume and page number of *The Complete Writings of Walt Whitman,* ed. Richard M. Bucke *et al.* (New York: G. P. Putnam's Sons, 1902).

This note suggests that Adam was to be the "central figure" in the entire section, even in those poems in which the Garden of Eden myth is not explicitly dramatized.[2]

But if the myth "informs" "Children of Adam," it is in turn reinterpreted and given new meaning in the process. The difficulty of the task that Whitman assumes may be realized when one notes that he does not rely on the ready responses to the Garden of Eden allegory. The story of Adam's fall has given Christian civilization its concept of the innate nature of man as evil: Adam through his disobedience degraded his original innocence and brought death into the world. Conceived in sin and born of flesh, each man must be born of the spirit anew to regain the paradise Adam lost for mankind. Whitman inverts this long-accepted and deeply imbedded interpretation: not Adam but his descendants ("children") have lost the garden through self-degradation of their innately innocent natures; to regain paradise, man must purge not the physical but the sense of the physical as sinful; he must be born again not through spiritual denial of the flesh but through spiritual transfiguration of the flesh. It is not man's shame but his glory that he is a child of Adam; and he must not suppress, but frankly acknowledge and accept, the Adamic in his nature.

In the opening poem of the section, the myth is ironically invoked:

> To the garden the world anew ascending,
> Potent mates, daughters, sons, preluding,
> The love, the life of their bodies, meaning and being,
> Curious here behold my resurrection after slumber.[3]

The world is ascending to the garden "anew," and associated with this return is the very element that, in inherited belief, has made it impossible for men to regain their lost paradise: the "life of their bodies." It is love, says the poet, that gives meaning to life, and it is the "life of their bodies" that gives men being, or existence: only

2. For a brilliant account of the importance of the Adam myth to American thought and American letters, see R. W. B. Lewis, *The American Adam* (Chicago: University of Chicago Press, 1955).

3. The quotations from *Leaves of Grass* may be easily located by poem title in any edition. All quotations have been checked with the text in the 1902 *Complete Writings*.

mates who are "potent" can "prelude" sons and daughters. Life to
the awakened Adam has a strange and singular beauty:

> Amorous, mature, all beautiful to me, all wondrous,
> My limbs and the quivering fire that ever plays through them,
>   for reasons, most wondrous,
> Existing I peer and penetrate still,
> Content with the present, content with the past,
> By my side or back of me Eve following,
> Or in front, and I following her just the same.

This Adam is "content" with past and present: he does not bemoan
his fall nor does he seek in the future but finds in the present his
paradise. He peers and penetrates "still" in all his original innocence. These are the Adam and Eve who looked upon each other's
nakedness and were unashamed; theirs is the innocence their "children" have lost.

The time image in the opening poem ("The revolving cycles in
their wide sweep having brought me again") is reintroduced in the
next poem developing the central myth (the eighth in sequence):

> Ages and ages returning at intervals,
> Undestroy'd, wandering immortal,
> Lusty, phallic, with the potent original loins, perfectly sweet,
> I, chanter of Adamic songs,
> Through the new garden the West, the great cities calling,
> Deleriate, thus prelude what is generated, offering these,
>   offering myself,
> Bathing myself, bathing my songs in sex,
> Offspring of my loins.

Whereas the first poem is a dramatic monologue, the speaker specifically identified as Adam, in "Ages and Ages" the "I" has become
the poet merged with Adam. The "revolving cycles in their wide
sweep" have become the recurring ages. And again it is implied that
Adam did not die: "Undestroy'd, wandering immortal." It is, of
course, the potentiality in man to achieve the innocence of Adam in
the garden that has not died; this potentiality has been realized at
intervals since Adam, perhaps in primitive societies, perhaps in individual men. In any case it has never completely disappeared. And
now, in the poet chanting his Adamic songs, the lusty, phallic songs
of "Children of Adam," the potentiality has again become realized.

The garden to which the world is ascending in the first poem becomes "the new garden the West, the great cities calling." The gar-

den is not a specific place, or even a place of a particular kind, but rather a state of mind. One of the rejected poems, which appeared in the 1860 edition just before "Ages and Ages" and which is concerned explicitly with the central myth, throws some light on the poet's concept of the "new garden":

In the new garden, in all the parts,
In cities now, modern, I wander,
Though the second or third result, or still further, primitive yet,
Days, places, indifferent—though various, the same,
Time, paradise, the Mannahatta, the prairies, finding me unchanged,
Death indifferent—is it that I lived long since? Was I buried very long ago?
For all that, I may now be watching you here, this moment;
For the future, with determined will, I seek—the woman of the future,
You, born years, centuries after me, I seek [III, 296].

The paradox of the garden becoming the "great cities" is surely intended. But there is also the implication of the importance of the role of the West in creating this new garden. Perhaps man's coming to terms with the frontier in the West, his brief return to the primitive state before the creation of the great cities, has enabled him to rediscover within himself an innocence long suppressed.

The poet become Adam is "deliriate," and "prelude[s] what is generated, offering these, offering myself." "Deliriate" implies unashamed acceptance of the mysterious, even religious, ecstasy of the sex impulse. But the poet does not generate; in his frank songs he merely preludes "what is generated," what has its own life, latent or virile, in every man. The Adamic poet offers his songs, offers even himself. The offering of self may have several senses: as the poems figuratively embody the poet, they are an offering of self; but there is also the implication of the offering of self freely in sexual union—the offer of the Adamic man to his Eve; and there is also the suggestion of sacrifice, the poet willing to accept the censure of the very society whose paradisiacal innocence he wishes to restore. There is implicit irony in the bathing metaphor that concludes "Ages and Ages." Bathing is associated with cleansing and even with the sacrament of baptism. But the poet's bathing is done in sex, the very element which necessitates, in the Christian tradition, a rebirth through baptism. The implication in "Ages and Ages" is that genuine baptism is in sex: both the Adamic poet and his songs are bathed in sex, are immersed and cleansed in sex. Sex thus becomes, in this metaphor, a sanctified and purifying element through which man regains his lost innocence.

In the last poem in "Children of Adam" there is a return to the central myth:

> As Adam early in the morning,
> Walking forth from the bower refresh'd with sleep,
> Behold me where I pass, hear my voice, approach,
> Touch me, touch the palm of your hand to my body as I pass,
> Be not afraid of my body.

The dramatic situation in this poem will recall the "resurrection after slumber" of the opening poem. But there the awakening occurred after the wide sweep of "revolving cycles"; here the awakening is after a night of sleep. There has been a complex progression in these three "myth" poems from Adam in the first, to the poet merged with Adam in the second, to, in the third, the poet who is simply "as Adam." Thus the poet concludes by identifying with himself Adam's shameless, even spiritual, acceptance of sexuality. But this last poem is to be taken more than literally. The night is ended; this poem represents the conclusion to "Children of Adam." One need but recall a line of "From Pent-up Aching Rivers"—"From the night a moment I emerging flitting out"—to associate the night from which the poet is awakening refreshed with the spiritual night he has illuminated, like a meteor, with his songs. The poet commands the reader to "Behold . . . hear . . . approach . . . touch." Beneath the bold invitation of the literal meaning lies the earnest plea for understanding and acceptance. Whitman says elsewhere in *Leaves of Grass:*

> Camerado, this is no book,
> Who touches this touches a man [II, 289].

The same figure is suggested in "touch the palm of your hand to my body as I pass." If *Leaves of Grass* is the whole man, "Children of Adam" is the man unclothed, unashamed in his nakedness.

Central to the poet's reinterpretation of the Eden myth is his inversion of the traditional concept of rebirth, touched upon in "Ages and Ages," but developed explicitly in the longest and probably the best of the "Children of Adam" poems, "I Sing the Body Electric":

Bridegroom night of love working surely and softly into the prostrate
  dawn,
Undulating into the willing and yielding day,
Lost in the cleave of the clasping and sweet-flesh'd day.
This the nucleus—after the child is born of woman, man is born of woman,
This the bath of birth, this the merge of small and large, and the outlet
  again.

The analogy between the sacrament of baptism and the "bath" of
sex, the "mystic deliria," is drawn in the midst of the delicate imagery of the sexual union of "bridegroom night of love" and "willing and yielding day," suggesting the rhythmic naturalness and
universal innocence of sexual fulfilment. Paradoxically, it is through
the sex experience, not by suppression of it, that man is reborn
("after the child is born of woman, man is born of woman"), that
he is to find his way back to the lost state of innocence of the
Garden of Eden. The "merge of the small and large" suggests the
identity of the experience of the child and man, both born of
woman; but more importantly it suggests the traditional mystical
experience: the "bath of birth," or rebirth, merges man with the
Transcendent. The first birth, the birth of the child, is an outlet into
life but an imprisonment in self; the rebirth through sex is the "outlet again"—the outlet from self to the greater-than-self. The function
of woman is no mean one: "Be not ashamed women, your privilege
encloses the rest, and is the exit of the rest." Through woman, the
child receives his body at birth; and through woman, the man realizes his soul in rebirth. One is reminded of the mystical function
of woman in the Christian tradition: the Virgin Mary, mother of
Christ, or the Beatrice of Dante, or the "lady of silences" of T. S.
Eliot.

The extent to which the Garden of Eden myth permeates and
informs "Children of Adam" can best be shown by close examination
of the poems, with particular attention to the central Adamic character. Although the "I" does not remain constant, as it never does
in *Leaves of Grass*, the association of the "I" with Adam, or the
Adamic man or poet, is never absent in any of the poems. Any
single poem, wrenched from context, dissociated from the informing
myth, loses importantly in meaning, if it does not become entirely
unintelligible. But the poems in "Children of Adam" are not merely
placed together; they are also placed in a significant order. We have

already noted a progression in the three poems given over entirely
to the central myth. There is progression also in the remaining
poems: a dramatic transition in the emotional state of the speaker,
from elation, to despair and defiance, to calm confidence.

This speaker reveals himself in "From Pent-up Aching Rivers"
as the Adamic poet setting forth to celebrate the divinity of sex:
"From time the programme hastening, (I have loiter'd too long as
it is)." The remaining poems are an attempt to fulfil this program,
to explore the "warp and woof" of sex in all its mystical complexity. "From Pent-up Aching Rivers" symphonically interweaves
the abundant and varied imagery by means of which the poet will
celebrate the "act divine," the "children prepared for," and the
"stalwart loins" in the poems to follow. The poem functions to set
forth the program in brief, leaving for later poems the task of full
development of individual themes. "From Pent-up Aching Rivers"
appears to be frenzied chaos unless read as the introductory fore-
runner and the emotional "outline" of the remaining poems.

"I Sing the Body Electric" dominates the entire section as it also
establishes a basic premise implicit in all the following poems: the
body is fundamental to the "mystic deliria," the central fact in the
Adamic poet's program. But, as the title of the poem indicates, the
poet celebrates the body *electric*, not the body alone, in isolation:

I sing the body electric,
The armies of those I love engirth me and I engirth them,
They will not let me off till I go with them, respond to them
And discorrupt them, and charge them full with the charge of the soul.
Was it doubted that those who corrupt their own bodies conceal them-
     selves?
And if those who defile the living are as bad as they who defile the dead?
And if the body does not do fully as much as the soul?
And if the body were not the soul, what is the soul?

The "electricity" is nothing less than the spiritual life of the body,
the soul. Those who have purged their bodies of the instinct of life
are like batteries gone lifeless. They must be "discorrupted," charged
full again with the "charge of the soul." This is the task the Adamic
poet assumes. And it is made all the more difficult because those
who corrupt their bodies do so in the name of their souls, unaware
that the soul takes its origin solely from the body, that the soul
and the body are inseparably one.

An acute awareness of the confusion which must be confronted gives "I Sing the Body Electric" its emotional coloring. The poet as Adam must *convince* the ignorant and the skeptical of the divinity of the body. He must affirm, he must shock, he must rhapsodize; and he must do all these for a subject which is at once infinitely difficult, yet absurdly simple:

> The love of the body of man or woman balks account, the body itself
> balks account,
> That of the male is perfect, and that of the female is perfect.

In the series of brief but vivid vignettes of people in various simple activities—the child at the mother's breast, the swimmers swimming naked, the apprentice boys wrestling, the firemen marching—the "I" becomes the Adamic spirit, always present when man engages in innocent physical action unself-consciously, without shame.

Following these brief glimpses is a longer picture of the "beautiful and vigorous" eighty-year-old farmer who is the father of five sons: "You would wish long and long to be with him, you would wish to sit by him in the boat that you and he might touch each other." The farmer represents primitive or Adamic man whose life of the body has been fulfilled—is, indeed, still being fulfilled. He is a man who has not corrupted his body, who is, even in old age, charged full with the "charge of the soul." That so long a portrait is drawn of a man of such advanced age is sufficient evidence that the poet's motive is more profound and his intent more serious than mere indulgence in a cult of youth. That the portrait of the old man was intended by Whitman to serve this purpose is borne out by his notebook jottings in preparation for the writing of "Children of Adam": "One piece presenting a vivid picture (in connection with the spirit) of a fully complete, well-developed, man, eld, bearded, swart, fiery,—as a more than rival of the youthful type-hero of novels and love poems" (IX, 150).

Physical nearness itself is a kind of fulfilment: "I have perceiv'd that to be with those I like is enough." The body "electric" is not the merely sensual body. It is the "beautiful, curious, breathing, laughing flesh"—the body that is primitive, natural, and innocent in its unawareness of corruption: "There is something in staying close to men and women and looking on them, and in the contact and odor of them, that pleases the soul well." This "something" is the Adamic spirit in all its complex simplicity. The casual contact, the mere bodily presence of another, "pleases the soul well." Thus a physical basis is given for man's spiritual craving for companionship. The physical is the foundation of the spiritual—from the pleasure of the body comes the pleasure of the soul.

The remainder of "I Sing the Body Electric" is given over to the ideal Adamic woman (section 5), the ideal Adamic man (section 6), society's corruption of a man's body at auction (section 7), its corruption of a woman's body at auction (section 8), and the final ecstatic catalogue of the body (section 9). There is some significance in the predominance of scientific imagery throughout the poem. For example, the female form "attracts with fierce undeniable attraction" and "mad filaments, ungovernable shoots play out of it." This imagery from electricity is paralleled by imagery from astronomy or physics in the section of the poem devoted to the male form:

Do you think matter has cohered together from its diffuse float, and the soil is on the surface, and water runs and vegetation sprouts,
For you only, and not for him and her?

Implicit in this fusion of scientific imagery, used to celebrate the body, and the Garden of Eden myth, used to present an ideal of the life of the body, is the suggestion that the primitive ideal may be realized in a complex, scientific society. The ideal is a matter of mind, of internal attitude, not a matter of place, of outward circumstance. The lost garden may be found in the "great cities" of the West.

The last section of the poem, presenting the exhaustive catalogue of the body, has frequently been cited as an example of failure in technique, perhaps even a grotesque caricature of the usually effective Whitman catalogue. It must be admitted that the modern reader is likely to be reminded of the endless "thigh bone connected to the hip bone" chant; but it must also be admitted that there is dramatic value in the minuteness of the detail. The body, the whole body, the body in all its parts, is to be celebrated, and not one part to the exclusion of the others. The well-balanced Adamic man accepts all, but he accepts more than the physical details: "O I say these are not the parts and poems of the body only, but of the soul." At the end of the poem, man is not left atomized but is gathered together again into a whole that is the soul.

This conclusion to the poem brings into sharp focus the concept of the body that has been insisted upon throughout: that the physical gives origin to the spiritual, that corruption of the body is in reality corruption of the soul. This concept is the essence of the meaning of the reinterpreted Adam myth. But, as noted before, it is the keen awareness of the society's rejection of this meaning that has given the poem its emotional tone. The Adamic poet alternately attempts to shock and convince or perhaps do both in such a delicately phrased line as "Ebb stung by the flow and flow stung by the ebb, love-flesh swelling and deliciously aching." In "I Sing the Body Electric" the Adamic poet, carried away by his own bright vision, has convinced himself that his ecstatic eulogy of the body will hasten, perhaps precipitate, his program; such confidence and self-assurance do not exist in all the later poems.

In "A Woman Waits for Me," the "I" is no longer the Adamic poet setting forth a program but rather the Adam in mankind, a representative Adamic man:

A woman waits for me, she contains all, nothing is lacking,
Yet all were lacking if sex were lacking, or if the moisture of the right man were lacking.

The woman who waits, containing all, is surely Eve, as, in the myth, in a literal sense, she contained all of us, her descendants. This conceit of sex containing the immortality of the race is developed throughout the poem. But the singular woman soon becomes the "warm-blooded and sufficient" women, and the image of Eve merges with womankind. The vision in the poem becomes a realization of the society urged in "I Sing the Body Electric," a society in which the body is accepted and celebrated without shame.

The basic idea on which the poem is constructed is contained in the ambiguity of the phrase "Sex contains all." In the romantic sense there is the commonplace meaning that fulfilment of sexual desire is the epitome of man's experience, that the entire meaning of life may be compressed within the one intense moment of sexual fulfilment. But, more literally, sex does contain all. It is only through sex that the procession of life continues. In the last stanza of the poem, the Adamic man addresses woman:

Through you I drain the pent-up rivers of myself,
In you I wrap a thousand onward years,
On you I graft the grafts of the best-beloved of me and America,
The drops I distil upon you shall grow fierce and athletic girls, new artists,
    musicians, and singers.
I shall count on the fruits of the gushing, showers of them, as I count on
    the fruits of the gushing showers I give now,
I shall look for loving crops from the birth, life, death, immortality, I
    plant so lovingly now.

The plant and river imagery, fused with the sexual, dramatically
portrays the vital function of sex. The "pent-up river" is the eternity
contained in man's sexual potential. But it is only a potential as
long as it is "pent-up"; used to nourish and make fertile the plant
(woman), the river becomes time itself—a "thousand onward years."
Not birth alone but "birth, life, death, immortality" are to result
from the "gushing showers." In this conceit, sex does indeed contain
all. The "pent-up rivers" are rivers of time flowing from the past,
from Adam, into the present, the Children of Adam, and, if they
do not remain pent up, into the future, into eternity.

"Spontaneous Me" introduces a new technique embodying a new
subject. The "I" in the poem, however, still takes its identity from
the central myth: "The oath of procreation I have sworn, my Adamic
and fresh daughters." The "I" is, again, Adamic man, not in a specific dramatic situation, as in "A Woman Waits for Me," but adrift,
"spontaneous." As the ideas in the poem are "natural" and unre-
strained, so the images are "beautiful dripping fragments, the negli-
gent list of one after another as I happen to call them to me or think
of them," and the finished poem is a "bunch," perhaps like a cluster
of grapes:

And this bunch pluck'd at random from myself,
It has done its work—I toss it carelessly to fall where it may.

In short, the fragments, the list, and the bunch are all one—the
randomly collected thoughts and images of a natural, "spontaneous,"
Adamic man who allows free rein to his uninhibited mind. The
technique is to convey the impression of the stream of consciousness
flowing on without obstruction.

The literary metaphor introduced in "From Pent-up Aching
Rivers" ("From the act-poems of eyes, hands, hips and bosoms")
and extended in "I Sing the Body Electric" ("I believe the likes of
you [the body] shall stand or fall with my poems, and that they are

my poems") reaches a climax in its development in "Spontaneous Me":

The real poems, (what we call poems being merely pictures,)
The poems of the privacy of the night, and of men like me,
This poem drooping shy and unseen that I always carry, and that all men carry,
(Know once for all, avow'd on purpose, wherever are men like me, are our lusty lurking masculine poems.)

"Men like me" are, of course, Adamic men to whom the phallus has all the spiritual attributes of the poetic. As genuine poetry "indicates the path" between reality and the soul, so the sexual offers the means to experience the spiritual.

"Spontaneous Me" abounds in rich images of nature: "The wet of woods through the early hours"; "The dead leaf whirling its spiral whirl and falling still and content to the ground"; "The walnut-trunk, the walnut-husks, and the ripening or ripen'd long-round walnuts." These vivid images, through subtle interaction in context, take on manifold and complex meanings. The Adamic man, filled with his "pent-up aching rivers," has a sexual vision of the natural world, a vision in which all objects assume an intense and significant coloring projected from his own emotional state. Such images as "The smell of apples, aromas from crush'd sage-plant, mint, birch-bark," suggest the emotional re-creation of a garden—that garden which existed before the fall.

The passionate outcry in "One Hour to Madness and Joy" betrays an intense desire for the garden: "O to return to Paradise!" "To ascend, to leap to the heavens of the love indicated to me!" recalls the opening poem: "To the garden the world anew ascending." But the emotional complexion of this poem differs considerably from the tone of the two previous, in which the garden seemed an achieved reality. When the poet cries, "O confine me not!" and speaks of "defiance of the world," he seems to be in a hostile society, a world in which the Adamic poet's program has been a failure:

O the puzzle, the thrice-tied knot, the deep and dark pool, all untied and illumin'd!
O to speed where there is space enough and air enough at last!
To be absolved from previous ties and conventions, I from mine and you from yours!

The "thrice-tied knot" is the stifling suppression, through "previous ties and conventions," of the body by the man, by the woman, and by society. Underneath the knot, when it is untied, lies the "deep and dark pool," the pool formed by the "aching river" when it is "pent-up."

The frenzied abandonment expressed in this poem is not mere sexual desire gone wild but an attempt to hint at the spiritual significance of the fulfilled experience: "O to drink the mystic deliria deeper than any other man!" Through the religious or mystical nature of the experience, one returns to paradise or leaps to the heavens:

> To rise thither with my inebriate soul!
> To be lost if it must be so!

In this extension of the drinking metaphor (from "O to drink") it is the soul that is inebriated. The physical experience is desired as a means of entry into the spiritual life. "To be lost if it must be so!" suggests that such abandonment as desired, the cutting of "previous ties and conventions," will result in loss of position or respectability in society; but, more significantly, the line recalls the "merge of small and large" of "I Sing the Body Electric": the individual is to be lost in the transcendent, the greater-than-self.

"Out of the Rolling Ocean the Crowd,"[4] with its abrupt change in emotional tone, may be considered as the converse of the preceding poem, or perhaps as its resolution. In "Out of the Rolling Ocean the Crowd" there is resignation to separation and an affirmation in loss. Association of the society of "ties and conventions" of "One Hour to Madness and Joy" with the "rolling ocean the crowd" is inevitable and surely intended. The Adamic woman has separated herself as a drop from the ocean "to look on you to touch you." And the Adamic man replies:

> Now we have met, we have look'd, we are safe,
> Return in peace to the ocean my love,
> I too am part of that ocean my love, we are not so
>   much separated.

There is an acceptance of the "thrice-tied knot" that is defied in "One Hour to Madness and Joy," a resignation to the "irresistible sea." Such resignation is prepared for in "I Sing the Body Electric," where an identical metaphor, the sea, is used: "I do not ask any

4. An interesting biographical interpretation of this poem is found in Emory Holloway, *Whitman: An Interpretation in Narrative* (New York: Alfred A. Knopf, 1926), pp. 232–33.

more delight [than 'to pass among them or touch any one'], I swim in it as in a sea." The resignation, however, is not to loss but to spiritual union after death: the ocean functions on three levels, as an actual sea, as a crowd, and as a universal soul that unites all in life as well as after life. The "irresistible sea" will not separate the two "diverse forever."

"We Two, How Long We Were Fool'd," which follows the "myth" poem "Ages and Ages," is remarkable for its accumulation of nature imagery—plants, fishes, birds, beasts, and celestial bodies—all connoting the ideal relationship of the natural or Adamic man and woman. The images fuse to suggest the many-sidedness of such a relationship: its quiet satisfaction in nearness (in the two oaks growing side by side), its fierceness of feeling (in the two predatory hawks and the "fang'd and four footed" beasts), its harmony and mutuality (in two "resplendent suns"), and its ecstatic union (in the "seas mingling"). But the poem is not a paean sung to wild lawlessness. In the context of the informing myth, the two who have been fooled so long become Adam and Eve, or modern man and woman who have rediscovered the Adamic spirit: "We are Nature, long have we been absent, but now we return." The return is, of course, a return to nature, but implied also is the return to paradise. When the poet says, near the end of the poem, "We have circled and circled till we have arrived home again, we two," the "circled and circled" suggests the hawks or the celestial bodies of the previous lines, but, more importantly, it recalls the "revolving cycles" of the immediately preceding poem ("Ages and Ages"). Such an association seems clearly intended; the home arrived at is the long-lost garden, and the two who have returned are the new Adam and Eve of the modern world.

After the fierce wildness of "We Two, How Long We Were Fool'd," two brief poems form a welcome interlude of relatively calm reflection. "O Hymen! O Hymenee!" is a query about the briefness of the "sting," with the suggested answer in "Is it because if you continued beyond the swift moment you would soon certainly kill me?" In context, the reply indicates that the merge of the "mystic deliria," if continued, would become permanent union with the Transcendent—death. "I Am He That Aches with Love" briefly extends the scientific imagery developed in "I Sing the Body Electric." As man can learn from nature, he can also gain insight into self through modern science: "Does the earth gravitate? does not all matter, aching, attract all matter?"

"Native Moments" reintroduces the emotional tone of "One Hour to Madness and Joy," with its resentment of the "previous ties and conventions" and the "thrice-tied knot." The Adamic poet who pleaded for unashamed acceptance of the body in "I Sing the Body Electric" comes to realize in "Native Moments" that his program is, at least for the present, rejected, that there has been no return to the garden. He therefore realistically accepts society's own mistaken terms, "life coarse and rank," "midnight orgies of young men," and places himself at the side of society's outcasts:

> O you shunn'd persons, I at least do not shun you,
> I come forth within your midst, I will be your poet,
> I will be more to you than any of the rest.

The Adamic poet does not declare in favor of lawlessness for its own sake; he merely rejects society's deluded conventions and declares for natural or Adam's law. As "Spontaneous Me" portrayed the free play of the mind and emotions of a natural or spontaneous Adamic man, "Native Moments" portrays such a man in the context of a hostile society, forced to choose between conformity to false social convention and conformity to the Adamic self. Choosing the latter, the spontaneous man naturally finds himself in conflict with society, consorting with society's outcasts but "Nature's darlings."

"Once I Pass'd through a Populous City"[5] and "I Heard You Solemn-Sweet Pipes of the Organ" are two poignantly drawn vignettes, dramatizing still different facets of the Adamic passion. Perhaps the "populous city" of the first is one of the "great cities calling," the "new garden the West," of "Ages and Ages Returning at Intervals." The "shows, architecture, customs, traditions" of the populous city fade into insignificance alongside the memory of the passionate, clinging woman. The fulfilment of experience not in nature but in a populous city again emphasizes that the garden is a matter not of place but of relationships of human beings. Cities are great because of the Adamic character of such relationships, not because of material or outward show. In "I Heard You Solemn-

5. See Emory Holloway (ed.), *The Uncollected Poetry and Prose of Walt Whitman* (Garden City, N.Y.: Doubleday, Page & Co., 1921), II, 102, for the original version of the poem addressed to a man. Although Holloway's discovery may be biographically revealing, the poem has the "meaning," surely, of its final version and derives further meaning from its context in *Leaves of Grass*.

Sweet Pipes of the Organ" there is a delicate association of music
with the pulse-beat of love, a transfiguration of the sensual into the
spiritual. The range of the music, from the "solemn-sweet pipes of
the organ," through the "winds of autumn," the tenor and soprano,
concluding with the delicate "still ringing little bells," suggests the
range in depth of feeling in human passion.

In "Facing West from California's Shores," the "I" is Adam, "a
child, very old," who faces west from California, toward the "house
of maternity," and meditates upon his long, "inquiring, tireless"
search for "what is yet unfound." The note of pessimism heard
clearly in "One Hour to Madness and Joy" and become defiant in
"Native Moments" is present but subdued:

> Now I face home again, very pleas'd and joyous,
> (But where is what I started for so long ago?
> And why is it yet unfound?)

The pleasure and the joy are in the progress of mankind in material
achievement, "the circle almost circled." The quiet but pervading
disappointment is for the lack of a parallel spiritual fulfilment, fulfilment of the "mystic deliria." The place "started for so long ago"
which remains unfound is the garden, Adam's "home," the "house
of maternity." The "new garden the West" remains but a promise,
a poet's dream. But the final question posed ("And why is it yet
unfound?") implies the eternal yearning for and determination to
find the long-lost paradise. "As Adam Early in the Morning," concluding the section, suggests the poet's continuation of the search
for modern man's Garden of Eden.

The interrelationship of the poems in "Children of Adam" is
subtle and complex. The alternating depths and heights of the emotional state of the central character, the "I," give dramatic significance to the order of the poems; and the recurring Garden of Eden
myth, of which the form is maintained but the substance transfigured, informs the entire section. The poet's intention, admirably
realized, was that the myth pervade those poems in which it was
not explicitly treated. It seems self-evident, in view of the function
of the myth, that criticism of the detached and isolated poem is
deprived of relevant data necessary for a valid interpretation or
judgment. "Children of Adam" has an integrity of form that cannot
be violated without sacrifice of much of its richly complex meaning.

CHAPTER THREE

"Calamus": The
Leaf and the Root

No section in *Leaves of Grass* has received so much close attention and been the center of so much discussion and controversy as "Calamus." Friends of Whitman, particularly the "hot little prophet[s],"[1] have indignantly defended the section against the charge of "indecency," usually by raising the opposite cry, "purity," and by citing Whitman's own saintlike, spiritual life as proof that the poems could not be unwholesome. William Sloane Kennedy calls "Calamus" "Whitman's beautiful democratic poems of friendship" and adds, "A genuine lover speaks in the Calamus pieces: a great and generous heart there pours forth its secret. Set side by side with these glowing confessions, other writings on friendship seem frigid and calculating."[2] At the opposite extreme is Mark Van Doren's recent judgment, which has been widely influential: "His [Whitman's] democratic dogmas—of what validity are they when we consider that they base themselves upon the sentiment of 'manly love,' and that manly love is neither more nor less than an abnormal and deficient love?"[3] To the serious reader of "Calamus," the "manly love" that recurs both as a term and as an idea is of such genuine poetic complexity as to render it a good deal more than "abnormal" and considerably less than "deficient."

It is indeed strange that the very element in Whitman's poetry that gained him nineteenth-century praise for his "purity" should

1. Bliss Perry, *Walt Whitman: His Life and Work* (Boston: Houghton Mifflin Co., 1906), p. 286.

2. *Reminiscences of Walt Whitman* (London: Alexander Gardner, 1896), pp. 133–34.

3. "Walt Whitman, Stranger," in his *The Private Reader* (New York: Henry Holt & Co., 1942), p. 82.

bring him twentieth-century condemnation for his "immorality." It is worthwhile examining "Calamus" in detail in order to test the validity of the prevailing belief that in it Whitman gave stammering utterance to a doctrine whose implications he did not fully comprehend. I would first like to glance briefly at data external to the poems that might shed light on their meaning; next I would like to search through Whitman's revisions of the poems; then I shall turn attention to the major themes in "Calamus"; and finally I shall explore Whitman's poetic technique, particularly the recurring leaf-root metaphor, for any illumination it might afford in interpretation.

I. *External Evidence*

Needless to say, the external evidence, evidence outside the "Calamus" poems themselves, has been sifted and resifted, and Whitman's life has been examined exhaustively in a series of studies, sympathetic and unsympathetic, for the clue, for the conclusive evidence, that will unveil the mystery of "Calamus." The search was begun in Whitman's lifetime by one of the most persistent students, John Addington Symonds. Horace Traubel's *With Walt Whitman in Camden* contains many fascinating accounts of Symonds' deep probing and Whitman's varied and puzzling reactions. At one time Symonds wrote: "What the love of man for man has been in the Past I think I know. What it is here now, I know also—alas! What you say it can and shall be I dimly discern in your Poems. But this hardly satisfies me—so desirous am I of learning what you teach."[4] That Whitman understood Symonds is revealed in the poet's complaints to Traubel that Symonds was "always driving at me about that"; "What does Calamus mean? What do the poems come to in the round-up? That is worrying him a good deal—their involvement, as he suspects, is the passional relations of men with men—the thing he reads so much of in the literature of southern Europe and sees something of in his own experience."[5] But more revealing than the letter of denial to Symonds ("That the Calamus part has even allowed the possibility of such construction as mentioned is terrible") and the notorious claim of parenthood ("Though unmarried,

4. *With Walt Whitman in Camden* (*March 28–July 14, 1888*) (Boston: Small, Maynard & Co., 1906), I, 75.

5. *Ibid.*, p. 73.

I have had six children")[6] is the admission to Traubel of uncertainty of intent: "I often say to myself about Calamus—perhaps it means more or less than I thought myself—means different: perhaps I don't know what it all means—perhaps never did know. My first instinct about all that Symonds writes is violently reactionary—is strong and brutal for no, no, no. Then the thought intervenes that I maybe do not know all my own meanings: I say to myself: 'You, too, go away, come back, study your own book—an alien or stranger, study your own book, see what it amounts to.' "[7]

The figure of Walt Whitman as alien to his own book is not so strange in an age of criticism that frequently asserts that the poet includes in his poems more than he knows, or in an age of Freud that is continually revealing that the artist exposes his inner being more than he intends. Did Whitman know his own meanings in "Calamus"? The question cannot, probably, be finally answered. But the problem as to what Whitman meant "Calamus" to mean can surely be solved. Abundant evidence as to the intended meaning of "Calamus" exists in Whitman's prose works, and, though not conclusive, as external data never is, such evidence is highly revealing and surely relevant. All the more valuable is this evidence in the case of "Calamus," in which intentional ambiguity—ambiguity used consciously as a poetic device—abounds, resulting in a language always something more or something less than appears on the surface. Wherever such ambiguity exists, a poet may always be quoted against himself.

It is surely significant that in his greatest prose piece, *Democratic Vistas*, Whitman does not silently pass over the "Calamus" emotion but rather dwells at length on it as central to the realization of his ideal democratic state. Of primary importance in understanding the distinctions Whitman would make in a precise definition of this emotion is the word he derived from phrenology, "adhesiveness."[8] In a passage in *Democratic Vistas* Whitman cites adhesiveness as one of the two halves that together constitute the essence—and tension—of

6. Whitman's letter to Symonds in Gay Wilson Allen, *The Solitary Singer* (New York: Macmillan Co., 1955), p. 535.

7. Traubel, *op. cit.,* pp. 76–77.

8. For a valuable account of Whitman's debt to phrenology for part of his key vocabulary, see Edward Hungerford, "Walt Whitman and His Chart of Bumps," *American Literature,* II (January, 1931), 350–84.

democracy: "It [democracy] is the old, yet ever-modern dream of earth, out of her eldest and her youngest, her fond philosophers and poets. Not that half only, individualism, which isolates. There is another half, which is adhesiveness or love, that fuses, ties and aggregates, making the race comrades, and fraternizing all. Both are to be vitalized by religion . . ." (V, 80).[9]

In another passage in *Democratic Vistas* Whitman returns to this fundamental concept of his democratic ideal: "Intense and loving comradeship, the personal and passionate attachment of man to man—which, hard to define, underlies the lessons and ideals of the profound saviours of every land and age, and which seems to promise, when thoroughly develop'd, cultivated and recognized in manners and literature, the most substantial hope and safety of the future of these States, will then be fully express'd" (V, 80). As, above, he opposes adhesiveness to individuality, so, in a footnote to this passage, he carefully distinguishes adhesiveness from "amativeness" (another phrenological term): "It is to the development, identification, and general prevalence of that fervid comradeship, (the adhesive love, at least rivaling the amative love hitherto possessing imaginative literature, if not going beyond it,) that I look for the counterbalance and offset of our materialistic and vulgar American democracy, and for the spiritualization thereof" (V, 80). The remainder of the footnote characterizes this "manly friendship" as "fond and loving, pure and sweet, strong and life-long," and again stresses the necessity of such "Calamus" emotion for democracy, "without which it will be incomplete, in vain, and incapable of perpetuating itself."

The purity, innocence, and spirituality of the "Calamus" concept as expressed in *Democratic Vistas* cannot be missed. The idea is not original with Whitman. As he states, the "Calamus" idea was expressed by all mankind's saviors and has frequently been expressed by the term "brotherly love." In short, it is a basic Christian concept Whitman has found indispensable to the democratic ideal. The "Calamus" emotion has two facets—personal and social: on the one hand, adhesiveness merges particular individuals in a deep-

9. Quotations from Whitman are where possible identified in the text by volume and page number of *The Complete Writings of Walt Whitman*, ed. Richard M. Bucke *et al.* (New York: G. P. Putnam's Sons, 1902).

ly personal, yet purely spiritual, attachment; on the other hand, a multitude of such attachments interpenetrating and binding a nation creates a democratic state rooted deeply in genuinely moral human character rather than in convention or law.

Although Whitman did not live to see his ideal state, he did experience the kind of personal attachment he celebrated. If further proof of the purity of Whitman's intended meaning is needed, it may be found in the series of letters he wrote to his Civil War companion, Peter Doyle, the unsophisticated Washington horsecar conductor. The letters have been published under the appropriate title *Calamus*, as they constitute a record of precisely the kind of relationship Whitman meant to describe by that title. The terms of endearment Whitman uses in these letters are lavish and suggest metaphorically the character of the emotion motivating his attachment: "Dear Pete, dear son, my darling boy, my young and loving brother . . ." (VIII, 42). It would be difficult to challenge the purity and spirituality of the feelings Whitman and Doyle had for each other, at least as they emerge in these letters, but, on the other hand, there can be no doubt that these feelings transcend those usual to friends or companions of the same sex.

The casual tone and genuine naïveté which Whitman uses in this correspondence to describe the depth of his friendship for "some of the pilots" in New York suggest that in his hands the symbols and language of love have become transfigured: "I have been out all the forenoon knocking around—the water is my favorite recreation—I could spend two or three hours every day of my life here, and never get tired—some, when we meet we kiss each other (I am an exception to all their customs with others)—some of their boys have grown up since I have known them, and they too know me and are very friendly" (VIII, 46). Such kissing, celebrated in "Calamus" as the signal of the genuine affection of comrades, is a physical token of a spiritual relationship. It is described also by another of Whitman's real-life comrades, John Burroughs, in his journal of January, 1864: "And so kind, sympathetic, charitable, humane, tolerant a man I did not suppose was possible. He loves everything and everybody. I saw a soldier the other day stop on the street and kiss him. He kisses me as if I were a girl."[10] Surely the innocence

---

10. Clara Barrus, *Whitman and Burroughs, Comrades* (New York: Houghton Mifflin Co., 1931), p. 17. For another example of Whitman's "Calamus" feelings

of such behavior on the conscious level cannot be questioned. One can but conclude, from the available evidence, that the love celebrated in "Calamus" had a genuinely personal—and pure—meaning for Whitman and that he advocated it for a serious social end—democracy.

II. *Revisions*

But all this external evidence does not dispose of "Calamus": the poems themselves must have the final say. A brief examination of the revisions Whitman made in the "Calamus" poems should indicate, at least in part, his intended meaning.

In a recent publication of *Whitman's Manuscripts*, Fredson Bowers has demonstrated that at an early stage of their growth the "Calamus" poems were twelve in number and had as their title and unifying symbol, "Live Oak with Moss." The twelve poems are listed below in the order in which Whitman originally arranged them but with the titles of the final edition (note that 5 and 8 were rejected in 1867):

1. Not Heat Flames Up and Consumes
2. I Saw in Louisiana a Live-Oak Growing
3. When I Heard at the Close of Day
4. This Moment Yearning and Thoughtful
5. (Rejected 1867—appeared in 1860 as No. 8, "Long I Thought That Knowledge")
6. What Think You I Take My Pen in Hand
7. Recorders Ages Hence
8. (Rejected 1867—appeared in 1860 as No. 9, "Hours Continuing Long")
9. I Dream'd in a Dream
10. O You Whom I Often and Silently Come
11. Earth, My Likeness
12. To a Western Boy[11]

For at least two of these poems (2 and 3) there are earlier holograph copies, with some variations, suggesting that the twelve-poem sequence might well have been organized (in the usual Whitman manner) from diverse poems related only thematically. Mr. Bowers' conjecture that "for some time Whitman may not have intended to

---

in his real as contrasted with his poetic life, see Allen, *op. cit.*, pp. 297–99, an account of the relationship of the poet and Thomas P. Sawyer reconstructed from letters written in 1863.

11. Fredson Bowers, *Whitman's Manuscripts: "Leaves of Grass" (1860)* (Chicago: University of Chicago Press, 1955), p. lxiv.

print these poems,"[12] implying that they are some kind of embarrassing personal revelation, does not seem consistent with Whitman's intention, clearly revealed in a manuscript note, to write a companion series: "A string of Poems, (short etc.) embodying the amative love of woman—the same as *Live Oak Leaves* do the passion of friendship for man" (X, 18).

Mr. Bowers finds in this twelve-poem series "an artistically complete story of attachment, crisis, and renunciation"[13] and speculates that this sequence "was motivated by some specific emotional experience."[14] With the aid of a suggestion from G. W. Allen concerning poem 3, Mr. Bowers even offers a conjecture of the date. Connecting a line in the poem ("When I heard at the close of the day how I had been praised in the Capitol, still it was not a happy night for me that followed") with a favorable review of *Leaves of Grass* that appeared in a Washington paper in February, 1856, Mr. Bowers offers the tentative guess that the "event recorded in this poem . . . may precede even the second edition of *Leaves*."[15] Observing that the poem describes the poet as rising early in the morning and bathing in the ocean, Mr. Bowers casts some doubt on the February dating.[16] He overlooks the fact that the connection the poet draws between the praise in the "Capitol" and the morning swim in the ocean is not a connection of time at all but of emotional intensity; the feeling of happiness on the one occasion is more intense than on the other: months or years might very well have separated the two events. And moreover, if one is allowed such speculation, why not guess, on the basis of poem 2, "I Saw in Louisiana a Live-Oak Growing," that the "emotional experience" of the sequence is somehow linked to the 1848 trip to New Orleans?

Perhaps the basic error in all this kind of speculation is the assumption that there must be an "event recorded" in a particular Whitman poem. Poems seldom "record" but frequently "transmute" events. The twelve-poem sequence seems to derive not from a single experience but from a multitude of fragments transfigured and

12. *Ibid.*, p. lxvii.
13. *Ibid.*, p. lxvi.
14. *Ibid.*, p. lxx.
15. *Ibid.*, p. lxvi.
16. *Ibid.*, p. lxx.

ordered thematically by a unifying sensibility. Although there are present all the emotions involved in "attachment, crisis, and renunciation," there is no clear narrative plot, as these words imply. And, indeed, the fact that all twelve of these poems were scattered throughout the "Calamus" section in 1860 suggests that the earlier sequence was somewhat tenuous. The "Live Oak with Moss" poems, although they contribute richly to our understanding of the evolution of "Calamus," do not provide the missing "clew": they are perhaps the infant but not the embryo. And to assume that the embryo is some specific emotional experience that may be accurately dated is to perpetuate in a new form the old biographical myth that Whitman discovered his transcendent poetic inspiration in an abortive Creole love affair in New Orleans.

Contrary to frequent implications by Whitman's critics, his revisions of "Calamus" over a period of some thirty years do not reveal that he was trying to "cover up" or change the original character of the group of poems. Perhaps the most significant and revealing revision made was in the poem now titled "Sometimes with One I Love," which ended originally: "Doubtless I could not have perceived the universe, or written one of my poems, if I had not freely given myself to comrades, to love."[17] Through revision this line became: "(I loved a certain person ardently and my love was not return'd, / Yet out of that I have written these songs").[18] Two highly significant conclusions may be drawn from this revision: first, changes in "Calamus" were not intended to make the poems less personal—indeed, in this instance, the poem has been made to appear more personal; and, second, and more important, biographical interpretation, the acceptance of Whitman's poetry at "face value," is highly dangerous and likely to be misleading. It would seem safe to assume that revision of "Sometimes with One I Love" from a statement of generalized experience to a suggestion of a highly personal and specific experience was made not for biographical but for poetic or dramatic reasons. How often has the first version of Whitman's poetry contained such seemingly specific references for similar

17. *Leaves of Grass* (Boston: Thayer & Eldridge, 1860), p. 376.
18. Quotations from the final or "deathbed" edition of *Leaves of Grass* may be easily located by title in any edition of the book. All such quotations have been checked with the text in the 1902 *Complete Writings*.

reasons? If, in "Sometimes with One I Love," the "certain person" loved ardently is a figment of Whitman's poetic imagination, it would seem the duty of the impartial critic to distinguish carefully, in the study of Whitman, his poetic from his real world and to refrain from passing so easily and superficially from one to the other on the naïve assumption that there is no difference.

The forty-five poems of the 1860 version of "Calamus" had, by the time of the appearance of Whitman's last edition, been reduced to thirty-nine. Three poems were rejected, four were transferred to other sections of *Leaves of Grass*, and one new poem was added. At first glance it might seem that the three poems were deleted because of their personal nature, because they revealed more than the author intended. But equally "personal" poems were allowed to stay. Close examination of the discarded poems reveals that there were other valid reasons for rejection. In "Long I Thought That Knowledge," the poet says that for a time he found the essence or meaning of life in a series of interests—obtaining knowledge, becoming the orator of America, emulating "old and new heroes," and, finally, composing the "songs of the New World"—but he discovered that he could be the "singer of songs no longer": "One who loves me is jealous of me, and withdraws me from all but love." This emotional dilemma becomes the central idea of the poem, which concludes: "I am indifferent to my own songs—I will go with him I love, / It is to be enough for us that we are together—We never separate again."[19] There are two good reasons for the deletion of this poem: it introduces the emotion of jealousy into "Calamus" love, an emotion which was avoided in the other poems and which Whitman probably decided was foreign to his concept of comradely attachment; and the poem contradicts certain basic ideas that recur throughout the "Calamus" section. It would be difficult to reconcile the poet's attitude of indifference toward his songs as expressed in this rejected poem with the determination, announced in the opening poem of "Calamus," to sing the songs of "manly attachment," to "celebrate the need of comrades." And it would be equally difficult to reconcile this indifference with the frequently expressed sentiment in "Calamus" that it was the love of comrades that initiated the poetic impulse and granted the poetic power.

19. *Leaves of Grass* (1860), p. 355.

Immediately following "Long I Thought That Knowledge" in the 1860 edition appeared another rejected poem, "Hours Continuing Long, Sore and Heavy-Hearted." The dominant emotion expressed is despair (rather than jealousy) over the defection of a "lover": "Hours discouraged, distracted—for the one I cannot content myself without, soon I saw him content himself without me." This poem takes on the character of a bashful, stammering confession: "Sullen and suffering hours! (I am ashamed—but it is useless—I am what I am;) / Hours of my torment—I wonder if other men ever have the like, out of the like feelings?"[20] The most facile interpretation of these lines is that they are a confession of abnormality and that the poem was rejected because Whitman wanted to suppress such an ill-advised revelation. Such an interpretation ignores the passages, equally confession-like, that remained in "Calamus": all the poems addressed directly to the reader, such as "Whoever You Are Holding Me Now in Hand," suggest that the poet is "far different" from "what you supposed." Again, a more probable reason for the rejection of "Hours Continuing Long" is that the emotional tone of despair and dejection is generally foreign to the "Calamus" section; and particularly is such an attitude, growing out of a dissolved friendship, in conflict with the oft expressed sentiment that such experience made possible the poetic expression. Similar reasons may be found for deletion of "Who Is Now Reading This?"—the third and last of the rejected poems. It would be contradictory for the poet, apparently on such sure footing elsewhere in "Calamus," to admit along with the reader that he is "puzzled" at himself. One may readily conclude, I think, that Whitman rejected these three poems not for personal but for poetic reasons, not to suppress anything they revealed but to achieve internal consistency in the "Calamus" cluster of poems.

Of the four poems transferred from "Calamus" to other sections of *Leaves of Grass*, three were transferred entire to "Whispers of Heavenly Death," and the other was divided into two parts, one of which was placed in "Whispers of Heavenly Death" and one in "Inscriptions." Inasmuch as the second poem of "Calamus," "Scented Herbage of My Breast," introduces the theme of the inseparability of love and death, the transfer of a number of these poems from

20. *Ibid.*

"Calamus" to a section whose title proclaims the subject as death is significant. As no poem in "Calamus" other than "Scented Herbage" develops the love-death theme, it might be assumed that Whitman, by shifting these poems, desired to modify this theme; or perhaps he considered treatment of it in "Scented Herbage" as adequate and requiring no further elaboration. Examination of these poems does not clearly reveal the poet's motives; in all of them there is an ambiguous or metaphorical treatment of death. In "Of Him I Love Day and Night" and "O Living Always, Always Dying," the words "death," "dying," "corpse," "burial-place," and others take on double meanings: "burial-places" become not merely the depository of the dead but the depository of all that is material, including the living; "corpses" become not merely the lifeless body but past personalities or attitudes of the individual now outgrown, changed—or dead. "That Music Always Round Me" takes on a significance that it could not have had in "Calamus," derived primarily from the title of its new section, "Whispers of Heavenly Death," but also from the poem that dominates the section, "Chanting the Square Deific." Poem 31 in the 1860 version of "Calamus," the first half of which became "What Ship Puzzled at Sea" in "Whispers of Heavenly Death," the second half, "What Place Is Besieged" in "Inscriptions," seems from the beginning to have been a "program" poem, celebrating the purpose and effect of *Leaves of Grass* as a whole rather than one of the themes peculiar to "Calamus."

One other extensive revision in "Calamus" should be noted. Poem 5 in the 1860 edition was a long poem emphasizing the social or democratic results of the "Calamus" emotion:

> States!
> Were you looking to be held together by the lawyers?
> By an agreement on a paper? Or by arms?[21]

Over half the poem was cut, the remaining portion being the poem now titled "For You, O Democracy," one of the best-known and most frequently quoted poems in *Leaves of Grass*. No one can doubt that Whitman's revision was an artistic improvement, pointing up much more dramatically and effectively his social theme than did the longer poem. The portion he trimmed from the poem was not

21. *Ibid.*, p. 349.

discarded but utilized in "Over the Carnage Rose Prophetic a Voice," in "Drum-Taps," a transfer that suggests the importance of the "Calamus" concept to the war poems. The war proved to be for Whitman a crucial national experience in which the social theories of "Calamus," untried on any large scale, could be tested and, as it turned out and as he recorded in "Drum-Taps," confirmed under fire.

Although the revisions here discussed are by no means all that Whitman made in "Calamus," they are the most extensive and significant, and they certainly do not reveal a pattern of suppression or concealment. In almost every instance, sufficient artistic reasons can be found to justify the change undertaken. By and large, the "Calamus" section remained in essence the same through some thirty years of revision. There exists no evidence that Whitman ever genuinely regretted the form "Calamus" had originally taken. Indeed, in 1874, in a review he prepared for John Burroughs' signature, Whitman singled out the "Calamus" emotion as a primary virtue of his *Leaves:* "Yet it [Walt Whitman's verse] is singularly emotional; probably no one has so daringly and freely carried 'manly attachment' into expression as this author."[22]

III. *Major Themes*

The germ of the principal theme in "Calamus" is found in a paper discovered among Whitman's manuscripts with notations indicating that the poet had at one time planned to develop a lecture on the topic: "Why should there be these modesties and prohibitions that keep women from strong actual life—from going about there with men? I desire to say to you, and let you ponder well upon it, the fact that under present arrangement, the love and comradeship of a woman, of his wife however welcome, however complete, does not and cannot satisfy the grandest requirements of a manly soul for love and comradeship,—The man he loves, he often loves with more passionate attachment than he ever bestows on any woman, even his wife.—Is it that the growth of love needs the free air—the seasons, perhaps more wildness more rudeness? Why is the love of women so invalid, so transient?"[23] Some of the ideas expressed in

22. Barrus, *op. cit.,* p. 108.
23. Clifton Joseph Furness (ed.), *Walt Whitman's Workshop* (Cambridge: Harvard University Press, 1928), pp. 63–64.

this crude early note become embodied in "Calamus" in Whitman's poetic expression of the distinction between the two kinds of love— amativeness and adhesiveness:

> Fast-anchor'd eternal O love! O woman I love!
> O bride! O wife! more resistless than I can tell, the
>   thought of you!
> Then separate, as disembodied or another born,
> Ethereal, the last athletic reality, my consolation,
> I ascend, I float in the regions of your love O man,
> O sharer of my roving life.

Critics have frequently noted that "Children of Adam" celebrates love of man for woman, while "Calamus" celebrates love of man for man; in the former, emphasis is on the physical or sexual aspects of love, in the latter on the spiritual. The above poem would bear out this distinction: love of man for man is "disembodied," "ethereal," "the last athletic reality." For Whitman, "athletic" had connotations of a desirable robustness or health: the "last athletic reality" would, surely, be a robustness of the soul or spirit that enables it to encompass more than self. Man is the "sharer" of the poet's "roving life," the companion on his spiritual journey.

In "Calamus" variations on the central theme are developed, dropped, reintroduced and treated from a fresh point of view, dropped again, echoed later, and so on, through the thirty-nine poems. This ebb and flow, or symphonic treatment of theme, suggests, as is natural in poetry, not a logical but an emotional development of ideas. In order to see the several aspects of the "Calamus" emotion, in order to understand its varied facets, it should prove useful to isolate and examine the major variations of the basic theme that thread their way through the section.

First, as in almost all sections of *Leaves of Grass,* is the announcement of the poetic program by the chanting poet:

> I proceed for all who are or have been young men,
> To tell the secret of my nights and days,
> To celebrate the need of comrades.

As "In Paths Untrodden" introduces this resolve, "Scented Herbage of My Breast" extends it and, later, it is reintroduced in "These I Singing in Spring" and elsewhere. In these poems the poet seems to consider himself in some way eminently fit, perhaps through experience, for the task he has assumed: "For who but I should understand lovers and all their sorrow and joy? / And who but I should be the poet of comrades?" And the resolution to celebrate "manly attachment" calls forth a renunciation of other interests, a dedication almost religious in its intensity in "Scented Herbage of My Breast":

I will sound myself and comrades only, I will never again utter a call only their call,
I will raise with it immortal reverberations through the States.

The hyperbole in the first line (Whitman did "utter" other "calls") is a poetic device used throughout "Calamus" for intensifying the felt or evoked emotion; such exaggeration must be taken into account in any honest interpretation of the poems.

Closely allied with these poems announcing the poetic intent are the poems, usually addressed directly to the reader, that are cast in the form of a warning:

I give you fair warning before you attempt me further,
I am not what you supposed, but far different.

The poet insists upon his "difference" in a number of poems, beginning with "Whoever You Are Holding Me Now in Hand" and including "Recorders Ages Hence," "Are You the New Person Drawn toward Me?" and "To a Western Boy." In "Recorders Ages Hence" the poet confides that he will take his future reader "underneath this impassive exterior" and reveal his genuine personality—"the tenderest lover." In "Are You the New Person Drawn toward Me?" the poet again admonishes, "To begin with take warning, I am surely far different from what you suppose." And in "To a Western Boy," he advises the lad that he cannot become an "eleve" of the poet's unless "blood like mine circle . . . in your veins."

The poet differs from others only in his capacity for "Calamus" love; his exterior, what he appears to be, gives no indication whatsoever of the depths possible to him in spiritual attachment to others. A large number of poems are devoted to portrayal of the impact and achievement of such attachments. In "Of the Terrible Doubt of Appearances," the poet asserts that, in the doubt and uncertainty about reality and "identity beyond the grave," such love grants "untold and untellable wisdom," a knowledge similar to the intuitive knowledge of the mystic: "He ahold of my hand has completely satisfied me." "When I Heard at the Close of the Day" dramatically portrays the importance of such love to the individual: the "plaudits in the Capitol" or the accomplishment of plans was as nothing to the knowledge that "my dear friend my lover was on his way coming." In this brief drama, the poet utilizes the language and conventions of romantic love in such details as "all that day my food nourish'd me more," and particularly in the vivid closing picture:

In the stillness in the autumn moonbeams his face was inclined toward me,
And his arm lay lightly around my breast—and that night I was happy.

Similar portraits, in which the physical comradeship becomes a token of deep spiritual attachment, are vividly drawn in "A Glimpse" and "We Two Boys Together Clinging."

In "Not Heat Flames Up and Consumes" the poet describes the "Calamus" love as even more intense and consuming than flames (called the "subtle electric fire" in "O You Whom I Often and Silently Come"), and as inevitable and mystical as sea waves. Indeed, the "Calamus" experience seems at some point to merge with the mystical: the "last athletic reality" becomes the reality of the spiritual as opposed to the material universe. The poet's soul is "borne through the open air, / Wafted in all directions O love, for friendship, for you." This image of the floating self, which appears also in "Fast-Anchor'd Eternal O Love!" ("I float in the regions of your love O man"), aptly suggests the spiritual merge of the mystic with the Transcendent. It is surely significant (and illuminating) that in "Song of Myself" God is conceived as the "great Camerado, the lover true for whom I pine." At the center of the "Calamus" emotion is a profound religious feeling, a feeling of spiritual identity and oneness with other beings.

Perhaps the most curious of these intensely personal poems cast in the language of romantic love is "Earth, My Likeness." In this poem one can imagine the poet contemplating a globe representing the earth:

Though you look so impassive, ample and spheric there,
I now suspect that is not all;
I now suspect there is something fierce in you eligible to burst forth.

The association of the earth with a relatively fragile balloon is inevitable upon the introduction of the term "burst forth." But more important than this secondary image is the implication of the object of the poet's contemplation—the earth, the world as we know it through our physical senses. Although the material globe seems "impassive, ample," in reality there is "something fierce" underneath ready to "burst forth." What could this "something" be but the spiritual reality behind the material illusion, "fierce" because it has been ignored or suppressed for so long? This interpretation seems mandatory if the remainder of the poem is to be coherent:

For an athlete is enamour'd of me, and I of him,
But toward him there is something fierce and terrible in me eligible to
   burst forth,
I dare not tell it in words, not even in these songs.

The spiritual reality, in this case a deep and agitated spiritual love, is "fierce and terrible" only in the sense that any spiritual passion could be when pent up for long without object on which to bestow its emotional intensity. If the language seems too intense for the spiritual meaning, one need but note Whitman's use of almost identical language in a prose context which leaves no doubt as to meaning: "To this terrible, irrepressible yearning, (surely more or less down underneath in most human souls)—this never-satisfied appetite for sympathy, and this boundless offering of sympathy—this universal democratic comradeship—this old, eternal, yet ever-new interchange of adhesiveness, so fitly emblematic of America—I have given in that book [*Leaves of Grass*], undisguisedly, declaredly, the openest expression" (V, 199). As the mystic cannot describe the source of his certainty, as it would be audacious for him to attempt to define the nature of the Transcendent with which he has merged, so the poet "dare" not attempt to convey the meaning of the feeling that possesses him. There is terror in an alien spirituality, a spirituality so long foreign to man's experience.

As it is dishonest to extract lines without regard to context, so it is misleading to discuss any single poem in "Calamus" without regard for the poems that surround it and modify or qualify its meaning. The poems in which the "Calamus" emotion appears to be a highly personal and intensely passionate spiritual attachment are informed and qualified by the many interspersed poems that celebrate the "Calamus" emotion as a social and democratic force. Indeed, poems of this latter kind make up the bulk of "Calamus." The poet thus finds in the "Calamus" concept the basic impulse necessary to the two conflicting elements in his ideal state, individuality and equality, or "one's-self" and "en-masse." The "Calamus" emotion provides, however, not only these contrary impulses but also their means of reconciliation: the same spiritual love that attaches one closely to an individual will also merge him with the mass. Whitman asserted in prose: ". . . important as they are in my purpose as emotional expressions for humanity, the special meaning of the 'Calamus' cluster of 'Leaves of Grass,' (and more or less running through the book, and cropping out in 'Drum-Taps,') mainly resides in its political significance. In my opinion, it is by a fervent, accepted development of comradeship, the beautiful and sane affection of man for man, latent in all the young fellows, north and south, east and west—it is by this, I say, and by what goes directly and indirectly along with it, that the United States of the future, (I cannot too often repeat,) are to be most effectually welded together, intercalated, anneal'd into a living union" (V, 199).

In "I Hear It Was Charged against Me" the poet seems to acknowledge the possibility of misinterpretation of his message:

I hear it was charged against me that I sought to destroy institutions,
But really I am neither for nor against institutions.

The only institution the poet is concerned with is one which, without "edifices or rules or trustees or any argument," he wishes to establish throughout "these States": "The institution of the dear love of comrades." In "The Base of All Metaphysics" the poet indicates, in stating the essence of all philosophies, the hierarchical relationship of the various kinds of love:

The dear love of man for his comrades, the attraction of friend to friend,
Of the well-married husband and wife, of children and parents,
Of city for city and land for land.

The "Calamus" friendship, conceived here as a kind of base on which all of the other relationships of society are constructed, is celebrated in one of the most famous "chants" as the magic ingredient that will transform America into the ideal indestructible state:

Come, I will make the continent indissoluble,
I will make the most splendid race the sun ever shone upon,
I will make divine magnetic lands,
    With the love of comrades,
        With the life-long love of comrades.

The "Calamus" message has, the poet insists throughout, particular application to America. The prairie grass itself, in "inland America," offers the symbolic example; the "spiritual corresponding" is to be the "copious and close companionship of men"—those with "sweet and lusty flesh clear of taint," "simple, never-constrain'd, never obedient." In "A Promise to California," the poet, noting that "these States tend inland and toward the Western sea," assures the West, "soon I travel toward you, to remain, to teach robust American love." The poet asserts in "To the East and to the West," "I believe the main purport of these States is to found a superb friendship, exalté, previously unknown." Although this kind of friendship has never been realized before, the "germs" for it "are in all men"; "it waits, and has always been waiting, latent in all men." But though America seems to have a special role to play in the evolution of this new relationship among men, the "Calamus" emotion knows no geographical boundaries; comradely attachment or brotherly love will bind and democratize not only the nation but also the world. In "This Moment Yearning and Thoughtful," the poet, in reverie about the men of Germany, Italy, China, Russia, and other lands, states: "It seems to me if I could know those men I should become attached to them as I do to men in my own lands." As Whitman has said elsewhere, in prose, "Perhaps the most illustrious culmination of the Modern and of Republicanism may prove to be a signal cluster of joyous, more exalted Bards of Adhesiveness, identically one in soul, but contributed by every nation, each after its distinctive kind."[24]

In direct emotional contrast to this broad social theme is a theme that delicately, almost shyly, threads its way through the section and that, in the way it is presented, seems almost a confession. The theme is introduced in the sixth poem of the section, "Not Heaving from My Ribb'd Breast Only," which, after a catalogue of the physical manifestations normally associated with romantic love (such as "husky pantings through clinch'd teeth" and "murmurs of my dreams while I sleep"), concludes:

Not in any or all of them O adhesiveness! O pulse of my life!
Need I that you exist and show yourself any more than in these songs.

24. *Ibid.*, p. 163.

In other words, the songs become the only *necessary* outlet for the poet's adhesiveness. The idea that the writing of the poetry offers emotional release is contained also in that strange poem, "Trickle Drops": "From my breast, from within where I was conceal'd, press forth red drops, confession drops." Particularly curious is the poet's calling upon the drops, "ashamed" and "blushing," to "glow upon all I have written."

We have already seen, in "Sometimes with One I Love," that Whitman relates the inspiration or motive for "these songs" to his love that "was not return'd." The poetry becomes the "pay" that is "certain one way or another" in the experience of love, the "pay" which confirms that, in reality, there "is no unreturn'd love." But the best known of these "confession" poems is "Here the Frailest Leaves of Me," which originally stood as the next to last poem in the section and whose first line ("Here my last words, and the most baffling")[25] was subsequently deleted. This short poem now appears near the middle of "Calamus":

> Here the frailest leaves of me and yet my strongest lasting,
> Here I shade and hide my thoughts, I myself do not expose them,
> And yet they expose me more than all my other poems.

All these poems suggest that the poet has found sufficient fulfilment in art for certain emotional needs in his personality frustrated in real life. There seems to be frank recognition by the poet that his poetry represents the sublimation of his adhesiveness. It is these poems that those who have sought so diligently for abnormality have seized upon as open admission by the poet. Why does he "shade and hide" his thoughts? The answer to this question must lie in an examination of "Calamus" not as rhetoric or philosophy but as poetry. The poet reveals here not his guilt but his poetic method—ambiguity.

IV. *Poetic Technique*

We have noted in a number of poems Whitman's use of the diction and tokens of romantic love to describe the "Calamus" comradeship. Such transference from the physical to the spiritual results, whether intentionally or not, in an ambiguity of meaning that gives rise to endless controversy. There is no doubt, however, that a good deal of the ambiguity in "Calamus" is intentional and is consciously

25. *Leaves of Grass* (1860), p. 377.

used to achieve certain poetic effects. Central to the section's ambiguity is the symbol introduced in the title—"Calamus"—and developed extensively in several key poems. Whitman himself, in one of his rare comments touching on specific meanings in his work, explains the symbol: "Calamus is the very large and aromatic grass, or rush, growing about water ponds in the valleys—spears about three feet high; often called Sweet Flag; grows all over the Northern and Middle States. The recherché or ethereal sense of the term, as used in my book, arises probably from the actual Calamus presenting the biggest and hardiest kind of spears of grass, and their fresh, aquatic, pungent bouquet."[26]

There is a fundamental value, of course, in the use of calamus as an extension of the metaphor, "leaves of grass," which in its common meaning has been elaborated more or less fully in "Song of Myself." Calamus is a very special kind of "grass" with unique connotations, just as "manly attachment" or "athletic love" is an emotion limited rather than universal, with distinct differences in its intense spirituality from other kinds of love. The calamus plant, in addition to having "the biggest and hardiest kind of spears of grass" and a "pungent bouquet," is found growing in clusters of several fascicles each, usually in out-of-the-way, secluded spots in and around ponds. As they are developed in "Calamus" each of these attributes of the plant suggests some aspect of the love of comrades: the size and toughness of the spears symbolize the depth and hardiness of such love; the distinctive odor suggests the spirituality of the attachments; growth in clusters suggests the twofold results of the realization of such emotion: personal attachment and democracy; the seclusion of the plant indicates the rarity of such revolutionary friendships.

Development of the calamus as a symbol is a part of the drama of the section. In the elaboration of the calamus image the poet achieves some of his most successful effects. Not only are all the attributes of the calamus plant utilized as symbolic, but the parts of the plant, the leaf and the root, are fully exploited in all their possible meanings. It is in such exploitation, where meaning on one level frequently expands to include meaning on another level, that

26. William Sloane Kennedy, *The Fight of a Book for the World* (West Yarmouth, Mass.: Stonecroft Press, 1926), p. 177.

ambiguity becomes a conscious poetic device. Although the resulting complexity makes for an enriched poetry, it is the kind of poetry easily open to distortion in interpretation. Such has been the fate of "Calamus."

In the opening poem of the section, "In Paths Untrodden," the untrodden paths by the pond waters quickly become more than the out-of-the-way places where the calamus grows: they become untried or infrequent patterns of human behavior, the action of the dissenter, the thought of the skeptic, the belief of the individualist. (Throughout "Calamus" the recurring image of the secluded, quiet pond is in significant contrast in its emotional connotations to the "pent-up aching river" that served as a basic image throughout "Children of Adam": the pond suggests a serene soul, the river a soul perturbed.) The long, sturdy blades of the fragrant calamus plant become "tongues aromatic" to which the poet responds "in this secluded spot." Here he has found something greater than the materialistic "pleasures" and "profits" and "conformities" he had been trying to feed his soul. He has found spiritual love ("manly attachment" or "athletic love"): the calamus blades (as tongues) "inform" by serving, in their fascicle clusters where "many" are brought together as one, as examples of close personal attachment as well as of broadly diffused love, and as examples of seclusion from the "clank of the world." That the "tongues" convey a spiritual message is indicated by their aroma: always in *Leaves of Grass*, odor or fragrance, a reality that has no apparent materialistic existence, symbolizes the spiritual, the ultimate reality that is impalpable and unknowable by any of the ordinary methods of knowing.

While the calamus blades are conceived as tongues in "In Paths Untrodden," they take on greater complexity in "Scented Herbage of My Breast." The title evokes a concrete, physical image of the robust, hirsute chest, an image that suggests the solidity and strength of the spiritual love symbolized. The herbage is scented; it is the spiritual emanation of the seat of love—the breast or heart. But the herbage is soon involved in further meanings:

> Leaves from you I glean, I write, to be perused best afterwards,
> Tomb-leaves, body-leaves growing up above me above death.

The herbage thus becomes first the grain (fruit of his being, thought) collected (gleaned) by the poet, and next the "leaves" of a book.

where the message from his heart can be preserved and "perused best afterwards"—after the strong emotional grip has passed. None of these meanings is abandoned even as new ones are sought out. "Tomb-leaves" are leaves that symbolize the immortality of man— man embodied in a book of leaves or, more literally, the "leaves of grass" that grow above one's grave (note section 6 of "Song of Myself"); "body-leaves" fuse the image of hair with the image of the grass growing above graves, out of the dead buried beneath.

But real death is denied: "Perennial roots, tall leaves, O the winter shall not freeze you delicate leaves." These physical details, applicable to the calamus plant, suggest the attributes of spiritual love. The root is the heart, the leaf the manifestation—the human as well as the poetic gesture (the poet exclaims later, "O blossoms of my blood! I permit you to tell in your own way of the heart that is under you"); the winter is the hostility of society toward the spiritual. Genuine spiritual love cannot be killed by such hostility. In its seclusion, in the life it finds withdrawn from society, such love flourishes: "O I do not know whether many passing by will discover you or inhale your faint odor, but I believe a few will." But spiritual love is not the source of mere pleasure: "O I do not know what you mean there underneath yourselves, you are not happiness." This elusive meaning takes on a mystical cast as the poet indicates the close relationship of love and death:

Yet you are beautiful to me you faint tinged roots, you make me think of death,
Death is beautiful from you, (what indeed is finally beautiful except death and love?)
O I think it is not for life I am chanting here my chant of lovers, I think it must be for death.

The "faint tinged roots" of the calamus plant, symbolizing on one level the heart, the organ from which love takes its origin, on another level suggests the phallus, in turn a token of "manly attachment." "Death is beautiful" from such roots: that is, death from a surfeit of spiritual love, from a yearning for the final merge with the great Camerado (as in "Song of Myself") is a beautiful experience. As death releases the confined soul for final and lasting union with other souls, death really becomes the genuine consummation of spiritual love: "I am not sure but the high soul of lovers welcomes death most."

At no time in this first part of "Scented Herbage of My Breast" is the central symbol dropped or are any of its meanings forgotten:

Indeed O death, I think now these leaves mean precisely the same as you mean,
Grow up taller sweet leaves that I may see! grow up out of my breast!
Spring away from the conceal'd heart there!
Do not fold yourself so in your pink-tinged roots timid leaves!
Do not remain down there so ashamed, herbage of my breast!

Throughout these lines, all the complex meaning of the symbol is operative. Never is the vividness of the actual calamus plant sacrificed or any of its natural attributes distorted for symbolic purposes. The leaves in this passage are, simultaneously, the leaves of the calamus plant, the hair on the chest (a suggestion utilized later when the poet asserts, "Come I am determined to unbare this broad breast of mine"), the grass growing atop the grave, pages of a book (*Leaves of Grass* itself), the outward manifestation of the hidden heart, and the capacity for spiritual love and the yearning for its return. The root is, of course, the calamus root with its distinctive color and odor; but at the same time it suggests the flesh where the hair is imbedded, the phallus in all its mystic associations (these meanings suggesting the vitality and virility of the "robust" spiritual love the poet describes), the buried corpse that feeds the grass above its grave, and the unseen heart as the source of the blood (passion) that has nourished the spiritual love.

The poet himself appears to admit that his symbol has become so burdened with meaning that it ceases to function effectively:

Emblematic and capricious blades I leave you, now you serve me not,
I will say what I have to say by itself.

After all the serious punning on "leaves," one might well read "I leave you" as a sly bit of humor into which the poet has been tempted as a farewell to the calamus, which has proved not only "emblematic" but "capricious." Perhaps the calamus is a capricious symbol because, although it was intended primarily to suggest the spiritual, it inevitably by the very nature of its form gave rise to physical associations: although these associations might in turn prove useful in suggesting attributes of the spiritual, they are also rather easily open to misinterpretation. After dropping the symbol, what the poet says "by itself" is a reiteration of what has been said through the symbol. He addresses death:

That you hide in these shifting forms of life, for reasons, and that they
  are mainly for you,
That you beyond them come forth to remain, the real reality,
That behind the mask of materials you patiently wait, no matter how
  long....

Here the poet glimpses the truth asserted by all mystics, that the physical world that we know through our senses is a "mask of materials," a "show of appearance," that the world beyond to which death brings us is the "real reality." Death, then, represents the only means to the consummation of genuine and deeply felt spiritual love. It is surely needless to point out that such love is not confined to males; it may exist wherever the physical is not the primary motive in close personal, passionate attachment.

The calamus image is reintroduced in "These I Singing in Spring" (note the ambiguity of the antecedent of "these"). The setting of this poem ("Now along the pond-side, now wading in a little, fearing not the wet") is essentially that of the opening poem, "In Paths Untrodden." In contrast with this secluded spot into which the poet has wandered is the place from which he has withdrawn: "Collecting I traverse the garden the world, but soon I pass the gates." One need but recall the opening poem of "Children of Adam" ("To the garden the world anew ascending") to realize that the garden through whose gates the poet has passed is Eden, the garden of innocent sexual love celebrated in "Children of Adam"; he has found Adamic love insufficient and searches for a love beyond it by the secluded pond side. Soon he is surrounded:

Alone I had thought, yet soon a troop gathers around me,
Some walk by my side and some behind, and some embrace my arms or
  neck,
They the spirits of dear friends dead or alive, thicker they come, a great
  crowd, and I in the middle.

There can be no doubt that the embrace of "spirits" must be spiritual. For these "dear friends" the poet plucks lilac, branch of pine, moss from a live oak, laurel leaves, and other "tokens"—all open and visible products of nature. But one token is reserved to be shared only with those "capable of loving" as the poet is capable:

And here what I now draw from the water, wading in the pond-side,
(O here I last saw him that tenderly loves me, and returns again never to
   separate from me,
And this, O this shall henceforth be the token of comrades, this calamus-
   root shall,
Interchange it youths with each other! let none render it back!)

It is of central significance that, of the products of nature enumerated
by the poet to serve as tokens to pass between friends, all are some
visible portion of the plant, tree, or flower with the single exception
of that which is reserved for tender, intimate love—the calamus root.
In this image all visible nature, with its pungent odor, vivid color,
and variety of form, symbolizes ordinary friendship, beautiful and
rewarding but relatively superficial; only that hidden from the eye,
only that which is the *source* of the visible manifestation, only the
fountainhead itself of the spirit—the heart—may serve to symbolize
spiritual love of the depth the poet conceives. The drawing of the
calamus root from the still pond water suggests the origin of "Calamus" love in the serenity and abundant spirituality of a great and
deep soul. If the "pink-tinged" root suggests the source of the procreative power, if it evokes a visual image of the "man-root," such
physical suggestion in turn serves to symbolize the virility and creativity of the poet's ideal love. These two attributes go far toward
explaining the poet's insistence in several poems on a relationship
between his capacity for the love of comrades and his capacity to
write poetry.

A number of poems scattered throughout the remainder of "Calamus" utilize the central vegetation symbol, exploiting the accumu-
lated multiplicity of meaning and the ambiguity of the key terms.
"I Saw in Louisiana a Live-Oak Growing" evokes a vivid image of a
lone live oak standing apart and "uttering joyous leaves of dark
green." The poet has broken off a twig, "twined around it a little
moss" (again, a highly suggestive physical symbol), and has kept
it as a "curious token" of "manly love." But there is obviously more
in the poem than a striking image: the tree is described in human
terms, particularly in its "uttering" of leaves. The tree, then, symbolizes a writer, perhaps a poet, isolated and astonishingly self-sufficient
in his isolation. As Whitman elsewhere in "Calamus" has indicated
that his own poems were possible only because of his "Calamus"
love, it should not be surprising that he stands amazed at the writer

who can utter "joyous leaves all its life without a friend a lover near." In "The Prairie-Grass Dividing," the poet demands the "blades to rise of words, acts, beings," a fusion of the three symbolic meanings of the spears of grass. Prairie grass, "copious and close," not confined to secluded spots, is a fit image to merge with the calamus upon the final attainment of the poet's ideal social state. The ambiguity of "leaf" is exploited in "Here the Frailest Leaves of Me" and "A Leaf for Hand in Hand": in the first the sturdiness, yet vulnerability, of the calamus spear renders possible the paradox essential to the poem—the "frailest," yet "strongest," leaves; in the latter, when the poet says, "I wish to infuse myself among you till I see it common for you to walk hand in hand," the "I" is, at the same time, the poet as his universal symbol—grass—and the poet as his compelling idea—athletic love.

"Roots and Leaves Themselves Alone" is one of the few poems in "Calamus" completely devoted to development of symbol, without lapse into direct statement or sheer assertion (as, for example, in "Scented Herbage of My Breast," where halfway through the poem the symbol is dismissed as "capricious"). The opening line (which originally read "Roots and leaves unlike any but themselves")[27] indicates, by the "alone," that the "Calamus" poems are as genuine and as authentic as nature itself, that the love expressed in them is as real, yet ethereal, as "scents brought to men and women from the wild woods and pond-side." The poet's basic technique is revealed symbolically in:

Gushes from the throats of birds hid in the foliage of trees as the sun is risen,
Breezes of land and love set from living shores to you on the living sea, to you O sailors!

As the breast-sorrel and pinks of love give rise to the "scents," as the birds originate their "gushes" of song, as the land sends breezes out to sea, so the physical and concrete always suggest the "spiritual corresponding." The almost systematic appeal to all the senses (the odor and sight of the flowers, the sound of the birds, the touch of the breeze, the taste of "frostmellow'd berries") suggests their important role in comprehending or achieving the spiritual. The "living shore" (the physical) sends forth breezes (a spiritual mes-

27. *Leaves of Grass* (1860), p. 359. This was line 3 in the original version.

sage) to the sailors on the "living sea" (those who live by the spirit). Thus the calamus plant, its leaf and root, offers an affirmation of spiritual love to those whose capacity for it is adequate. The "love-bud," "put before you and within you," will unfold "on the old terms":

If you bring the warmth of the sun to them they will open and bring form, color, perfume, to you,
If you become the aliment and the wet they will become flowers, fruit, tall branches and trees.

You can receive no more love than you are capable of giving: the largeness of your spirit determines your return in spiritual love. After all, a vessel can contain no more than its capacity.

Throughout "Calamus" ambiguity is used to create drama. Doubtless, Whitman has introduced the physical image into his poems in such a way as to multiply his meaning or to blur it. One vividly sees, hears, smells, tastes, or touches, and if he does no more he is prepared to question the poet's motives and psychology. If, however, the reader understands that the suggestive or symbolic image is, in Whitman's belief, the essence of poetry and that only the physical (what is knowable through the senses) can be imaged, he may then realize that the tokens of amative love in "Calamus" are but metaphors, a poetic attempt to associate with spiritual love the intensity and personal passion of traditional romantic attachment. Mark Van Doren widely misses the mark when he questions Whitman's "democratic dogmas" because of their basis in "abnormal" love. In the first place, Whitman did not proclaim "dogmas" but rather suggested an ideal. In the second place, there exists no evidence that Whiman's ideal is grounded in abnormality. Outside of "Calamus," in his prose, Whitman indicated rather clearly that his belief in adhesiveness was an intense belief in the Christian concept of brotherly love. There are only two ways of reading "Calamus" as a proclamation of the unwholesome: superficially, without going beneath the surface meanings, without attention to the intentional ambiguity; or psychoanalytically, with no attention whatever to either surface or symbolic meaning, but with intensive (and wild) speculation as to personal motives and unintended revelations. Surely neither of these methods is valid in the reading and interpretation of poetry. But even if one grants the as yet unproved charge against the poet, there is still the necessity of showing that such a biographical fact is relevant to an evaluation of Whitman's ideas or his poetry. Should knowledge of Keats's tuberculosis modify or condition in any way our response to "Ode to a Nightingale"?

CHAPTER FOUR

"Brooklyn Ferry" and Imaginative Fusion

"Crossing Brooklyn Ferry" achieves, in triumph over space and time, an imaginative fusion of the poet and the reader. The gradual accomplishment of this fusion is the central drama of the poem and may be traced through three distinct stages: sections 1–3, sections 4–6, and sections 7–9. Emotional climaxes are reached in sections 3 and 6, and the dramatic climax is reached in section 8, in which the poet asserts that he has achieved direct interpenetration. Readers of "Crossing Brooklyn Ferry" have frequently had the eerie feeling that, as they read, Walt Whitman is peering over their shoulders. This feeling is precisely what the poet wished to evoke. The reader not only should feel the poet's presence but, finally, should feel that he and the poet are *one*. Whitman utilizes all the devices of poetry to evoke this emotional response. But the feeling of oneness with the poet may be considered the emotional recognition of a philosophical truth. Instead of attempting to persuade the intellect through logic of a truth intuitively felt, the poet has persuaded the emotions. The reader's feeling, at the end of the poem, that he and the poet are interfused represents his emotional insight into the world of spiritual unity.

I. *Sections 1–3: Flood Tide and Ferry*

Sections 1 through 3 represent the initial "cycle" of the poem. In them the first stage of identification is achieved through persistent exploitation of the setting introduced in the title. Subsequent sections of the poem are no longer primarily concerned with the crossing of Brooklyn Ferry.

One might well begin his reading of the poem with a close examination of the title. The presence of the non-finite verb "crossing" suggests neither past nor future but an eternal present. The ferry connotes not only progressive movement forward but, more importantly, cyclic movement, a going and a return, a beginning and an end, and a new beginning. Both land and water are a necessary part of the total image of the crossing ferryboat. The two form a duality symbolic of the physical and the spiritual, body and soul, life and death. It is only through insistence on recognition of this dualistic nature of the universe, a recognition of the existence of a transcendent spirituality, that the poet evokes a sense of unity in his readers. Another significant attribute of the ferryboat is its involvement with masses of people. These people, unknown to one another, come together for a brief period of time during which their destinies are joined. They come together from scattered points, they have in common only their common lot as people, and they scatter from their arrival to sundry destinations. It is Brooklyn Ferry in transit, *crossing*, that brief period in the lives of the people when their individual and separate lots are all cast in together, that the poet portrays as symbolic of the spiritual unity of all mankind.

The opening section of "Crossing Brooklyn Ferry" introduces the setting, both place and time, and the main characters of the drama. The place is the boat in transit; the time late afternoon; and the characters are the objects (the flood tide, the clouds, the sun) that make deep impressions on all those who see and feel, the poet and the men and women on the boat with the poet—those who, in spite of their attirement in the "usual costumes," are still "curious" to the poet; and, finally, the reader himself: "You that shall cross from shore to shore years hence are more to me, and more in my meditations, than you might suppose." It is through manipulation of the characters, the "objects" and people about him, that the poet is to effect his union with the reader.

The first seven lines of section 2 of the poem contain a series of substantives that seem to be loosely connected images floating through the poet's mind and bearing primarily on the curious nature of his relationship to others. This passage opens:

The impalpable sustenance of me from all things at all hours of the day,
The simple, compact, well-join'd scheme, myself disintegrated, every one
    disintegrated yet part of the scheme.

Out of such concepts as these has grown the poet's conviction of spiritual unity. The first line suggests the role of the objects impressed on the poet's senses from outside: they contribute as "impalpable sustenance" to the spiritual nourishment of the poet. This thought on the basic nature of the poet leads naturally to the thought on the basic nature of the universe. Not chaos but order prevails. There is a "simple, compact, well-join'd scheme" that constitutes the latent unity of all mankind. Individuals, though they are "disintegrated," though they assume individuality, remain "yet part of the scheme." It is through prevailing over the "disintegration" and by emphasizing the "scheme" that the poet is to evoke in the reader a sense of identification. The second half of section 2 represents the poet peering into the future, noting that the people "fifty years hence" or "a hundred years hence, or ever so many hundred years hence" will engage in the same activities and will view the same sights as he and those about him take part in and watch. Others in the future, even the distant future, will "enjoy the sunset, the pouring-in of the flood-tide, the falling-back to the sea of the ebb-tide." One senses beneath the surface of these lines the poet's own intense feeling of the "ties" between him and the "others."

Section 3 opens with the simple, almost impertinent, dismissal of the great *apparent* obstructions to unity: "It avails not, time nor place—distance avails not." And the poet asserts, quite simply and directly, his immediate presence: "I am with you, you men and women of a generation, or ever so many generations hence." Throughout these first sections the poet manipulates his verb tenses to serve his poetic purposes. In section 1 he is with the people of his time and his actions are actions of the present: "Flood-tide below me! I *see* you face to face!" (italics mine). The first part of section 2 contains no finite verb; the second part is couched entirely in the future tense ("Others will watch the run of the flood-tide"). In section 3, what was future tense in section 2 becomes present, and what was present tense in section 1 becomes past. The sum effect is to move the poet out of the past, over the barrier of time, into the present *with* the reader. When the poet says, "Just as you feel when you look on the river and sky, so I felt," he conveys the impression of being at the reader's side looking back with the reader to the poet's past. Repetition of this construction, "Just as you [present] . . . I [past] . . . ," serves to reinforce the impression of oneness of poet and reader.

Section 3 represents the climax in the first stage of the poet's approach to the reader. After the opening seven lines or so, the poet drops the "Just as you . . . I" construction and focuses attention on himself, and by now all his actions are *past* and he can look upon them with the same curiosity as can the reader. The long passage beginning "I too many and many a time cross'd the river of old" is filled with a richness of imagery rarely equaled in *Leaves of Grass*. In this passage the poet re-creates the experience of the Brooklyn Ferry crossing. And there is an orderly progression, both spatial and temporal, in the appearance of the imagery. The point of view is that of the poet on the ferry in passage. The poet first observes the "Twelfth-month sea-gulls" making "slow-wheeling circles" in the sky. This observation leads to his noting the "reflection of the summer sky in the water," and he watches the sunbeams reflected and he looks at "the fine centrifugal spokes of light round the shape" of his head in the water (a halo suggesting the "divinity" that connects him with all others). Next the poet's observation of the "haze on the hills southward" leads to his long notation of the varied and multiple activity in the lower bay: the "vessels arriving," the "white sails of schooners and sloops," the "sailors at work in the rigging," the "large and small steamers in motion," the "white wake left by the passage," "the scallop-edged waves." From this flurry of activity of the bay the poet turns to the river and its shores and watches the "fires from the foundry chimneys burning high" and "casting their flicker of black contrasted with wild red and yellow light over the tops of houses, and down into the clefts of streets." This brilliant, almost lurid, color cast over the shore-scene contrasts sharply with the yellows and violets and whites of the preceding scenes. At the same time that the poet proceeds from sky to water, to lower bay, to, finally, river and shore, the time fades from late afternoon (the sun is still up, perhaps "half an hour high," at the opening of this passage) to sunset, to twilight, through the deepening shades of gray to the blackness of night fully arrived.

II. *Sections 4–6: The Old Knot of Contrariety*

Sections 4 through 6 shift the "argument"; instead of emphasizing that reader and poet saw and experienced the same sensuous world while crossing Brooklyn Ferry, no matter the length of time that has elapsed between their existence, the poet now argues primarily from the universality of emotions, particularly the common feelings and impulses generally considered evil. The argument thus moves from the special or particular to the general and is no longer dependent on the "accident" of the reader's, like the poet's crossing Brooklyn Ferry. Section 4 is little more than transitional in nature, looking backward as well as forward. But, although the opening sentences seem similar to those that have appeared before, the verbs have changed. Instead of expressing sensuous perception, they express emotion:

> I loved well those cities, loved well the stately and rapid river,
> The men and women I saw were all near to me.

And when the poet says, "Others the same—others who look back on me because I look'd forward to them," that casual "the same" means that the poet feels as close to his reader, both physically and emotionally, as he does to those actually surrounding him. He concludes with the parenthetical prophecy, "The time will come, though I stop here to-day and to-night."

Section 5 opens with the posing of the rhetorical questions:

> What is it then between us?
> What is the count of the scores or hundreds of years between us?

Already in these questions lurks the assumption that there is no insurmountable barrier between poet and reader, that complete identification is imminent. And when the poet begins again to present his "proof," he is no longer confined to Brooklyn Ferry: "I too lived, Brooklyn of ample hills was mine, / I too walk'd the streets of Manhattan island." No longer restricted to a particular place, the poet soon discontinues limiting his "argument" to *place*. Following the emphasis placed on the interior life—emotions—in section 4, the poet focuses on his life within, his intellectual speculations: "I too felt the curious abrupt questionings stir within me." And what were the answers? A clear formulation of what had been somewhat disconnected and "floating" ideas in the first half of section 2:

> I too had been struck from the float forever held in solution,
> I too had receiv'd identity by my body,
> That I was I knew was of my body, and what I should be I knew I
>   should be of my body.

In many ways these three lines may be considered the heart of the poem. The chemical figure evokes a vivid picture of the abstract concept that underlies the entire poem. As when in a chemical solution the addition of some particular new element causes a precipitation, so the poet has been "struck from the float forever held in solution." There is the implication in the figure that the poet, or, indeed, any individual, comes from and returns to the same spiritual or divine source. What figure could better suggest the spiritual inseparability and unity of all mankind than the "solution"? Also implicit in the figure, behind the "struck," is a "Striker"; precipitation, the poet indicates, is no chance happening but is caused. There is, too, a curious, but necessary, paradox in the "forever." Even though the individual is precipitated or "struck," he is still "held in solution"—he does not become completely separate. What remains in solution is the soul; the body is precipitated and gives "identity." Since the spiritual source is common to all, since we are all united, interfused, inseparable spiritually, our only "identity" is physical. When the poet says, "That I was I knew was of my body," he means that the only element that granted him individuality was his physical nature; his spiritual nature did not separate him from, but joined him to, the mass of mankind.

In section 6 the poet continues his examination of the "bonds" his interior life creates between him and the reader. Emphasis is placed not only on the emotions but on the dark and sometimes sinister feelings that frequently engulf the individual. The poet asserts:

> Nor is it you alone who know what it is to be evil,
> I am he who knew what it was to be evil,
> I too knitted the old knot of contrariety. . . .

That "old knot" is, surely, Satan's knot; and, in view of the catalogue of the basic and apparently universal sins of mankind ("[I] was wayward, vain, greedy, shallow, sly, cowardly, malignant, / The wolf, the snake, the hog, not wanting in me") so near the passage emphasizing that man's individuality exists solely in his body, one might well conclude that the poet meant to imply that the physical existence of the body itself made inevitable many and varied sins. But, though the poet's list of sins is long, he seems to feel no sense of guilt. On the contrary, the tone of robust joy in the multiple and complex activities of life and pleasures of the body dominates the section. When the poet asserts that he, too,

Play'd the part that still looks back on the actor or actress,
The same old role, the role that is what we make it, as great as we like,

the reader concludes that, if that list was a list of "sins," these "sins" were an inevitable, universal, perhaps immediately painful but nevertheless ultimately enjoyable, part of assuming a physical identity. As the poet says, the role we play in reality "looks back" (that is, far excels in "drama") on the role of the mere actor in a play.

III. Sections 7–9: Fusion

The last part of "Crossing Brooklyn Ferry," sections 7 through 9, achieves that identification prepared for in the first two parts. And when the fusion comes, it arrives as a semimystical venture of this nature should, almost unheralded. Sections 7 and 8 express the final achievement of that fusion; section 9, the last section of the poem, recapitulates all the major images by which that identification was brought about and concludes the poem with a song of praise in their behalf.

Section 7 opens with the simple assertion, "Closer yet I approach you," suggesting that the final stage of complete identification is fast approaching. The "proof" is no longer dependent on an identity of place, as in the first part, or on the common "knot of contrariety," as in the second, but rather on a mutual psychic experience: "What thought you have of me now, I had as much of you—I laid in my stores in advance." Although these "stores" are the poet's "long and serious" thoughts of the reader before he was born, there is the suggestion also that they constitute the poet's abundant spirituality, stored in advance of the reader's simply because the poet achieved identity before the reader. At any event the section ends with the startling question: "Who knows, for all the distance, but I am as good as looking at you now, for all you cannot see me?" This suggestion of the poet's physical presence, perhaps meant to shock with its novelty, is surely intended to imply the imminence of spiritual union.

The chief characters in this drama are reintroduced in section 8 in the same order as that in which they first appeared in section 1.

First, the objects that impress themselves on the senses are reviewed in brief. In the three lines devoted to them, there can be only a representative selection of those that appeared in section 1 and, more particularly, in section 3. But the details of setting that the poet does repeat seem precisely those called for to re-create for the reader in its entirety the previous scene: "mast hemm'd Manhattan," "river and sunset and scallop-edg'd waves," sea gulls, "hay-boat in the twilight," and the "belated lighter." Not only do we observe the scene reset, but also once more we see the symbolic passage of time from sundown to night. As in section 1, section 8 introduces next the people of the poet's own time, whether those on the Brooklyn Ferry with him or those who, as described in section 6, call him by his "nighest name by clear loud voices." The poet asks: "What is more subtle than this which ties me to the woman or man that looks in my face?" This spiritual love that binds man to man, first given emphasis in section 4, now becomes the bridge that allows the poet to move swiftly and unostentatiously from the people of his own time to his reader with nothing more substantial than a subordinate clause: "Which fuses me into you now, and pours my meaning into you?" It is at this point that the poet dramatically achieves that identification with the reader that he had steadily aimed at from the first. The poet assumes that by now the reader *feels* instinctively the spiritual ties that bind. He asks: "What I promis'd without mentioning it, have you not accepted?" And he indicates that the miracle he has accomplished has been beyond logic or philosophy: "What the study could not teach—what the preaching could not accomplish is accomplish'd, is it not?" The knowledge of one's spiritual identity with all mankind is, like all mystic knowledge, beyond the reach of the mind because it is a knowledge of the soul.

Section 9 is a recapitulation in miniature of the poem in its entirety. The first two-thirds of this section is a direct address made by the poet to the major images that have appeared previously, beginning, "Flow on, river! flow with the flood-tide, and ebb with the ebb-tide!" Such a series of commands, one "exploding" after the other (all the verbs receive major emphasis as they begin each line), lends major significance to the objects; one feels that their role is, or has been, the most important in the poet's achievement in imaginative fusion. This series of images represents in itself a fusion of a selection of those that have appeared in previous sections; one can trace the poet as he collects them from sections 3, 5, 6, and 7, and then back to section 3 again.

At the end of this long series of images, the poet says:

> Appearances, now or henceforth, indicate what you are,
> You necessary film, continue to envelop the soul,
> About my body for me, and your body for you, be hung
>   our divinest aromas.

This passage is crucial in defining the relationship of the objects to the spiritual fusion achieved in the poem. The *appearances* surely refer back to the vivid visual images that have been tumbled forth in the immediately preceding lines. When the poet commands, "Appearances . . . indicate what you are," he is asking for a revelation as to the nature of reality. The very word "appearances" suggests doubt in the poet's mind as to the objective existence of these outward "shows." When the poet commands the "necessary film" to "continue to envelop the soul," he seems to be addressing some kind of spiritual counterpart to those "appearances." Both the "film" and the "aromas" are metaphors that embody the spiritual in the physical. The film that envelops the soul is the "float forever held in solution"—the oversoul or spiritual world or the world of eidolons. Those "divine" aromas surround the body because of the soul that exists within. The poet thus seems to be implying a relationship between objects (shows, things) and oversoul similar to the relationship of body and soul.

When the poet asserts that there is "none else more lasting" than "objects," he is speaking of the objects themselves not as they exist independently but rather as they exist spiritually within the souls of men—an existence that, after all, may be their primary existence or, in the language of the mystic, the real reality. The objects are the "dumb, beautiful ministers," *dumb* because they do not have the voices of men, *beautiful* because they speak appealingly to the senses, *ministers* because they minister finally and ultimately, like the minister of religion, to the spiritual life or soul. Once we have discovered, as we have discovered in "Crossing Brooklyn Ferry," the vital spiritual role of the objects, we of course receive them "with free sense at last." As elsewhere in Whitman, we discover the paradox of the spiritual attained through acceptance, not denial, of the physical or material. When the poet says of the objects, "We plant you permanently within us," he is indicating directly their contribution to the identification achieved in the poem. Their spiritual manifestation within the poet and within the reader has brought the "knowledge" of spiritual fusion. In this way the objects, as they exist not without but within, furnish their "parts toward eternity," their "parts toward the soul."

CHAPTER FIVE

The "Broad-Axe":
Arising Shapes

"Song of the Broad-Axe" demonstrates Whitman's ability to exploit fully and dramatically an intricate and complex symbol. Although the poet in this poem gives the central role not to himself but to the ax, he still employs dramatic principles of construction in the making of his poem. It is merely the ax and not the poet that assumes the dramatic pose. And the total cast of characters includes the infinite number of "Shapes" created by the busy broadax.

It would have been easy to allow the broadax to symbolize simply the creativity of the pioneer, and, indeed, it is some such function as this that the reader expects. Perhaps the frequent failure in fulfilment of such expectations has caused this poem to be less read and admired than it deserves. But as in "Pioneers! O Pioneers!" Whitman is celebrating not the "westering" movement in this country but rather the continuous unfolding of "mystic evolution," so in "Song of the Broad-Axe" the American frontier is only one part of a much broader subject the poet celebrates. That subject may be best defined by the opening lines of *Leaves of Grass:*

> One's-self I sing, a simple separate person,
> Yet utter the word Democratic, the word En-Masse.

In brief, the broadax develops in the poem into a complex symbol embodying individuality yet equality, separateness yet togetherness, one's-self yet "en-masse." Thus the broadax becomes a symbol of unity in variety. It should be no wonder, then, that the poet associates this symbol closely with America, where, he believed, the greatest stride forward yet in history had been made in the reconciliation of these paradoxical elements. It should be no wonder, too, that finally the ax, like the "westering" movement in "Pioneers! O Pioneers!" becomes identified with mystic evolution, Whitman's own poetic concept of time as purposeful and oriented progression. The broadax comes ultimately to symbolize, then, the final goal or fulfilment of mystic evolution. The element of individuality is dominant in sections 1 through 6 of "Song of the Broad-Axe"; the counterpart, "en-masse" or democracy, is dominant in sections 7 through 12. But the poem can best be analyzed in four parts: sections 1–3, pageantry of the ax; sections 4–6, executive deeds; sections 7–8, what always served; sections 9–12, the shapes arise.

I. *Sections 1–3: Pageantry of the Ax*

Like Joseph Conrad and Ford Madox Ford, who believed that the protagonist of a story should be got in at the beginning with a strong impression, Whitman opens his poem with a vivid presentation of his main character. In one of the most unusual passages in all of *Leaves of Grass*, in which both conventional rhyme and rhythm are marked, the ax is introduced:

> Weapon shapely, naked, wan,
> Head from the mother's bowels drawn,
> Wooded flesh and metal bone, limb only one and lip only one,
> Gray-blue leaf by red-heat grown, helve produced from
>   a little seed sown,
> Resting the grass amid and upon,
> To be lean'd and to lean on.

Both the trochaic tetrameter (the third and fourth lines are extended by simply doubling the lines) and the solitary, repeated rhyme, bring the ax on stage in such an impressive and stately fashion, in what seems a bardic chant, that one is properly prepared for the dominant role of the ax in the sweeping pageant to follow. But the sound is only one aspect of these striking opening lines. There is a rapid progression of successive views of the ax in various roles, focusing finally on not the ax but the human being's relation to the ax. In the first line the ax is seen as ax, as a weapon; but, paradoxically, this weapon is "naked, wan," attributes suggesting that the ax is not primarily designed as a weapon, perhaps is only secondarily a weapon. In the next two lines the ax is viewed as human; in a brilliant metaphor the ax's head is described as drawn from the "mother's bowels" (earth's interior); the wood is both flesh and limb, the metal bone and lip. In the next following two lines, the ax loses its human attributes and assumes those of a product of nature. The head is now a "gray-blue leaf" grown by "red-heat," and the helve is the product of a "little seed." The ax is next given a natural setting, amid the grass. And finally, in the last line of the passage, a use of the ax is portrayed, but it is a use far different from that which opened the passage: no longer a weapon, the ax is "to be lean'd and to lean on." The ax *leaned on* suggests not the heat of battle or even of creative construction but man's moment of specu- lation or even dream. The passage ends, then, with the focus on man's relation to the ax.

Following these opening lines of section 1, in which the ax is introduced with a strong impression, there appears a short passage containing hints of the nature of the construction of the poem:

Strong shapes and attributes of strong shapes, masculine trades, sights and sounds,
Long varied train of an emblem, dabs of music,
Fingers of the organist skipping staccato over the keys of the great organ.

When one arrives at the latter part of the poem, beginning in sec- tion 9, and encounters the frequently repeated refrain, "The shapes arise," he perhaps recalls that the visual image, "shapes," was as- sociated with the ax in the opening section of the poem. And here in the beginning the shapes are "strong," the shapes of "masculine trades." One cannot help assuming that these shapes and their "attributes" are the shapes not only of the created but also of the creators, not only of objects but also of the people who create the objects. This line concerning the "strong shapes" may be considered as the poet's announcement that a part of his poem is to consist of clusters of these shapes re-created for the reader to look on and admire. But there are to be both "sights and sounds"; the reader will be asked both to look and to listen, for the ax may be heard as well as seen. The sound the reader will hear, however, will be some- thing more than the sound of the ax chopping the trees of the forest; this sound will be the "long varied train of an emblem" and will consist of "dabs of music." The sound will be, then, not the sound of the ax as ax but the sound of the ax as "emblem" of "executive deeds" or, finally, as emblem of the progression of mystic evolution. It is the spiritual overtones of the ax that will be heard, an ax whose representation of physical vigor but symbolizes a spiritual vigor. Throughout *Leaves of Grass,* music is symbolic of the spiritual (see, for example, "Proud Music of the Storm" or "That Music Always Round Me"). The image of the "organist skipping staccato over the keys of the great organ" is, surely, ultimately a spiritual image, suggesting the order and harmony of the universe as it is unfolded in mystic evolution; the staccato sounds, or "dabs of music," are but the partial and incomplete glimpses man has of this whole and complete plan of the universe.

Sections 2 and 3 of "Song of the Broad-Axe" represent the pageant of the ax. The poet skips "staccato" over the "train" of the ax to present a composite picture of its origins and uses. Section 2 is concerned solely with the origins of the ax. The poet dwells on the strange nature of those "mother's bowels" from which the head of the ax is drawn: it is indeed a paradox that such a creative and fruitful instrument should originate in a land so seemingly desolate. Such a paradox is surely nature's graphic demonstration of the truth of mystic evolution—that the good apparently engulfed in evil will emerge and become triumphant. The poet points up the paradox central to his meaning by bidding welcome first to the romantic and fruitful lands of pine and oak, gold, wheat, and grape, and even of "the white potato and sweet potato." But welcome just as much as these are "the other more hard-faced lands":

> Lands of mines, lands of the manly and rugged ores,
> Lands of coal, copper, lead, tin, zinc,
> Lands of iron—lands of the make of the axe.

The poet appears here as indiscriminate in his inclusion of all lands as he appears elsewhere in his inclusion of all people. But the poet's all-inclusiveness is not indiscriminate but rather represents an insight into the nature of a unity beneath the surface that belies the superficial but more apparent diversity. Thus the poet's inclusion of all may be best described as highly discriminating. These "hard-faced lands," in spite of their sterile appearance, are the lands of the virile, creative ax. This vivid visual imagery representing the poem's central paradox is reintroduced in the middle of the poem, at the beginning of section 7, and serves to anounce the poem's major structural division.

Section 3, the poem's longest section, seems to result literally from the poet's skipping staccato over the "long varied train" of the broad-ax. Like other Whitman catalogues, this section gives the impression of great variety and multiplicity, the impression of a poet over-whelmed by the abundance he has discovered and so anxious to convey it that he loses artistic control over his material. And as with other Whitman catalogues, when this one is examined closely, an order is discovered underlying the apparent chaos, and there seems to exist the calculated and deliberate intention of evoking the impression of disorder so as to create the illusion of limitless ma-terial. This pageant of the ax opens with a series of pictures begin-ning with a woodpile and "sylvan hut" with a "space clear'd for a garden," moving next to "ships stuck in the storm" and the "cutting away of masts," and including the "founding of a new city" and the "voyage of those who sought a New England." Suddenly there ap-pears the striking line, "The beauty of all adventurous and daring persons," followed shortly by "The beauty of independence, depar-ture, actions that rely on themselves." In this fashion is introduced the major theme of the section, one whose impact is to be conveyed not by repetitive assertion but through innumerable scenes. After these thematic lines, focus shifts from the ax and from the act or product of the ax to the ax's user. We see next the "butcher in the slaughter-house" and the "lumbermen in their winter camp." And, with the introduction of the "housebuilder at work in cities or any-where," we have a series of comparatively long portraits of work-men busily at work in creative activity. Following the building of the house comes the construction of the "huge storehouse." The poet focuses in quick succession on the various workmen in typical activity, from the framing-men to the hod-men. Next come the spar-makers: "The swing of their axes on the square-hew'd log shaping it toward the shape of a mast." The next scene of the firemen bat-tling a raging fire in the "closepack'd square" injects a new note: "The crash and cut away of connecting wood-work, or through floors if the fire smoulders under them." Ironically the ax is used here to destroy that which it helped to create in previous scenes. Following the fire scene is a brief account of the making of the ax: but, throughout, attention is focused not on the ax (as in sec-tions 1 and 2) but on the *men* who make the ax, from the "forger at his forge-furnace" to the "one who clean-shapes the handle and sets it firmly in the socket."

Next the poet presents the "shadowy processions of the portraits of the past users" of the ax, from the "primal patient mechanics" to the "antique European warrior with his axe in combat." The "processions" end with a full picture of the "sack of an old city in its time," with its "roar, flames, blood, drunkenness, madness." Like the fire scene before it, this scene of the sack of a city balances with its destructiveness the creativity implicit in the earlier building scenes. The long section concludes:

> The hell of war, the cruelties of creeds,
> The list of all executive deeds and words just or unjust,
> The power of personality just or unjust.

Thus by the end of this section, the meaning of the broadax has been infinitely extended. The poet capitalizes on the association of the ax with both construction and destruction, with creativity and destructivity, with making and breaking. The broadax has come to symbolize "executive deeds and words just or unjust, / The power of personality just or unjust." This identification of the ax with "executive deeds" is but a step toward the identification of the ax with the unfolding of mystic evolution; for it is the "executive deeds" of powerful personalities, both good and bad, just and unjust, that constitute that orderly unwinding of time that is mystic evolution.

II. *Sections 4–6: Executive Deeds*

Sections 4 through 6 sing the praises of "executive" or "defiant" deeds. Although these sections are an outgrowth of the emphasis in section 3 on the "power of personality," they have their own unity in that they constitute a kind of digression from the story of the ax (the ax is not mentioned once throughout) and they revolve around the single idea of the "electric" deed that creates its own law in the act itself. Thus these sections carry to the utmost extreme the poet's doctrine of individuality, and the ax is implicitly associated with the doctrine. A balance is achieved in the later sections of the poem by emphasis on democracy and "en-masse."

The opening of section 4 seems to be an attempt by the poet to justify his acceptance of both the just and the unjust act:

Muscle and pluck forever!
What invigorates life invigorates death,
And the dead advance as much as the living advance.

"Muscle and pluck," which lie behind the executive deed, exist "forever" in the sense that all qualities have their spiritual manifestation in the world of eidolons. In this same sense, the deed that "invigorates life" (by definition the executive deed) also "invigorates death" —the physical vigor has its counterpart, in the world of eidolons, in a spiritual vigor. When the poet says that the "dead advance as much as the living advance," he seems to be making direct reference to progress in the unfolding of time. In mystic evolution, there is a spiritual progression paralleling the material progression of the spiral. In this progression and viewed from its perspective, events are not good or bad, just or unjust; rather they are executive and defiant or conforming and acquiescent: the former loom large in the progression, the latter are almost lost from view. For, says the poet, "the roughness of the earth and of man encloses as much as the delicatesse of the earth and of man." This image, embodying and "justifying" the poet's paradoxical acceptance of both the just and the unjust, recalls the poem's central paradox of the production by the "hard-faced lands" (here the "roughness of the earth") of the fruitful ax. As in the preceding section, focus shifts from materials and objects to the human being. In a passage that seems aimed directly at his own country, the poet, in answer to the question as to what endures, asserts that it is not "a teeming manufacturing state" or a "prepared constitution" or "hotels of granite and iron":

The show passes, all does well enough of course,
All does very well till one flash of defiance.

The "flash of defiance" is, of course, an executive deed, and such a deed endures. But only human beings can do such deeds. Great cities, then, exist not in the material show but in great men and women capable of great deeds.

In section 5 the poet explores fully the factors that make a great city. Such a city is not "the place of stretch'd wharves, docks, manufactures, deposits of produce merely," nor could it be a place of mere material plenty or numerical strength, a place of size or quantity. Things can never constitute a city; only people—and people of a particular kind—can transfigure a place into a city. One can find in the traits ascribed to the people who constitute the great city a recapitulation in brief of the earlier pages of *Leaves of Grass*. There are the intense feelings for equality side by side with feelings for self-reliance, as in "Song of Myself": "Where the slave ceases, and the master of slaves ceases" and "Where outside authority enters always after the precedence of inside authority." There is the "Calamus" emotion: "Where the city of faithfulest friends stands." And there is the "philosophy" of "Children of Adam": "Where the city of cleanliness of the sexes stands." There, the poet concludes simply, "the great city stands."

The "executive deeds" of the latter part of section 3 and the "one flash of defiance" of section 4 merge at the opening of section 6: "How beggarly appear arguments before a defiant deed." It is interesting to note that an earlier adjective modifying "deed," "electric," had reiterated the "one flash" rather than the "defiance" of the phrase of section 4. This earlier adjective casts some light on Whitman's meaning: the deed which is electric (or defiant) must be a deed that originates in the soul; such a deed, by the very nature of its spirituality, must be a deed in opposition to the generally prevailing materialism. In the second line of section 6, just such a conflict is envisioned: "How the floridness of the materials of cities shrivels before a man's or woman's look!" The poet's "defiant deed," then, is not a ruthless, senseless deed, nor is his "strong being" a mere tyrant:

A strong being is the proof of the race and of the ability of the universe,
When he or she appears materials are overaw'd,
The dispute on the soul stops,
The old customs and phrases are confronted, turn'd back, or laid away.

This "strong being" is one who is not dominated by, but dominates, materials and one who, by the very abundance and assertion of his spirituality, "proves" the soul beyond argument. This kind of non-conformity, which confronts, with "defiance," "customs and phrases," "money-making," "respectability," and much more, is the non-conformity of a genuine spirituality to gross materiality. Such non-conformity is the essence of the poet's concept of individuality or self-reliance. Deeds of such non-conformity are *executive* deeds because they rest solely on the spiritual authority from within. It is in section 6 that the poet reaches the climax in his development of the broadax as a symbol of individuality.

III. *Sections 7–8: What Always Served*

There is an immediate transition at the opening of section 7: "A sterile landscape covers the ore, there is as good as the best for all the forbidding appearance." Abruptly the reader is returned to section 2, and the "hard-faced lands" of the ax. And the very paradox dwelt upon in the earlier section is re-emphasized in section 7; there, dominating this "sterile landscape," the fruitful product of it, is the broadax—"What always served and always serves is at hand." This sudden movement from the delineation of an ideal individuality to the vivid image of the barren land of the ax serves to announce a major division in the poem. The ax was developed as a symbol of individuality only after the striking visual representation of the lands of the ax in section 2; before developing the ax as a symbol of democracy, the poet returns to that same visual image. By this device he succeeds in making the ax qua ax dominate the poem.

After the reintroduction of the "hard-faced lands," the poet launches a rapid-fire history of the ax, "skipping staccato" over the distant past. As section 3, with its emphasis on the multiple and varied uses of the ax in places both near and far, familiar and remote, explored the relation of the ax to space, so section 7 and succeeding sections explore the relation of the ax to time. In a sense, the ax is found coeval with time and space. Certainly each of these "identifications" is significant in relating the ax to mystic evolution. Most of section 7 is devoted to identifying the ax with the dawn of history. A series of brief, "staccato" images evokes a picture of the remote and far-distant past—a picture in which the broadax plays an important role. The ax served the "subtle-sensed Greek," the "most ancient Hindustanee," the "mound-raiser on the Mississippi," "those who time out of mind made on the granite walls rough sketches of the sun, moon, stars, ships, ocean waves," and many more. The section concludes with a series of pairs of opposites which the ax also serves:

> Served the making of helms for the galleys of pleasure and
> the making of those for war,
> Served all great works on land and all great works on the sea,
> For the mediaeval ages and before the mediaeval ages,
> Served not the living only then as now, but served the dead.

As the ax in section 3 served to unify space, here it serves to unify time. But the ax that serves both pleasure and war, land and sea, living and dead, is rapidly becoming a symbol of unity in contrast with the ax as a symbol of individuality in the entire first half of the poem. How, one might ask, can the ax serve the dead? The ax is involved, of course, in the making of coffins, and in this sense serves the dead (this use of the ax is mentioned in section 10). But there is another sense in which the ax serves the dead: it can become the instrument of their martyrdom.

It is this sense that is developed in section 8. The section opens with the vivid image of the "European headsman," "clothed in red, with huge legs and strong naked arms," leaning on his "ponderous axe." In his vision of the pageant of the past the poet says, "I see the clear sunsets of the martyrs." The broadax thus becomes associated with the terrible, but gradually successful, struggle of the world toward democracy:

> I see those who in any land have died for the good cause,
> The seed is spare, nevertheless the crop shall never run out,
> (Mind you O foreign kings, O priests, the crop shall never run out.)

This unfolding struggle for the "good cause" and the supreme confidence in eventual success constitute the nineteenth century's myth of inevitable progress, or Whitman's poetic version of that myth, mystic evolution. No doubt the perspective in the nineteenth century seemed clearer than it does in the twentieth. At any rate, there was the fact of America as a living proof that the "crop" would not only "never run out" but would produce fruit. When the poet says, "I see the blood wash'd entirely away from the ax," he seems to be readying it for transport across the sea to its "clean" work of clearing a wilderness. And the last line of section 8 confirms that the ax is now ready for its new work in the next evolutionary stage: "I see the mighty and friendly emblem of the power of my own race, the newest, largest race."

IV. Sections 9–12: The Shapes Arise

Two elements give sections 9 through 12 of "Song of the Broad-Axe" an obvious unity. The sections are drawn together by the constantly recurring refrain, "The shapes arise!" This phrase allows the poet not only to speak of the historic development of America but also to prophesy a future fulfilment of the democratic ideal. The second element is the subject of America and democracy, the two fused as one. The total effect of these sections is complex: the diversity of America is drawn together in a unity, with emphasis placed on the "en-masse" rather than on individuality; and at the same time a sense of evolutionary movement, evoked in part by the refrain, in part by the quality and tone of the sections, is conveyed. Section 9 opens with a curious parenthetical statement:

> (America! I do not vaunt my love for you,
> I have what I have.)

This statement seems to anticipate and warn against any expectations the reader might have that the poem will disintegrate at this point into a chauvinistic chant. Indeed, the poet *has* what he has and, presumably, *knows* what he has. No chant will change the reality, and it is the reality with which the poet is concerned.

There are three distinct segments within section 9, each devoted to a separate aspect of America. The opening line of the first, "The axe leaps!" suggests not only the leap across the Atlantic Ocean but also the leap in the air in preparation for clearing the wilderness:

> The solid forest gives fluid utterances,
> They tumble forth, they rise and form.

The first of these lines is typical of the densely packed lines which appear so casually placed in *Leaves of Grass* that one is likely to rush past without noticing. In this line a wealth of meaning focuses in the opposed adjectives "solid" and "fluid," the first suggestive of the material, the second of the spiritual, a duality of which the poet is extremely fond. The material gives way in the wake of the ax (as symbolic of mystic evolution) and makes a creative contribution to the spiritual. Although the forests "tumble forth," they rise again and take the form imposed by the spirit of man. In the first segment of section 9, emphasis throughout is placed on fixed structures, such as hut, citadel, exhibition-house, library, capitols, and hospitals, but the very last line suggests movement: "Manhattan steamboats and clippers taking the measure of all seas." The second segment of the section, introduced by the refrain "The shapes arise!" shifts attention from objects to individuals, from the "shapes of the using of axes" to the users. "Cutters down of wood and haulers of it" as well as "seal-fishers, whalers, [and] arctic seamen" are included. But it is the word "dwellers" that best enables the poet to encompass the geography of the New World, from the "Californian mountains" to the St. Lawrence, from "Kanada" to the Rio Grande. Following the shapes of fixed objects and the shapes of men, in the last segment of the section introduced by repetition of the established refrain, appear the shapes of the means of travel. There are the shapes of the "two-threaded tracks of railroads" and the shapes of the "sleepers of bridges, vast frame works, girders, arches," and the shapes of shipyards and "live-oak kelsons." These three segments of section 9 seem logical in progression, from the homes or establishments or places of the New World, to the people who inhabit it, and, finally, to the means of transport that connect the places and make a unity out of the great diversity.

In section 10 the poet continues to envision the rising of shapes made possible by the broadax. The first part of the section associates the ax with the complete life-cycle, beginning, paradoxically, with death: "The coffin-shape for the dead to lie within his shroud." But following immediately are "the bedstead posts . . . the posts of the bride's bed"; and again almost immediately, "The shape of the little trough, the shape of the rockers beneath, the shape of the babe's cradle." Throughout this first part, the picture is that of contentment, peacefulness, goodness—an idealized simple life: "The roof over the supper joyously cook'd by the chaste wife, and joyously eaten by the chaste huband, content after his day's work." In sharp contrast with this scene of happiness is the next segment introduced by the refrain "The shapes arise!":

The shape of the prisoner's place in the court-room, and of him or her seated in the place,
The shape of the liquor-bar lean'd against by the young rum-drinker and the old rum-drinker,
The shape of the shamed and angry stairs trod by sneaking footsteps.

Through this dramatic contrast of evil and good, unhappiness and happiness, and the association of the ax with both, the poet develops the ax as a complex symbol of the ultimate unity not only of diversity but of opposites strongly opposed. The final stanza of the section increases the complexity of the symbol by the introduction of the door as an emblem of human life, of all kinds, quality, and degree: "Shapes of doors giving many exits and entrances." In section 10 the ax thus becomes symbolic of the reconciliation of good and evil, symbolic, that is, of an all-inclusiveness that is the essence of mystic evolution.

The portrait of the idealized, nonchalant woman in section 11 is striking and, in view of the context, must ultimately be discovered to be symbolic. It is interesting to find that Whitman cut a large section of the poem at about this point that paralleled section 11 in subject: a portrait of an idealized, independent, democratic man.[1] The poet must have realized that deleting the portrait of the man would point up the symbolic quality of the woman. Section 11 begins with only a slight variation on the refrain: "Her shape arises." She is, then, like the forms listed in the previous sections, a product of the ax. Throughout, it is her equanimity that is stressed:

Oaths, quarrels, hiccupp'd songs, smutty expressions, are idle to her as she passes,
She is silent, she is possess'd of herself, they do not offend her,
She receives them as the laws of Nature receive them, she is strong,
She too is a law of Nature—there is no law stronger than she is.

On one level this woman is the ideal New World woman, as much a product of a conquered and transformed wilderness as the "live-oak kelsons" or the "family home." On another level this woman *is* the New World fused with its ideal of democracy. The poet uses the contrast between her and her environment as a device by which to suggest the contrast between the ideal democracy and the present reality. The poet's faith resides not in the "quarrels, hiccupp'd songs, [and] smutty expressions" but rather in the democratic ideal that is "possess'd of" itself and is in its own right "a law of Nature." Ultimately, then, inasmuch as she represents perfection in an imperfect present, she merges with the ax in symbolizing mystic evolution.

The last section of the poem opens with still another variation on the refrain: "The main shapes arise!" The "main shapes," however, are not of the past or present but of the future. Section 12 looks to the future to the final, climactic fulfilment of mystic evolution:

Shapes of Democracy total, result of centuries,
Shapes ever projecting other shapes,
Shapes of turbulent manly cities,
Shapes of the friends and home-givers of the whole earth.

1. *The Complete Writings of Walt Whitman,* ed. Richard M. Bucke *et al.* (New York: G. P. Putnam's Sons, 1902), III, 164–65.

Here is the myth of inevitable progress in all its glory. "Democracy total" will be achieved in the future merely through the passage of time—the "result of centuries." But this concept is, too, that of mystic evolution—the spiraling of time purposefully. Perhaps this concept is perfectly embodied in the line, "Shapes ever projecting other shapes": there is the movement of time, the present and future formed out of the past; and there is the presence of purpose, implied by the word "shapes" itself (as contrasted with formlessness). In the future, at some distant stage of mystic evolution, there will be "shapes bracing the earth and braced with the whole earth." This vision of the globe intricately crossed and bound and braced, made whole and one, represents that final unity the ax has come to symbolize in the entire second half of the poem. This braced globe is a vision of the earth with "Democracy total," its "manly cities" built on the "Calamus" ideal, and its "home-givers" founded on the "Children of Adam" philosophy. The fabulous broadax, made coeval with place and time, comes finally to symbolize the realization of man's brightest dream and fondest ideal.

CHAPTER SIX

The "Rocking
Cradle" and a Reminiscence

"Out of the Cradle Endlessly Rocking" is a vivid, imaginative re-creation by the mature poet of the primary childhood experience that determined him to be a poet and granted him poetic (or spiritual) insight. In understanding the structure of the poem it is important to note the "time" frame within which the action of the drama is set. The poet is "A man, yet by these tears a little boy again" and he is "borne hither," back to the scene of the unforgettable boyhood experience by recollection of all the images of nature that played such important roles in the experience. But in addition the poet remembers the experience so vividly because he recalls "the thousand responses of my heart never to cease," the "myriad thence-arous'd words," and "the word stronger and more delicious than any." All the poet's poems are reminders of that one crucial experience and carry him back, almost against his will. Indeed, with the onrush of all the lines of the opening section, lines tumbled onto each other by the swiftly moving "out of," "over," "down," "up from," "out from," "from," the poet is apparently overwhelmed with recollections that spring out at him from all directions at once. Possessed by an insistent memory, the poet finds himself helpless as he is transported imaginatively back into the past of his childhood. He curiously looks upon the words of this poem as somehow detached from and uncontrolled by him:

> From such as now they [the words] start the scene revisiting,
> As a flock, twittering, rising, or overhead passing.

The metaphor of the flock itself suggests that the poet's will has been subverted by his overpowering memory and the experience is, in a sense, forcefully re-creating itself.

Although the poem in the main is the boy's experience, the reader is not allowed to forget throughout that that experience is re-created out of a man's memory, the recollection of a mature poet, and the experience has its greatest significance in relation to the man as poet. When the he-bird first discovers his mate missing and sends forth his first anguished cry, the poet confides, "He pour'd forth the meanings which I of all men know." And when the poet reveals, "I have treasur'd every note," he is suggesting to the reader that the bird's song has a significance far beyond what is apparent in the dramatic incidents of the poem. At the end of the poem, too, the poet reminds the reader that the experience of the poem is not immediate but recalled, and recalled primarily because the experience reveals the source of the mature man's poetic vision. As the bird sang to the boy "in the moonlight on Paumanok's gray beach," the song evoked, like that "flock, twittering, rising," a "thousand responsive songs at random"; the poet says simply, "My own songs awaked from that hour." In this line lies the key to the primary meaning of "Out of the Cradle Endlessly Rocking."

This frame, of the adult poet re-creating in his imagination a boyhood experience, serves not only to inclose and give form to that experience but also to endow it with its primary significance. The boy is not just an ordinary boy but an "outsetting bard." The man recalling the boy is the accomplished bard. The "meaning" of the poem, if it is to have a meaning separate from the drama, is the "meaning" of the experience for the poet's songs. What are the "meanings" that the poet "of all men" knows? Why were his songs "awaked from that hour"? Perhaps one of the secrets of the triumph of this poem is that its "meaning" is nowhere explicitly stated but is imaginatively and emotionally evoked. The reader, like the boy in the poem, lives the experience and through that experience comes intuitively to *know*.

In order to discover the meaning closest to that intended by the poet, it is perhaps best to examine closely the dramatic action of the poem. The characters of the action as well as the setting function symbolically, and the action itself becomes ultimately symbolic. There are three stages in the drama of the re-created experience. In the first the dominant characters are the two mockingbirds, the "two feather'd guests from Alabama," who in their carol of bliss sing the song of ideal love and happiness. In the second stage, introduced with the sudden disappearance of the she-bird, the male mocking-bird becomes the central character and sings his powerful, anguished lament for his lost love, a carol of "lonesome love." In the final stage of the experience, the ocean becomes the main character and sings its song. Compared to the preceding carols, the ocean's song is barren, for it has only one word—death. But that word is the missing "clew."

Though these "characters" successively assume center stage in the drama, it must be remembered that what is happening is doubly seen and heard. It is filtered first through the consciousness of the boy who is there; it is filtered next through the memory of the boy become man and poet. The reader is thus twice removed from the actual experience. It is this indirect point of view in the poem that constitutes its realism. Only the brilliant imagination of the boy could translate the music of the birds and the sound of the sea into words; only the poet could fuse these "messages" into a profound insight into the nature of man's fate. In reality, then, the central character throughout is the boy, shadowing forth the man-poet he is to become, and attention is focused not on the birds and sea but on the boy-man's deepening understanding wrought by the impingement of these elements of nature on his sensitive consciousness. Each of the stages outlined above broadens the boy-poet's awareness of the nature of life and death. In the first stage the protagonist learns something of the nature of fulfilled love. While the two mockingbirds are together, they sing "all time" and mind "no time" in their bliss; out of their transfiguring love they create their own eternity. After the she-bird becomes lost, "may-be kill'd, unknown to her mate," the protagonist gains insight into "lonesome love," a love deprived of its beloved, an anguished love of the spirit, a love that has nothing to sustain it except the spiritual.

Finally, after the aria of the he-bird "sinks," the protagonist cries out: "O if I am to have so much, let me have more!" And as the sea sends forth its single word, "death," as the ocean chants the word "death," the protagonist responds with the emotional fervor of a deep and intuitive insight. He "fuses"

> . . . the song of my dusky demon and brother,
> That he sang to me in the moonlight on Paumanok's gray beach,

> With the thousand responsive songs at random,
> My own songs awaked from that hour,
> And with them the key, the word up from the waves.

This fusion is not a fusion of logic in the intellect but rather a fusion of the emotions in the soul. The meaning of the aria of the bird has been "deposited" in his soul ("the ears, the soul, swiftly depositing"), and the sea's word has been a response to the "boy's soul's questions." The fusion, then, of his songs, the bird's carol, and the sea's chant is a fusion in which the soul acts as catalyst. The poetry of this "outsetting bard" is to be forever spiritually tinged with the lament of lonesome love and the "strong and delicious word," death. There is the inevitable suggestion of the spiritual fulfilment of lonesome love in death, a concept dominant in the "Calamus" poems. The sea is described as "hissing melodious" its word of death. Such a phrase, a conscious juxtaposition of words whose connotations clash, suggests the paradoxical nature of death: "hissing" connotes all the horror aroused at the thought of death; "melodious" connotes all the happiness and harmony resulting from the spiritual fulfilment of death. It is an intuitive understanding of this paradox, an insight into the relationship of death and love, death as the spiritual fulfilment of love, that is the "meaning" of the poem and that informs the "thousand responsive songs" forged in the soul of the mature poet.

But the most important elements in "Out of the Cradle Endlessly Rocking" have so far gone almost unnoticed; these are the elements that bring about or "precipitate" the protagonist's insight into love and death. Whether they are regarded as mere elements of the setting or as highly charged symbols, surely there can be no doubt that the sun and moon, the day and night, the land and sea, the stars and waves play significant roles in convincing or persuading through the logic of emotion. At least there can be no disagreement that the *poetry* of "Out of the Cradle Endlessly Rocking" exists primarily in the dramatic use of these vividly created images.

It is no accident that in the first part of the poem, when the two mockingbirds are described in their wedded bliss, Paumanok is pictured in brilliant colors. The "lilac-scent" is in the air and "Fifth-month grass" is growing. In the bird's nest among the briers are "four light-green eggs spotted with brown." Amid all this color and all these images suggestive of life, fertility, and love, the two birds together sing out their paean of joy:

> Shine! shine! shine!
> Pour down your warmth, great sun!
> While we bask, we two together.

The sun is the great life-giver, and to it the birds pay tribute for their supreme happiness. But the tone of the joint song of the birds is one of defiance—

> Winds blow south or winds blow north,
> Day come white, or night come black

—a defiance of the elements as long as the birds remain "two together."

Those very winds defied by the two birds in their song of happiness are invoked by the he-bird as he searches for his lost mate: "Blow! blow! blow!" The meter of the stark line, recalling the opening of the previous carol ("Shine! shine! shine!"), brings into dramatic focus not only the change of fortune of the singer but also the transformed setting. Instead of the sun pouring down its great warmth, now the stars glisten, the waves slap the shore, and the moonbeams intertwine with the shadows. Day has become night. Attention is gradually shifted from the land (the sea is not even mentioned in the bird's opening carol) to the ocean. And such images as "the white arms out in the breakers tirelessly tossing," suggestive of unassuageable grief, reflect the tragic turn that events have taken.

The he-bird's carol of lonesome love, which forms in more senses than one the real heart of the poem, is justly celebrated for its incomparable marriage of sound and image. The three heavy beats of the previous songs are repeated not only in the opening line ("Soothe! soothe! soothe!") but also at intervals throughout, strong reminders of the tragic transformation. As the he-bird in his song scans the ocean, the land, and the sky for any sign of his beloved, he re-creates a world after his own emotional image. The breakers and waves of the sea, the brown-yellow, sagging moon, the land, and the rising stars—all reflect the he-bird's dejected and despairing state. These objects of the setting emerge vividly as symbols. When the bird cries out—

O brown halo in the sky near the moon, drooping upon the sea!
O troubled reflection in the sea!   ˙

—both moon and sea are symbols. But it is well to remember that they are not functioning directly as such for the reader. The reader sees both moon and sea as the man-poet remembers, when a boy, having imagined their appearance to the grieving bird. From this circuitous route these natural objects emerge charged with complex meanings by the minds through which they have filtered. The very universe comes to reflect like a mirror the emotional turbulence disturbing the bird, the boy, and the poet.

The opening duet of bliss and the he-bird's lament introduce a series of opposites suggestive of the duality of nature: sun and moon, day and night, land and sea. These pairs indicate not only a dual but also a rhythmical universe, a universe whose patterned unfolding must be the result of some unrevealed purpose. But there is additional significance to these symbols. The sun, day, and land are associated with the blissful, fulfilled life of the birds—"two together." The moon, night, and sea are associated with unfulfilled, lonesome love, a love deprived of its object. In short, one set of these symbols is associated with physical love, the body, and life; the other with spiritual love, the soul, and death. Out of these associations comes the suggestion that life and death too, like day and night, are merely a part of the rhythmical evolution of the universe.

When the he-bird in his anguished lament cries out—

O madly the sea pushes upon the land,
With love, with love

—it is, surely, with some understanding of the land and sea as symbols of body and soul. The sea "loves" the land as the spirit is attracted to the body, gains its identity through the body, finds its fulfilment only through the physical. With the land and sea established as symbols of the material and spiritual (they have been established as such in earlier sections of *Leaves of Grass*), the point of contact, the shore, inevitably develops special significance. It is symbolic of death itself, that point where the material life ends and the spiritual begins. The poet has exploited this special symbolic significance by using as the setting for his drama the seashore, with the he-bird singing his lament from the land to the she-bird lost over the sea. The poet makes explicit use of this symbolic significance of the seashore near the end of the poem, when he portrays the boy as crying out for the "clew":

> Are you whispering it, and have been all the time, you sea-waves?
> Is that it from your liquid rims and wet sands?

It is the sound of the wave dashing the shore's wet sands that the boy translates into the "low and delicious word death."

The "clew," then, is provided not by the sea but rather by the seashore, by the sea and the land jointly. "Liquid rims and wet sands" vividly suggest the land and sea inextricably intermingled or, symbolically, the conjunction of the physical and the spiritual. The sea waves, "delaying not, hurrying not," repeat their single word, "Death, death, death, death, death." The slow and funereal march of the stress ironically recalls the preceding lines of repeated heavy stresses, lines of both joy and sorrow. The sea waves' line not only recalls but also reconciles or merges the joy with the sorrow, for the hypnotic effect ("Creeping thence steadily up to my ears and laving me softly all over") precipitates in the soul of the protagonist not terror but the ecstasy of mystic insight and affirmation. Something of the nature of that insight is suggested parenthetically at the end of the poem. Those sea waves striking unceasingly and rhythmically against the shore, forming the spiritually fertile "liquid rims," are "like some old crone rocking the cradle." The poem ends as it began ("Out of the cradle endlessly rocking"), and the cycle of the experience, like the cycle of life, is begun again. Life and death are not the beginning and end, but rather ceaseless continuations. Death is birth into spiritual life. The sea, as it sends its waves unceasingly to the seashore, is the "cradle endlessly rocking," just as the spiritual world, through the mystic experience of death, provides the "cradle" for man's spiritual birth.

CHAPTER SEVEN

"Lilacs": Grief and Reconciliation

"When Lilacs Last in the Dooryard Bloom'd" is an expression of grief at the loss of a beloved national leader and a dramatization of the reconciliation to that loss that becomes ultimately a reconciliation to all death. Although the elegy does not mention Lincoln, it appears in a section of *Leaves of Grass* entitled "Memories of President Lincoln." One can experience a full appreciation of the poem, however, without extensive knowledge of Lincoln's death. Like Milton's elegy "Lycidas," Whitman's poem is only incidentally about its subject. The real subject is death, as the poet insists parenthetically in section 7:

> Nor for you, for one alone,
> Blossoms and branches green to coffins all I bring,
> For fresh as the morning, thus would I chant a song for you
> O sane and sacred death.

Like the cradle figure in "Out of the Cradle Endlessly Rocking," the dominant images of these lines—blossoms, green branches, morning—suggest that "sane and sacred death" is not darkness but light, not the end but the beginning, not death but life.

The discovery of this knowledge is the dramatic focus of the poem. For the poem is a drama representing within the protagonist the gradual transformation of uncontrollable grief into emotional reconciliation and acceptance. The course of this transformation is not a straight line from the pole of one extreme to the pole of the other; the movement is cyclic, not smooth but halting, not logical but emotional. The poet's emotions revolve about the major elements of the setting of the poem—the star, lilac, and bird. The first four sections of the poem constitute the first cycle, as the western star, lilac bush, and hermit thrush are introduced in the second, third, and fourth sec-

tions, respectively. The second cycle is made up of the next five sections, 5 through 9, as all the elements are reintroduced, with the last
section, as in the previous cycle, devoted to the thrush. The third
cycle is made up of sections 10 through 13, and again the last section
dwells primarily on the bird. The final sections of the poem (14, 15,
and 16) represent the climax of the action, the final insight and
reconciliation; and in these the bird plays the central role. These
"cycles," which in themselves suggest rhythm and recurrence, are
symbolic of that rhythmic pattern in the universe suggested in the
opening lines of the poem—"ever-returning spring." Moreover, when
placed together, one merging with another in the emotional progression of the poem, these cycles form a figure similar to the spiral
movement Whitman frequently conceived for the concrete representation of his concept of mystic evolution. The pattern of the
cycle or spiral is accentuated by the use of the bird as the climactic
element in each circle and, indeed, as the major element in the
climax of the poem.

I. *Sections 1–4: First Cycle*

The first part of "When Lilacs Last in the Dooryard Bloom'd"
(sections 1–4) not only introduces the major elements of the setting
but also establishes their basic roles in the poem. In the opening
section, symmetrically proportioned in two three-line stanzas, with
the last words of the first stanza ("ever-returning spring") used as
the first words of the second stanza, the lilac and the star are joined
with the "thought of him I love" to form for the poet a "trinity"
that will return every spring. In section 2 the uncontrollable grief
of the speaker is given full portrayal, and it is a grief directed at
the star of the west:

> O powerful western fallen star!
> O shades of night—O moody, tearful night!
> O great star disappear'd—O the black murk that hides the star!

All the lines of this section begin with the "O"—a vivid visual representation of the protagonist's grief (the letter suggests the inevitable
shape of the mouth in expressing great pain). Within the section
the outline of a celestial drama is drawn. It is a "harsh surrounding
cloud" that obscures the star as well as holds the speaker powerless.
The cloud "will not free" the speaker's soul. Each of the adjectives

applied to the star, "powerful," "western," "fallen," is also applicable to Lincoln: the poet identifies the star with Lincoln and the black cloud's act of obscuring the star with Lincoln's death. The celestial drama is a re-enactment of the earthly tragedy. The drama of the poem is not Lincoln's death, however, but the protagonist's grief at the death. When the speaker exclaims, "O helpless soul of me! / O harsh surrounding cloud that will not free my soul," he is revealing his imprisoned state created by his grief—a state whose change the poem traces, portraying, finally, the poet's release.

The instruments of that release are introduced in sections 3 and 4. The lilacs have already been met, not only in the title, but also in the first section of the poem as a part of the poet's "trinity." In section 3 the lilac bush is introduced in the full glory of its blossoms and is given a specific setting. The rich color of this section—the "white-wash'd palings" of the dooryard, the lilac bush with its "deli-cate-color'd blossoms," the "heart-shaped leaves of rich green"—con-trasts vividly with the "black murk" of the preceding section, a contrast as sharp as that between life and death. But in spite of the extensive and rich description of section 3, its single sentence is so constructed as to focus attention on the simple act revealed in the last line: "A sprig with its flower I break." This small gesture is an advancement of the poem's central action; and inasmuch as the lilac bush is a sym-bol of life, love, or affection (the strong "perfume" suggests spiritual love), the breaking of the twig is the beginning of a symbolic act of love (and of the bestowal of life), which is to be consummated in a later section.

In section 4 the hermit thrush is introduced for the first time in the poem. Although the action involving the sprig of lilac is to be a "working out" of his heartache by the poet, only his involvement with the thrush can bring about a complete purge of the grief. Un-like the lilac bush, which, symbolic of life, is in the midst of life in a dooryard, the thrush is "shy and hidden" and is "withdrawn to himself, avoiding the settlements." The lilac bush, with its rich color and strong perfume, represents physical life, and the hermit thrush, through the song that he sings by himself, represents spiritual life:

> Song of the bleeding throat,
> Death's outlet song of life, (for well dear brother I know,
> If thou wast not granted to sing thou would'st surely die.)

The bird's song is "death's outlet song of life" in that it is a song in celebration of death as an "outlet" (or rebirth) into the spiritual life. If the thrush could not sing—if there were no spiritual world— the bird would indeed "surely die" (the voice of the spirit would be stilled). There is the implication throughout section 4 that the poet is pulled toward the bird by its mystic song, but he is held by the strong attraction of the lilac bush; physical life is at this point dominant over the spiritual in attracting the protagonist, and he must allow himself more time to spend his grief for the physical departure of Lincoln.

II. *Sections 5–9: Second Cycle*

In the opening of the second "cycle" of the poem (sections 5–9), the act begun in section 3 is consummated. Both sections 5 and 6 (like section 3) are composed of periodic sentences in which copious description precedes a terse account of action. The contrast noted earlier is repeated in sections 5 and 6: in section 5 the coffin travels "over the breast of spring" amid all the fertility and growth of nature—amid the "yellow-spear'd wheat," the "dark-brown fields," and the "apple-tree blows of white and pink"; in contrast with this bright, suggestive color, the route of the coffin in section 6 is marked by somber tones—"the great cloud darkening the land," the "crape-veil'd women," the "flambeaus of the night"—shades of gray and black that recall the star-cloud drama of section 2. In short, the journey through the natural setting seems a journey through life; the journey through the mourning cities seems a journey through death. The closing lines of section 6 terminate the act begun in section 3:

> Here, coffin that slowly passes,
> I give you my sprig of lilac.

The bestowal on the coffin of this "delicate-color'd" blossom with its strong perfume is more than an act of affection; it is an act symbolic of the bestowal of life on the dead, the gift of eternal spiritual life to the physically dead. In section 7 the symbolic nature of the act is emphasized through generalization: the poet asserts that he comes "with loaded arms" for the "coffins all of you O death." Whether they be roses, lilies, or lilacs, he bestows these tokens of "ever-returning spring" (tokens of rebirth or immortality) on all the dead.

The poet turns next to the star and bird. In section 8 the poet recalls a past act of the star that he now realizes was a prophecy of the tragedy he mourns. A "month since," the star "droop'd from the sky low down" as if it had something to confide. The poet remembers how full of woe the star seemed and how it became "lost in the netherward black of the night." In this section the star, the "western orb sailing the heaven," if symbolic of Lincoln, seems also symbolic of something more. The star, in its sadness and woe, its shock and grief at an approaching loss, seems to be an interested celestial observer of man's fate—like a deity who foresees and mourns but is helpless to prevent the approaching tragedy. (This aspect of the symbolic nature of the star will be examined more fully later.) In section 9 the poet acknowledges the strong attraction of the bird's song, tells the "bashful and tender" singer to sing on, asserts that he understands the bird's song and will come presently:

> But a moment I linger, for the lustrous star has detain'd me,
> The star my departing comrade holds and detains me.

Here the poet makes the direct identification of the star with Lincoln. And the central conflict of the poem is reintroduced: the poet is still held in the grip of the cloud of his grief for the loss of the physical Lincoln and is not yet ready to accept reconciliation through intuitive knowledge of Lincoln's spiritual existence.

III. *Sections 10–13: Third Cycle*

Sections 10 through 13, which constitute the third "cycle" of "When Lilacs Last in the Dooryard Bloom'd," is made up in the main of a description of the gifts the poet presents his departed comrade—his song, perfume, and pictures. Like the symbolic gift of the sprig of lilac, these gifts serve to express a binding affection. The act of their presentation not only serves to alleviate the poet's grief but, in addition, symbolizes the act of bestowal of life. The perfume is to be the sea winds "blown from the Eastern sea and blown from the Western sea, till there on the prairies meeting." The pictures to "adorn the burial-house" are to be, like the lilac, pictures of "growing spring"; in these pictures are to be depicted scenes of nature in all its glorious and colorful and endless abundance as well as "scenes of life and the workshops" drawn from the dense cities. With the depiction (in section 12) of the "varied and ample land" and the "far-spreading prairies," a sense of Lincoln's breadth of vision and amplitude of soul is conveyed; and with the portrayal of the "violet and purple morn" followed by the "fulfill'd noon" and, finally, the "coming eve delicious, the welcome night and the stars," the endless cycle of day suggests Lincoln's immortality. In section 13 (as in 9 and 4) the poet exhorts the "gray-brown bird" to continue its song from the swamps. But though the poet responds with the ecstatic response of the mystic ("O wild and loose to my soul"), he is still not ready to leave the star:

> You only I hear—yet the star holds me, (but will soon depart,)
> Yet the lilac with mastering odor holds me.

The lure of the bird's "loud human song" is stronger now than previously, and the poet can delay his full response for only a little longer.

IV. Sections 14–16: Reconciliation

That response comes at last in section 14 as the cloud, "the long black trail" (the images of the cloud and funeral train merged), falls upon and envelops the nation, the poet with the rest. In fleeing forth "to the shores of the water" to hear the gray-brown bird, the poet is accompanied by two companions: "the knowledge of death as walking one side" of him and "the thought of death close-walking the other side." These two comrades are personifications of the basic conflict that has been present throughout the poem. The "thought of death," death conceived as the cruel depriver of life, has held the poet in his grief, reluctant to leave the star; the "sacred knowledge of death," insight into death as a spiritual rebirth, has through the bird's song attracted the poet to the swamp cedars. The poet's joining hands with both these companions symbolizes his reconciliation of a love of life and a love of death, each a fulfilment of its own kind. This reconciliation is stated explicitly near the opening of the poet's spiritual "tally" of the thrush's song:

> Prais'd be the fathomless universe,
> For life and joy, and for objects and knowledge curious,
> And for love, sweet love—but praise! praise! praise!
> For the sure-enwinding arms of cool-enfolding death.

Praise of life needs little defense; praise of death needs explanation. The bird's song offers such explanation in its conception of death as a "dark mother," a "strong deliveress": death paradoxically bestows birth—a rebirth into a spiritual life. The bird's song creates for the poet a mystical state that bestows (in section 15) mystical insight. In his "long panoramas of visions" in which he sees the chaos of the battlefield and the myriads of "white skeletons of young men," the poet discovers that the slain are "fully at rest" and that it is the living, not the dead, who suffer. In the final section of the poem the poet reintroduces the major images and weaves them together in an incantatory chant hypnotic in its rhythmical repetition and powerful in its restrained but intense emotion.

V. *Symbolism*

In this close examination of the dramatic structure of "When Lilacs Last in the Dooryard Bloom'd," the meaning of the poem's several symbols has not been sufficiently explored. The identification of the star as Lincoln, the lilac as love, and the bird as the voice of the spirit seems only superficially valid. The star at times seems to include more than Lincoln, the lilac to be greater than love, and the bird more complex than the soul's voice. And the black, murky cloud, frequently neglected by critics, is surely an important symbol in the poem. "Chanting the Square Deific," from the "Whispers of Heavenly Death" section of *Leaves of Grass*, illuminates the four dominant symbols of "When Lilacs Last in the Dooryard Bloom'd." The four sides of the "square entirely divine" are Jehovah, Consolator, Satan, and Santa Spirita. These figures represent a consolidation of all myth and a distillation of its imaginative truth.

"When Lilacs Last in the Dooryard Bloom'd" represents an emotional drama in which each of these four basic instincts of the universe plays a part in the guise of an element of nature. The symbols in the poem are not fixed, however, but operate on several levels. The following "chart" suggests some of the complexity of the symbolic significance of the star, lilac, cloud, and thrush:

Jehovah (Time)	Star	Comrade	Thought of death
Consolator (Affection)	Lilac	Love	Remembrance of the dead
Satan (Defiance)	Cloud	Grief	Deprivation by death
Santa Spirita (Soul)	Bird	Insight	Knowledge of death

In one direction beyond the concrete objects (and the star, lilac, cloud, and bird exist first as such in the poem) lies the "eternal" significance of the symbols; in the other direction lies their relevance to the immediate experience that is the subject of the poem. There exists that balance or tension between the universal and the particular in the multiple significance of the symbols that is the essence of all great art.

The individuality of the symbols is striking. The star is a celestial body, eternal, yet disappearing and reappearing nightly; this eternal recurrence or cycle is most intimately connected with that unit of time, the day, with which man is most immediately concerned and to which his every activity is related. The most notable attribute of the star is light; indeed, it is only by its light that we know that the remote and unknowable star exists. The lilac, on the other hand, is a plant of the earth, immediately knowable through the senses of sight, smell, and touch: its overpowering characteristics are its delicate color and its palpable odor. The lilac, too, is associated with time, larger than the unit of the star—the season of the year. But the recurrence of the lilac differs importantly from that of the star: the lilac dies and is born again each spring, passing through a life-cycle of growth, fruition, and decay similar to, though more telescoped than, man's.

The cloud, like the star, is also without man's reach in the heavens, but, unlike the star, it is irregular in its form, shape, and movement and capricious in its time of appearance. As the star is light, so the cloud, when it appears, is an obstruction to light. The bird also is irregular in its movement and, like the cloud, is not intimately associated with time. Of all the symbols in the poem, the bird is closest to man, warm-blooded, endowed with sense perceptions, and, above all, gifted with song. Although the bird is, like man, subject to death, its song, like that of the nightingale in Keats's ode, is immortal. Of significance, too, is the ability of the bird to settle in the swamp or soar into the heavens at will, to be near man like the lilac, or, like the cloud and star, to become a distant object in the sky.

These attributes of the four dominant symbols may be related to the sides of the "Square Deific." Jehovah (or Brahm or Saturnius) states, "Not Time affects me—I am Time, old, modern as any." His most pronounced feature is his relentlessness, "ever with those mighty laws rolling." What more appropriate symbol for him than the star, relentless in its cyclic return, ceaselessly numbering the days through which man progresses toward "extinction." The mild Consolator (the Lord Christ, Hermes, or Hercules), on the other hand, is the deity become human, absorbing "sorrow, labor, and suffering," wending his way through "the homes of men, rich or poor, with the kiss of affection." "For I am affection . . . and my sweet love bequeath'd here and elsewhere never dies." The lilac, blooming in the common dooryard, with its delicate perfume and its purple color of the passion of the Crucifixion ("I [have] been rejected, taunted, put in prison, and crucified, and many times shall be again"), symbolizes not only the lasting love embodied in the Consolator but also his destined early death and periodic return.

Satan, "with sudra face and worn brow, black" is "full of guile, full of reminiscences, brooding, with many wiles" and is defiance personified. The cloud, opaque, a "black murk," defying the star by obscuring it, shutting it from man's view, symbolizes this eternal side of the square that neither "time nor change shall ever change." Santa Spirita completes the square and bears a unique relation to the other sides:

Santa Spirita, breather, life,
Beyond the light, lighter than light,
Beyond the flames of hell, joyous, leaping easily above hell,
Beyond Paradise, perfumed solely with mine own perfume.

The thrush bears precisely the same relationship to the star, cloud, and lilac that Santa Spirita bears to Jehovah, Satan, and Consolator. The attributes delineated in this quotation are similar to the attributes of the symbols in "Lilacs": the light of the star, the murkiness (smoke resulting from flame) of the cloud, and the perfume of the lilac. And the thrush's song has its counterpart in the Santa Spirita:

. . . I, the general soul,
Here the square finishing, the solid, I the most solid,
Breathe my breath also through these songs.

The breadth of the Santa Spirita performs the same function in "Chanting the Square Deific" as do the thrush's "deliberate notes spreading filling the night" in "When Lilacs Last in the Dooryard Bloom'd." The drama of Whitman's masterpiece is not just the drama of Lincoln's death but the eternal drama of the motive-forces of the universe.

CHAPTER EIGHT

"India" and
the Soul's Circumnavigation

"Passage to India" is no more *about* its "subject" than "When Lilacs Last in the Dooryard Bloom'd" is *about* Abraham Lincoln. But, as one begins with Lincoln's death in comprehending "Lilacs," so in understanding "Passage to India" one begins with the "great achievements of the present" celebrated in the opening lines: the Suez Canal, the transcontinental railroad, and the transoceanic cable. These modern accomplishments furnish the basic impulse from which the poem takes its origin, but the poem goes far beyond them.

The real subject of "Passage to India" is stated explicitly in section 8 of the poem:

> O soul thou pleasest me, I thee,
> Sailing these seas or on the hills, or waking in the night,
> Thoughts, silent thoughts, of Time and Space and Death, like
>   waters flowing,
> Bear me indeed as through the regions infinite.

"Passage to India" is created out of the poet's "silent thoughts" on time and space and death. But the poem is not about these large philosophical problems in some blurred, abstract sense. The structure of the poem reveals a dramatic progression. The nine sections of the poem may be grouped as follows: sections 1–3, space: the earth spanned; sections 4–6, time: the slopes of history; sections 7–9, death: the soul's circumnavigation. "Passage to India" is a dramatization of the poet's voyages through space and time until, at the end, he arrives at his destination outside both. The meditations on space and time lead to mystical insight into death and an affirmation similar to that in "Out of the Cradle Endlessly Rocking" and "When Lilacs Last in the Dooryard Bloom'd."

I. *Sections 1–3. Space: The Earth Spanned*

Emphasis throughout sections 1 through 3 is placed on space as, paradoxically, the annihilator of time. The achievements of the present which the poet sings are man's contemporary achievements in spanning the globe and bringing the heretofore separated worlds together. Three geographical areas, identified by the poet with the three dominant eras of history, are finally linked: Asia with Europe by the Suez Canal; Europe with the New World by the Atlantic cable; the New World with Asia by the transcontinental railroad. Although Whitman celebrates in section 1 this mastery of space, he does so by emphasizing that such mastery, which has brought mankind back to the place of its birth in Asia, constitutes a spiritual return to the past. Although the poet sings his "days" through singing their material achievement, the greatness of the present paradoxically lies in the return to the past that the present has made possible. This past is a past that exists in space rather than in time. The tendency of the entire first section of the poem is, through exploitation of the modern miracles that have diminished space, to diminish time, to connect closely and inseparably past and present. The section concludes with one of the most vivid of Whitman's metaphors:

> As a projectile form'd, impell'd, passing a certain line, still keeps on,
> So the present, utterly form'd, impell'd by the past.

The impact of this figure demolishes the differences between present and past: time is conceived as movement through space. What is present was once past and will be future: all are the projectile that carries within itself its impulse onward.

Section 2 of "Passage to India" continues the identification of time with space. The past, "the dark unfathom'd retrospect," eulogized in the opening section, turns out to be, in section 2, not a temporal but a geographical reference to Asia and Africa; but the reference is, ultimately, not really geographical but spiritual: the poet uses the past symbolically to mean "the far-darting beams of the spirit, the unloos'd dreams" of Asia and Africa. The refrain, which opens section 2 and, in variations, several subsequent sections and gives the poem its title, "Passage O soul to India," demonstrates the poet's achievement in identifying space with time, in merging the two and making them indistinguishable for the spirit. Some of Whitman's

richest imagery appears in his identification of spirituality with the
source of "the deep diving bibles and legends":

O you fables spurning the known, eluding the hold of the known, mounting
to heaven!
You lofty and dazzling towers, pinnacled, red as roses, burnish'd with gold!

It is the past as the spirituality of long-ago and far-away India that
is, paradoxically, reached through the present's shrunken globe. But
the main point is that this spirituality, presumably remote in time
and space, is actually confined to neither but is outside both and is
knowable here and now. The first of the two brief stanzas that close
section 2 indicates that the modern miracles the poet celebrates,
resulting in "the distance brought near" and the "lands . . . welded
together," are a part of "God's purpose from the first." In the closing
stanza the poet reveals explicitly why he has chosen to sing "a
worship new," a worship of those captains and engineers and others
who have made possible the spanning of the globe, the conquering
of space: "in God's name, and for thy sake O soul."

Section 3 is devoted in its entirety to this "worship new," to the
celebration of the achievements of the present through the depiction
of "tableaus twain." But throughout these two elaborate pictures of
material accomplishment the poet insists that their ultimate service
is for the soul ("Lo soul for thee of tableaus twain"; "yet thine, all
thine O soul, the same"). As the poet has insisted elsewhere, the
route to the spiritual lies through the material; in order to get beyond space and time, one must first be embodied within space and
time. These two vignettes—one the opening of the Suez Canal, the
other a train ride over the New World's western landscape—serve
to memorialize these accomplishments in man's mastery over the
world's distances and, at the same time, to suggest the possibility
of corresponding spiritual accomplishments. Both these tableaus
evoke a sense of movement through space. In the first the poet moves
from watching the "procession of steamships" through the Suez
Canal to a point on one of them: "I mark from on deck the strange
landscape, the pure sky, the level sand in the distance." These observations convey a sense of the vastness of space, but it is a space
brought to focus in the poet; instead of space shrinking the poet
into insignificance, the poet seems to dominate (if not, indeed, to
create) the space. Similarly, in the next tableau the poet moves from

a point of observation of the train to a point on the train as it moves swiftly across the continent. And the rugged landscape, instead of appearing formidable and unconquerable, seems rather to be within man's power and subject to his wish as the train rushes swiftly across mountain and plain. Such power comes, paradoxically, from the "duplicate slender lines" of the railroad. And the real significance of the road is that it ties "the Eastern to the Western sea" and serves as "the road between Europe and Asia." This first part of the poem closes with a parenthetical exclamation on Columbus' dream—a dream of the past that envisioned the discovery of a passage to India. The poet sees in these modern engineering feats the fulfilment of the dream of Columbus: "The shore thou foundest verifies thy dream." America itself has become a passage to India.

II. *Sections 4–6. Time: The Slopes of History*

As the first part of "Passage to India" is devoted to the minimizing of space and uses time or the timelessness of time (the presence of the past) to that end, so the second part of the poem is devoted to the minimizing of time and uses a space now vastly reduced and under man's control to this end. Section 4 of the poem is transitional:

> Struggles of many a captain, tales of many a sailor dead,
> Over my mood stealing and spreading they come,
> Like clouds and cloudlets in the unreach'd sky.

These visions of history now stealing over the poet's mood are, significantly, linked by metaphor to space: events of time are like clouds of the "'unreach'd sky." Time is equated with space not only in this figure but also in another that immediately follows:

> Along all history, down the slopes,
> As a rivulet running, sinking now, and now again to the surface rising,
> A ceaseless thought, a varied train—lo, soul, to thee, thy sight, they rise.

The ceaseless events of history are here envisioned as a rivulet running down the slopes of a mountain. Time is conceived in spatial images, and the events of time become visible outside time—to the soul. Time as a barrier is destroyed, once it is penetrated as the poet now spiritually penetrates it: all time is spread out before him as on a landscape. One should note that by implication the rivulet of time running down the slope of history must pour eventually into the sea of spirituality—the world of eidolons. The events of history to be singled out by the spiritual eye of the poet are voyages and expeditions, explorations and discoveries, and particularly those that advanced mankind in its steady onward march. Vasco da Gama is the only individual singled out for mention, for it was he who discovered the sea route to India. As section 4 closes, again there is mention of a "purpose vast" and a reminder that the history to be reviewed has resulted in the "rondure of the world at last accomplish'd."

Sections 5 and 6 constitute the poet's spiritual view of the slopes of history. The first of these sections might be described as a poet's-eye view of history in contrast with the more orthodox historical view of section 6. Section 5 opens with a vivid picture of the earth:

> O vast Rondure, swimming in space,
> Cover'd all over with visible power and beauty,
> Alternate light and day and the teeming spiritual darkness.

The poet has begun with the beginning, for the earth is here described from the point of view of God. One might even imagine the Creator as standing off to admire his handiwork and examining closely the "manifold grass and waters, animals, mountains, trees" and deciding that they are good, keeping meanwhile to himself his "inscrutable purpose" and "hidden prophetic intention"—which will be revealed in due time after this curious "vast Rondure" is finally spanned by a curious creature called man. The poet seems to identify himself with God as he says, "Now first it seems my thought begins to span thee." Next in this train of events mankind appears on the scene:

> Down from the gardens of Asia descending radiating,
> Adam and Eve appear, then their myriad progeny after them,
> Wandering, yearning, curious, with restless explorations.

This poet's history of the creation of the world and the origin of man comes from the Bible, one of those "deep diving bibles" that India symbolizes, to which a spiritual "passage" has been made possible by modern-day achievements.

Throughout all section 5 no realistically "historical" event is related or mentioned. Yet the poet seems to encompass all time in his sweeping view of the world's total existence. After peopling that "vast Rondure" with the "myriad progeny" of Adam and Eve, the poet speculates on the enigmatic relationship of earth and man: ". . . what is this separate Nature so unnatural? / What is this earth to our affections?" Although no human answer can satisfy man's restless questions, "Yet soul be sure the first intent remains, and shall be carried out." Continuing his sweeping survey of history, the poet passes swiftly from the far-distant past to a distant future. After the explorers and engineers and scientists have done their work and the physical and material are encompassed and stand revealed,

> Finally shall come the poet worthy that name,
> The true son of God shall come singing his songs.

The works of this poet are to accomplish in the spiritual world what the works of the engineers have achieved in the material world. When he appears on the scene,

All affection shall be fully responded to, the secret shall be told,
All these separations and gaps shall be taken up and hook'd and link'd together,
The whole earth, this cold, impassive, voiceless earth, shall be completely justified.

This poet as the "true son of God" is one of the kind of poets who wrote the "deep diving bibles and legends" of Asia. In hooking and linking the "separations and gaps," he will be doing spiritually what the explorers and scientists have done materially. The purpose for which this son of God "shall double the cape of Good Hope" will be to discover a spiritual India in which "Nature and Man shall be disjoin'd and diffused no more."

Although section 6 lacks the breath-taking sweep from the past into the future of the previous section, the events related are the "actual" events of history. The poet begins, however, with the events of the present, the events of the "year at whose wide-flung door" he sings, the year of the "marriage of continents": "The lands, geographies, dancing before you, holding a festival garland." From this bright, if incongruous, image the poet passes to the remote historic past, and what follows is a fusion of the familiar and the unfamiliar, the Euphrates, Indus, and Ganges, Alexander, Tamerlane, and Marco Polo—all evoke a sense of the swift passage of time. Saved for full treatment is the "sad shade" but "chief histrion," "the Admiral himself." It was Columbus who, in his search for a passage to India, discovered, instead, America, a discovery that constituted an important link in the chain of events that led to the modern spanning of the globe. It was the Genoese's dream that, the poet noted at the end of section 3, was verified by the modern achievement. It is natural that in his brief survey of history the poet should dwell on Columbus' discovery, fame, and misfortunes, his "dejection, poverty, death." Like the first part of the poem (at the end of section 3), this middle part closes with a parenthetical aside to the reader. The poet abandons his historical survey and comments:

> Curious in time I stand, noting the efforts of heroes,
> Is the deferment long? bitter the slander, poverty, death?

For the poet to say almost casually that he stands "in time" is for him to imply his capability of standing outside time. This same careful placement of the poet "in time" as he surveys history's happenings and dwells on Columbus' misfortunes suggests that the "deferment" is only as long as time. Outside time, in eternity, the "seed unreck'd for centuries in the ground" (like the "seed perfection" of "Song of the Universal") will, on "God's due occasion," rise, sprout, and bloom and fill the "earth with use and beauty." When time becomes timeless, the deferment will end in spiritual fulfilment.

III. *Sections 7–9. Death: The Soul's Circumnavigation*

After the triumph over space in Part I and the mastery of time in Part II, the poet and his soul are ready in Part III to launch a voyage both spaceless and timeless. Throughout section 7 there is the almost ecstatic realization of both the poet and his repressless soul that they may return, go "back, back to wisdom's birth." The highly charged metaphoric language of this section suggests several levels of meaning. That to which the poet and his soul may return might be any one of four—or all four—places. First, there may be a physical "return" to the East, the cradle of mankind. The material spanning of the globe has made such a return possible. Next, there may be a return in spirit to the time of civilization's birth in the Orient. This time, which coincides with the flourishing "realms of budding bibles," is historically valid. Again, there may be a return to "reason's early paradise," "back to wisdom's birth, to innocent intuitions." This time, the time of Adam and Eve, is not historically but mythically or imaginatively valid. Finally, there is the suggestion in such phrases as "the young maturity of brood and bloom" and "fair creation" that the poet and his soul may long to return, if not to the womb, at least to the "time" before birth—a time of pure, innocent, spiritual existence, a world of spirit whence we come and to which we go. The poet and his soul long for the mystic's experience in his union with God—a union in life identical with the union before and after life.

Sections 8 and 9 represent the poet, in excited anticipation of imminent discoveries, exhorting his soul to begin the voyage. There is in these last two sections the fervency of the evangelist, almost a mystical ecstasy:

> O we can wait no longer,
> We too take ship O soul,
> Joyous we to launch out on trackless seas.

This note of urgency and joyousness that opens section 8 rises gradually to its highest emotional pitch at the close of the poem (a poetic technique Whitman has used elsewhere, particularly in "Starting from Paumanok" and "Song of the Open Road"). In section 8 comes the climax of "Passage to India." After comparing himself and his soul to two lovers in restless, reckless exploration, the poet attempts to re-create the mystic's experience of union with God and to convey some impression of the nature of God's divinity. The poet exclaims:

> Bathe me O God in thee, mounting to thee,
> I and my soul to range in range of thee.

This point in the poem might be recognized as the culmination of the poet's imaginative union with God. Immediately following, the poet seems to be groping for language, however inadequate, to embody his apprehension of Deity. In his search for words, the poet moves quickly from metaphor to metaphor: God is "Thou transcendent," "the fibre and the breath," "Light of the light," center of universes—and more:

> Thou mightier centre of the true, the good, the loving,
> Thou moral, spiritual fountain—affection's source—thou reservoir.

But this imaginative apprehension of God does more than bestow impressions of the Deity; it grants the poet insight not only into himself but also into those allegedly complex philosophical concepts of time, space, and death, concepts that, in more senses than one, he has in the earlier parts of the poem penetrated. When the poet exclaims, "Swiftly I shrivel at the thought of God," he evokes in his reader a vivid visual impression of his acute sense of insignificance. But it is the physical self that shrivels. The poet says, "I, turning, call to thee O soul, thou actual Me." The "actual" poet is his soul, and his soul, instead of shriveling, infinitely expands:

> . . . thou gently masterest the orbs,
> Thou matest Time, smilest content at Death,
> And fillest, swellest full the vastnesses of Space.

The soul, because it is eternal, mates with Time, and, because it is infinite, swells "full the vastnesses of Space"; having become equal to time and space, having, in a sense, *become* time and space, the poet's real self, his soul, may in its triumph smile "content at Death." Section 8 concludes with the poet, his imaginative mystical experience concluded, speculating on the nature of the real event that lies ahead, when, "the time achiev'd," "the voyage done," he will finally confront God. He imagines the experience—

> As fill'd with friendship, love complete, the Elder Brother found,
> The Younger melts in fondness in his arms.

The use of the image of melting or dissolution, like "Bathe me O God in thee" and the "spiritual fountain" of a few lines before, conforms to the use of water imagery as symbolic of spirituality throughout *Leaves of Grass*. And the paradoxical element in this figure impresses a paradoxical truth: although there is spiritual interfusion and inseparability of the individual soul and the oversoul, both retain their identity—the Elder Brother his and the Younger his.

The entire last section of the poem is given over to a dramatization of the poet's questioning, pleading with, and exhorting his soul. As the previous section envisioned the ecstasy of mystical union with God, section 9 portrays both poet and soul looking forward with supreme faith to the time when death will precipitate a permanent union with the Transcendent. Both bird and ship serve as images: "Are thy wings plumed indeed for such far flights?" And, immediately following: "O soul, voyagest thou indeed on voyages like those?" Flight or voyage, the "passage" is to more than "India": it is to "ye aged fierce enigmas!" and to "ye strangling problems" and to the "secret of the earth and sky!"—as, indeed, we have already learned in the mystical union portrayed in the previous section. As section

9 progresses, the pleading becomes more fervent, the tone more ecstatic, and the poet cries out, "Passage, immediate passage! the
blood burns in my veins!" But even in the ecstatic fervency there is
order. The poet exclaims:

Have we not stood here like trees in the ground long enough?
Have we not grovel'd here long enough, eating and drinking like mere
    brutes?
Have we not darken'd and dazed ourselves with books long enough?

The progression in this passage is not chaotic but systematic, from
one end of the scale of life to the other, from plant to animal to man.
As the poem closes, the exclamations become more frequent, the
lines shorter, until, in the last, the hypnotically repeated words suggest complete ecstatic, but spiritual, abandonment: "O farther, farther, farther sail!"

CHAPTER NINE

"The Sleepers"
and the World of Dreams

"The Sleepers" deserves to be more widely known and appreciated than it is, not only because it ranks high in Whitman's poetry, but also because of its innovations in dramatic technique. A previous title, "Night Poem" (1856), suggests the central symbol and theme: the night symbolizes the world of spirituality, and sleep represents death's release of the soul. In the realm of spirituality all mankind merges and becomes one, "averaged" and "restored." In that world is achieved a spiritual fulfilment impossible in the world of matter. The achievement of the poem, however, lies in the poet's technique that embodies the theme with imaginative impact. Another former title, "Sleep-Chasings" (1860), suggests the main element of that technique: psychological dramatization of a flow of images with only eccentric relationships one to another, closely resembling the stream-of-consciousness technique of a later era. The key to understanding the method of the poet appears in the opening lines:

> Wandering and confused, lost to myself, ill-assorted, contradictory,
> Pausing, gazing, bending, and stopping.

Perhaps the primary words are "confused" and "ill-assorted," for such is the way the ordering of the images seems; but to achieve this effect in itself requires the control and order of the accomplished artist. "The Sleepers" is a portrayal of a night of dreams, representing the poet entering the confused night of sleep, his experiences once he is plunged deeply into the world of dreams, and, finally, his return to the world of awakened day. The parts of the poem may be grouped thus: sections 1–2, identification; sections 3–4, ocean and death; sections 5–6, time and love; sections 7–8, union.

I. *Sections 1–2: Identification*

In the first two sections of the poem there is a continuous progression paralleling the erratic character of the thinking processes, half-rational, half-dream, of one falling off to sleep. At the beginning the poet, wandering "all night in" his "vision," is observer of the human scene. He observes "the little children in their cradles," "the livid faces of drunkards," the "sick-gray faces of onanists," "the insane in the strong door'd rooms"; in short, he observes the whole range of human life from birth to death: "the new-born emerging from gates, and the dying emerging from gates." And in the poet's vision the covering darkness acts as a soothing or healing agent: "The night pervades them and infolds them." Next the poet observes the various kinds of love brought paradoxically to a fulfilment by sleep: he sees "the married couple sleep calmly in their bed," "the sisters sleep lovingly," "the men sleep lovingly," and "the mother sleeps with her little child carefully wrapt." He observes, too, that society's misfit, deviate, or outcast sleeps: the blind, the deaf and dumb, the prisoner, the runaway son, the murderer. Even the male and the female who love "unrequited" sleep, the "money-maker that plotted all day sleeps," the "enraged and treacherous . . . all, all sleep." Suddenly the poet assumes a Christlike role:

> I stand in the dark with drooping eyes by the worst-suffering
>   and the most restless,
> I pass my hands soothingly to and fro a few inches from them,
> The restless sink in their beds, they fitfully sleep.

The poet seems to envision himself as helper and healer as he identifies himself with the pervading and "infolding" night whose descent has brought with it sleep and release from pain.

Immediately following this projection of self, the poet cries out the achievement of a more penetrating insight:

> Now I pierce the darkness, new beings appear,
> The earth recedes from me into the night,
> I saw that it was beautiful, and I see that what is not the earth is beautiful.

This insight, like the mystic's, is intuitive and instinctive; it penetrates through the material world into the spiritual and grants a reassuring but incommunicable knowledge of both matter and spirit. These lines suggest the basic symbolism of the poem: when the poet pierces the night, he is looking into the world of spirit and the "new beings" that appear are spiritually transfigured. More deeply submerged in his dreams, the poet abandons himself to the fantasies of the unreal world of night. He no longer merely observes, but sleeps with all the sleepers, dreams their dreams, and, finally, enters their identity. In this state he first *becomes* a dance: "I am a dance—play up there! the fit is whirling me fast!" Reduced to pure motion, the poet seems flung through the night fully prepared to enter the very beings of those he meets. Throughout the remainder of this first section of the poem, the imagery becomes increasingly sexual in implication and in fact. The poet identifies himself with the "journeymen divine," the youthful, virile day-workers, and accompanies them in their wild exploits: "Onward we move, a gay gang of blackguards! with mirth-shouting music and wild-flapping pennants of joy!"

After becoming quickly in turn actor, actress, voter, politician, "the emigrant and the exile," the criminal, and more, the poet identifies himself with a young woman expecting her lover:

> I am she who adorn'd herself and folded her hair expectantly,
> My truant lover has come, and it is dark.

There follows one of the most tender passages in all of *Leaves of Grass*, containing all the emotional impact of the sexual embrace presented from the point of view of the woman with whom the poet has identified himself. But there are not two but three in the cast of characters: the woman, her lover, and the darkness:

> Double yourself and receive me darkness,
> Receive me and my lover too, he will not let me go without him.

There follows an intentional confusion of pronoun antecedents ("I roll myself upon you as upon a bed, I resign myself to the dusk") which parallels the woman's confusion of her lover and the darkness. Ultimately it is the darkness that assumes the place of the lover: "He whom I call answers me and takes the place of my lover." In comparing the two, the poet-as-woman suggests the superiority of the darkness: "Darkness, you are gentler than my lover, his flesh was sweaty and panting, / I feel the hot moisture yet that he left me." In these scenes the poet is dramatizing the almost simultaneous occurrence of two experiences, one between the woman and her phys-

ical lover, the other between the woman and her spiritual lover—
darkness. On the narrative level this act suggests a surrender to
sleep or the world of dreams. On the symbolic level it suggests surrender to the world of spirit, a loss of identity in an all-encompassing spirituality.

The spiritual experience is described in physical terms:

> I thought my lover had gone, else darkness and he are one,
> I hear the heart-beat, I follow, I fade away.

This image of the poet dispersing himself in the night and becoming one with it, as a woman loses herself in the identity of her lover,
is striking and was once followed by a passage that merits examination. It seems quite likely that misunderstanding of the passage
caused Whitman's withdrawal of it. The psychological experience
of the poet's identification with the pervading and penetrating darkness is described vividly as the harrowing experience of being seen
naked by the world: ". . . my clothes were stolen while I was abed, /
Now I am thrust forth, where shall I run?"[1] And again, "I feel
ashamed to go naked about the world, / And am curious to know
where my feet stand—and what is this flooding me, childhood or
manhood—and the hunger that crosses the bridge between."[2] As in
previous passages, there is ambiguity: is the hunger physical or spiritual? Perhaps both, the one leading to the other. The sensation of
"flooding" would suggest the spiritual.

The four succeeding lines are filled with a startlingly vivid physical imagery:

The cloth laps a first sweet eating and drinking,
Laps life-swelling yolks—laps ear of rose-corn, milky and just ripened;
The white teeth stay, and the boss tooth advances in darkness,
And liquor is spilled on lips and bosoms by touching glasses, and the
    best liquor afterward.[3]

It was no doubt these lines that were the primary consideration in
cutting the entire passage, but placed in context the sexual imagery
seems innocent enough. The "cloth" is, surely, the "folds" of woman
(cf. "Unfolded out of the folds of the woman man comes unfolded, and

1. *The Complete Writings of Walt Whitman,* ed. Richard M. Bucke *et al.*
(New York: G. P. Putnam's Sons, 1902), III, 234.
2. *Ibid.*
3. *Ibid.*

is always to come unfolded").[4] The "cloth laps," then, introduces two metaphors: the "cloth," itself a metaphor, is conceived in turn as "lapping" or "eating and drinking." To maintain consistency, what is lapped is conceived as food—to be sure, food closely associated with fertility: "life-swelling yolks" and "ear of rose-corn, milky and just ripened." These are, unmistakably, semen and phallus. The "white teeth" that "stay" must be the fancied teeth of the cloth that laps; and the "boss-tooth" which advances must be that which dominates the lapping cloth, the "ear of rose-corn"—the phallus itself. Its advance in the darkness of the womb parallels the poet's advance in the darkness of night, itself conceived as a womb at the end of the poem. In the last line of the rejected passage, the entire sexual experience is associated with drinking, as "touching glasses" spill liquor on lips and bosoms. This spilling no doubt suggests the sexual climax, but the lips in the one case are (like the "white teeth") the lips of the cloth that laps. The "best liquor afterward" is, surely, the exhilarating aftermath, the feeling of peace that follows fulfilment. But throughout this passage one must keep in mind that the primary point is the parallel between the poet's identification with night and the sexual experience. One must remember, too, for better or worse, that Whitman rejected this passage in the final version of his poem.

In section 2 the poet continues his identification with the darkness:

> I descend my western course, my sinews are flaccid,
> Perfume and youth course through me and I am their wake.

The darkness itself takes its "western course," and the perfume and youth belong to the night as much as to the poet. He not only contains these elements but is their "wake" also. The poet next identifies himself with a "yellow and wrinkled" old woman who sits "low in a straw-bottom chair" and with "the sleepless widow looking out on the winter midnight." And, finally, in the climax of this series of identifications, the poet becomes a shroud, wraps a body, and lies in the coffin: "It is dark here underground, it is not evil or pain here, it is blank here, for reasons." The section closes with a parenthetical aside:

4. *Ibid.*, II, 166.

(It seems to me that everything in the light and air ought to be happy,
Whoever is not in his coffin and the dark grave let him know he has
   enough.)

The poet, penetrating in his night vision to a dramatic knowledge of
death, finds darkness and blankness there; and, although he finds no
"evil or pain," his knowledge is sufficient to inform him of the immense value of the "light and air" of life. The poet does not necessarily elevate one above the other but implies that the individual
should value that state in which he discovers himself.

II. *Sections 3–4: Ocean and Death*

The intimate association with death that ends section 2 is an apt
transition to the next two sections, each concerned with some aspect
of death. The poet enters a new stage in his penetration into the
world of sleep and dreams. Throughout the first two sections of the
poem, the poet seemed on the edge of that world, neither completely in nor completely out and deprived of the clearness of vision of
either the fully awake or the fully asleep. He seemed to be in that
murky in-between state, which invited a rapidly shifting and merging imagery. In sections 3 and 4 (and also 5 and 6) the poet seems
to have penetrated to a state of lucidity, a state in which the images
are more vivid and logical and fixed—a state of deep and undisturbed
dream-vision. The poet has won his way to this state by his identification with (or diffusion in) darkness. No longer does he identify
himself with what he sees; he observes with unobstructed vision.

In section 3 the poet portrays himself on the seashore (physical
symbol of the line separating life and death throughout *Leaves of
Grass*) observing a "beautiful gigantic swimmer swimming naked
through the eddies of the sea." Two aspects of the sharply drawn
picture stand out: the swimmer is a handsome physical specimen of
mankind: "His brown hair lies close and even to his head, he strikes
out with courageous arms, he urges himself with his legs"; and the
swimmer's death comes only after great courageous struggle:

He is baffled, bang'd, bruis'd, he holds out while his strength holds out,
The slapping eddies are spotted with his blood, they bear him away, they
   roll him, swing him, turn him.

The battle of the finest of human specimens (the "courageous giant") against the sea and the resulting triumph of the sea are im-

pressive, but throughout the passage there lurks a meaning beyond the literal. There is the suggestion of man's universal battle with death, and his final capitulation; but the capitulation is to the *sea*, always the world of the spirit in *Leaves of Grass*. In the closing lines of the section there is a tone of contemplative calm highly suggestive of an emotional reconciliation:

> His beautiful body is borne in the circling eddies, it is
>   continually bruis'd on rocks,
> Swiftly and out of sight is borne the brave corpse.

This tone could spring only from a knowledge granted by spiritual insight.

As the special instance is represented in section 3, so the general situation is portrayed in section 4. One man is the focal center in the one section; an entire ship becomes the center in the other. But the scene does not shift. The poet is still on the seashore, observing death in the ocean. He says at the opening:

> I turn but do not extricate myself,
> Confused, a past-reading, another, but with darkness yet.

The brief phrase, "with darkness," recalls the poet's dispersion in the night at the end of section 1, an act of "surrender" that has resulted in the lucid vision of his dream. He seems to be informing the reader that he still remains engaged, that he is so deeply submerged that he is unable to "extricate" himself. The wreck of the ship in the tempest is vividly described from the perspective of one on the seashore: "I look where the ship helplessly heads end on, I hear the burst as she strikes, I hear the howls of dismay, they grow fainter and fainter." The poet's only gesture is his "wringing fingers": "I can but rush to the surf and let it drench me and freeze upon me." The close of the section, like the close of that preceding, exhibits a quality of restraint suggesting mystic reconciliation: "In the morning I help pick up the dead and lay them in rows in a barn."

III. *Sections 5–6: Time and Love*

In sections 5 and 6, the poet seems to remain in the same deep, undisturbed state of sleep that characterizes the two previous sections. And this state grants, again, a clear and penetrating insight that results in lucid and sustained, rather than shadowy and fleeting, images. As in sections 3 and 4 the poet, through his identification with darkness and transport to the side of the sea, triumphed over space, so in sections 5 and 6 he triumphs over time. Both sections go back in time, section 5 portraying an episode from the nation's history, section 6 representing an event from the poet's history. As in the two previous sections, the poet does not identify himself with the persons portrayed but reports as an observant onlooker. Section 5 re-creates an incident that involves close, almost inexplicable, ties that bind men together. George Washington is presented first in defeat, at the height of his emotional involvement in the loss of his men: "He lifts the glass perpetually to his eyes, the color is blanch'd from his cheeks." The Commander is next observed "when peace is declared," again at a time of emotional intensity, as he says farewell to his men:

The chief encircles their necks with his arm and kisses them on the cheek,
He kisses lightly the wet cheeks one after another, he shakes hands and bids
    good-by to the army.

The encircling of the neck is a ritualistic act of democracy in *Leaves of Grass* signifying spiritual love of the "Calamus" kind. In this scene the poet is projecting his own private American myth back in time, giving it the authority of identification with the primary Founding Father. But the focal point in both scenes in section 5 is the spiritual love that exists between man and man.

Section 6 also portrays a deep spiritual love, but, in contrast with the male comradeship of section 5, involves two women. The poet, in defiance of time, re-creates a scene out of his mother's past. The use of precise details makes the portrayal impressively realistic:

A red squaw came one breakfast-time to the old homestead,
On her back she carried a bundle of rushes for rush-bottoming chairs,
Her hair, straight, shiny, coarse, black, profuse, half-envelop'd her face.

The poet's mother discovers, to her "delight and amazement," that the squaw is a classic primitive example of "beauty and purity": "The more she look'd upon her she loved her." But, as with Washington and his army, there came a time for parting. After the departure of the red squaw, the poet's mother felt a great loss and a deep longing:

All the week she thought of her, she watch'd for her many a month,
She remember'd her many a winter and many a summer,
But the red squaw never came nor was heard of there again.

The parallel between the emotion felt by Washington at the loss of his men and that of the poet's mother felt at the absence of her primitive visitor is clear and pointed: the spiritual relationship that exists among human beings, characterized fully in the "Calamus" section of *Leaves of Grass,* is fundamental and lasting. These two sections, coming, as they do, after the two sections expressing a calm restraint in the face of death, clearly imply the fulfilment of a frustrated spiritual attachment in death, when the spirit is released for return to that spiritual world (signified, in this poem, by the night) whence it derived.

IV. *Sections 7–8: Union*

The opening of section 7 portrays the poet emerging from his dream. He is again, as in sections 1 and 2, in that halfway stage in which images fade and merge. But the poet's return from his deep and lucid dream world is suggestive of an emergence from a mystical experience:

> A show of the summer softness—a contact of something
>   unseen—an amour of the light and air,
> I am jealous and overwhelm'd with friendliness,
> And will go gallivant with the light and air myself.

The emphasis on light in this section is in pointed contrast with the emphasis on darkness in the opening sections of the poem. In the earlier sections, the poet was on his way *in,* toward an identification with darkness; in sections 7 and 8 the poet is on his way *out,* toward the light of day. But the light is also suggestive of illumination, the kind of illumination granted by the poet's penetration of the world of night (or spirit).

The technique through these last two sections resembles closely that used in the first two: the impression of chaos and disorder is conveyed through a rapid succession of images only obscurely related. Although the images first presented seem selected at random, as they accumulate they evoke a sense of the basic cyclic quality of human life:

> O love and summer, you are in the dreams and in me,
> Autumn and winter are in the dreams, the farmer goes with his thrift.

At one point the poet seems consciously to reveal his method: "Elements merge in the night, ships make tacks in the dreams." Many of the images in the passage which follows are images of return, the return of the sailor, the return of the exile, the return of the fugitive. But there is more than mere travel through space involved in these *returnings;* there is also travel through time. For example, "the immigrant is back beyond months and years, / The poor Irishman lives in the simple house of his childhood with the well-known neighbors and faces." From these merging elements of the night, in which both space and time lose their significance as barriers, one gains the impression of an entire world *returning* to its origins. The "Dutchman voyages home, and the Scotchman and Welshman voyage home," "the Swede returns, and the Dane and Norwegian return." All, all return; and the physical return seems but a symbol of some kind of spiritual renewal.

The next passage of this section, beginning "The homeward bound and the outward bound," is a summary recapitulation of the major images that appeared in previous sections, from the "beautiful lost swimmer, the ennuyé, the onanist, the female that loves unrequited, the money-maker," to the "laugher and weeper, the dancer, the midnight widow, the red squaw." The poet, out of the depths of his newly acquired intuitive knowledge, comments:

> The antipodes, and every one between this and them in the dark,
> I swear they are averaged now—one is no better than the other,
> The night and sleep have liken'd them and restored them.

The effect of night and sleep—or submergence in the mystical state of the spiritual world—is twofold: there is a leveling and there is a healing. But the likeness that all acquire in sleep is of a supreme quality: "Every one that sleeps is beautiful, every thing in the dim light is beautiful." Beauty in darkness can be only a spiritual beauty. The poet makes the explicit connection between night and spirituality through what he calls the "myth of heaven":

> The myth of heaven indicates peace and night.
> The myth of heaven indicates the soul.

But this soul indicated by the "myth of heaven" comes bodied forth in the physical. The soul

> . . . comes from its embower'd garden and looks pleasantly on itself and
> encloses the world,
> Perfect and clean the genitals previously jetting, and perfect and clean
> the womb cohering,
> The head well-grown proportion'd and plumb, and the bowels and joints
> proportion'd and plumb.

The divine soul by its very presence makes "perfect and clean" the physical processes that produce the body it inhabits. It is because of the presence in it of the spiritual that the physical commands a due respect. But the primary point the poet makes in these closing lines of section 7 is his supreme faith, gained perhaps from his spiritual experience, in the existence of a divine plan that makes life meaningful: "The universe is duly in order, everything is in its place." This universe is recognizable as the universe created out of the poet's theory of mystic evolution. The last lines of the section embody this abstract theory in concrete terms:

The sleepers that lived and died wait, the far advanced are to go on in
   their turns, and the far behind are to come on in their turns,
The diverse shall be no less diverse, but they shall flow and unite—they
   unite now.

The simple phrase "in their turns" implies order and plan and purpose, the central element in mystic evolution. The poet is fully aware of the paradoxical nature of his poetic vision of evolution, and, as in his view of democracy (balanced delicately between individuality and "en-masse"), he asserts the reconciliation, without injurious modification of either, of diversity and unity in mystic evolution.

In section 8, the poet appears to be waking from his night of dreams. But at the beginning he is not fully awake, for there is still an unreal quality attached to the images:

The sleepers are very beautiful as they lie unclothed,
They flow hand in hand over the whole earth from east to west as they
   lie unclothed.

The sleepers have become naked not merely by divesting their clothes but by divesting their material nature in their sleep. Their "flow" is a flow of spirit that unites one with another. And the catalytic element in this union is spiritual love:

The bare arm of the girl crosses the bare breast of her lover, they press
   close without lust, his lips press her neck,
The father holds his grown or ungrown son in his arms with measureless
   love, and the son holds the father in his arms with measureless love.

But the "flow" represents also a dissolution of pain and suffering: "The felon steps forth from the prison, the insane becomes sane, the suffering of sick persons is reliev'd." And it is the "invigoration of the night and the chemistry of the night," symbolic of the spiritual, that achieves such miraculous restoration.

At the end of this section (also the end of the poem) the poet returns to an examination of self:

> I too pass from the night,
> I stay a while away O night, but I return to you again and love you.

The night is conceived not as a segment or unit of time but as a place and, ultimately, as a person. The poet envisions the night as his progenitor: "I love the rich running day, but I do not desert her in whom I lay so long." The poet's knowledge as to his origins and destiny, like the mystic's, is, although uncertain, full of the certainty of faith: "I know not how I came of you and I know not where I go with you, but I know I came well and shall go well." Throughout these last lines, the poet identifies the night with the spiritual and the day with the material world, and there is the suggestion that his birth from night, or awakening, parallels his actual birth into life and that his return to night, or sleep, parallels his actual death. Death, then, becomes a birth into the spiritual world or, in the poet's conceit, a return to the mother: "I will duly pass the day O my mother, and duly return to you." The womb of that dark, gliding mother lurking behind many of the pages of *Leaves of Grass* is not only the poet's origin but also his destiny. Man comes from the womb and man returns to the womb. And the womb is the teeming world of spirit, the ultimate and real Reality.

CHAPTER TEN

The
Smaller Leaves

So much critical attention has been paid to Whitman's long poems that it is frequently forgotten that much of *Leaves of Grass* is made up of short poems, some of them ranking with the best of Whitman's poetry. Although it is probably true that Whitman's expansive temperament was best fitted for poems of some length, it is equally true that his genius enabled him at times to create brilliant short lyrics. Perhaps one of the reasons for the nature of Whitman's reputation is that the longer poems are more easily "detachable" from the whole of *Leaves of Grass* and are less dependent on their context for their fulness of meaning. Whitman's short poems frequently refer and have application to the entire body of his work. But a critical treatment of *Leaves of Grass* would be incomplete without some attention to the short poems. The attention of this chapter, though inadequate (as all criticism is, ultimately, inadequate), is meant to account for a few of the flashes of brilliance the reader of *Leaves of Grass* perceives in the short lyrics as he browses through the volume.

I

One of the most notable elements of many of the short "leaves" is what might be termed their cryptic quality, a quality of ambiguity, even evasiveness, which suggests an abundant complexity of meaning. This quality, a deliberate technique consciously developed by the poet, perhaps reaches its maximum use and effectiveness in "Calamus," but it appears throughout *Leaves of Grass*. When Whitman asserts, somewhat defiantly, in one of his prefaces to his book,

"I have not been afraid of the charge of obscurity" (V, 202),[1] he not only aligns himself with the dominant tradition in twentieth-century poetry but also reveals an important element of his poetic technique. Whitman's "obscurity" was motivated by the poet's realization that there was a good deal of "obscurity" about the ultimate nature of things. One could have assurance, could be certain, but such *emotional* insight was not necessarily accompanied by *philosophical* insight. That the emotions were not confirmed by the intellectual understanding made them no less valid, particularly as subjects of poetry. Perhaps it was precisely in this area that poetry found its most appropriate subject matter; for the rich language of poetry could suggest, could hint at what existed beyond man's understanding.

In an "Inscriptions" poem ("Poets To Come"), Whitman asserts the philosophical inadequacy of his poetry:

I myself but write one or two indicative words for the future,
I but advance a moment only to wheel and hurry back in the darkness
    [I, 15].

It is clearly this attitude, acknowledging the inadequacy of language to embrace systematically the complexity of "reality," that underlies Whitman's technique of the cryptic, the ambiguous, the suggestive, in poetry. This technique emerges in such a short poem as "For Him I Sing," in which no antecedent for the crucial pronoun is ever revealed:

For him I sing,
I raise the present on the past,
(As some perennial tree out of its roots, the present on the past,)
With time and space I him dilate and fuse the immortal laws,
To make himself by them the law unto himself [I, 9].

The reader may go back to the opening "Inscriptions" poem, "One's Self I Sing," for the antecedent, modern man. Or perhaps today's man, the common man of modern democracy, will suggest itself from this single poem. In any event it is certain that a good deal of pleasure in reading the poem, as the poet must have known, derives from the gradual realization of the answer to a question of meaning posed at the outset.

1. Quotations from Whitman are where possible identified in the text by volume and page number of *The Complete Writings of Walt Whitman,* ed. Richard M. Bucke *et al.* (New York: G. P. Putnam's Sons, 1902).

There is at least one example of the poet's deliberately directing his reader's attention to this element of ambiguity as the central element of his poem—in "A Riddle Song," a poem which links directly the ambiguity of language with the infinite complexity of ultimate reality. "That which eludes this verse and any verse" is "Open but still a secret, the real of the real, an illusion." Whitman teases the reader:

> Two little breaths of words comprising it,
> Two words, yet all from first to last comprised in it [II, 259].

"A Riddle Song" employs directly that technique that is present indirectly in nearly all Whitman's poetry. The two words of "God's riddle" may be "the ideal," as William Sloane Kennedy suggests,[2] but the reader will want the intellectual and emotional pleasure of solving the riddle in his own terms.

One of the notable short poems that provide the reader with a certain amount of pleasurable intellectual toughness is "Beginners," an "Inscriptions" poem, in which a good deal is said, and a good deal more hinted, about the nature and fate of—beginners:

How they are provided for upon the earth, (appearing at intervals,)
How dear and dreadful they are to the earth,
How they inure to themselves as much as to any—what a paradox appears their age,
How people respond to them, yet know them not,
How there is something relentless in their fate all times,
How all times mischoose the objects of their adulation and reward,
And how the same inexorable price must still be paid for the same great purchase [I, 10].

The central poetic device of this brief poem is the repetition of the "How" construction in every line, so that, finally, no statement is made, but merely a series of exclamations tumbled forth, dramatically characterizing the implied speaker as caught up in a spell halfway between musing and wonder. The effect conveyed is that of an overpowering insight somewhat haltingly in search of adequate language, truths glimpsed and pursued with hints and indirections.

But the poem's central ambiguity is introduced in the title. It is likely that, at first glance, the reader will assume that "beginners" refers to novices—those who are just "starting" in some area of life.

2. William Sloane Kennedy, *The Fight of a Book for the World* (West Yarmouth, Mass.: Stonecroft Press, 1926), p. 188.

But as he progresses in the poem, the reader discovers that Whitman's "beginners" are quite rare, in that they appear at "intervals"; that they are unusual, in that they are both "dear and dreadful"; and (in a curiously involved phrase) that these beginners "inure to themselves as much as to any" (find their adjustment to their own marked difference as momentous as their adjustment to the difference of others). Clearly these beginners are not all men as novices but rather the great, original minds, the fabulous, if sometimes currently unnoticed, innovators, the intellectual revolutionists. They are "dear" in that they are precious to man's development, but they are also "dreadful" in that they bring an inevitably painful change from things as they are. People respond, unaware that they do so, because the idea or will or attitude of the great innovator detaches from him as an individual and permeates all areas of life and society. The final irony about beginners is that they go unrecognized: "all times mischoose the objects of their adulation and reward." The really great innovators have, the poet asserts, gone unrecognized. The last line of the poem seems to shift the focus from the people and the times to the "'beginners" themselves—it is they who must pay the "same inexorable price" (lack of recognition, perhaps even poverty, exile, or execution) for the "great purchase" that is their achievement.

This simple, innocently titled poem turns out, on close examination, to be a compact commentary on the effect, the contribution, the influence, the neglect, and the fate of the great geniuses who "began" or launched movements of ideas that affected profoundly the course of history—such figures, perhaps, as, on one level, Christ or, on another, Joan of Arc. Or, on still another, in the area of literature and particularly poetry, perhaps Whitman is obliquely referring to himself, his work, and the nineteenth century's neglect of both.

II

Another dominant device present in many of the fine short poems is the catalogue. Perhaps this device is more tolerable in the brief than in the long poem because it appears to be under a stricter control. In any event in the best of the short-poem catalogues, the function or purpose of the "list" of swiftly succeeding images is sharply

pointed. Like the cryptic element in Whitman's poetry, the catalogue, really an ecstatic and extended engagement with—delight in
—the physicality of the universe, derives from a fundamental point
of view held by the poet. Whitman confesses in one of his "Inscriptions" poems—"Beginning My Studies":

> Beginning my studies the first step pleas'd me so much,
> The mere fact consciousness, these forms, the power of motion,
> The least insect or animal, the senses, eyesight, love,
> The first step I say awed me and pleas'd me so much,
> I have hardly gone and hardly wish'd to go any farther,
> But stop and loiter all the time to sing it in escstatic songs [I, 10].

This confession goes far toward explaining the nature of and the
cause for the catalogues in *Leaves of Grass*. But if there is a realization in this poem of the difficulty of getting beyond the physical,
there is also an acute awareness that "mere fact consciousness" is
only the "first step." This awareness is elevated to the level of a car-
dinal principle in Whitman's poetics.

The principle was proclaimed in the 1855 Preface: "The land and
sea, the animals fishes and birds, the sky of heaven and the orbs, the
forests mountains and rivers, are not small themes . . . but folks expect of the poet to indicate more than the beauty and dignity which
always attach to dumb real objects . . . they expect him to indicate
the path between reality and their souls."[3] Pleasant though it might
be to construct poems only of images, Whitman affirms the necessity
for the poet to go beyond, to perceive relationships and probe connections, to discover and convey the spiritual significance of the
physical fact. In this step lies the supreme act of perception of the
poetic process, as difficult as it is rewarding.

Whitman appears at his best when he allows his mind free play
over a seeming multitude of "physical facts," ferreting out submerged relationships and illuminating imbedded significances. Three
brilliant short poems may serve as examples of Whitman's adaptation
of the catalogue technique to the brief lyric: "I Hear America Singing," "The World Below the Brine," and "I Sit and Look Out."

One of the most frequently reprinted poems in *Leaves of Grass*,
"'I Hear America Singing" presents an image of America that Amer-

3. Facsimile of 1855 text of *Leaves of Grass* (New York: Columbia University
Press, 1939), p. v.

ica would like to believe true—an image of proud and healthy in-
dividualists engaged in productive and happy labor. Mechanic,
carpenter, mason, boatman, deckhand, shoemaker, hatter, wood-
cutter, plowboy—from city to country, from sea to land, the "varied
carols" reflect a genuine joy in the day's creative labor that makes
up the essence of the American dream or myth. After the catalogue
of the men of the various crafts and occupations, the poet turns to
the women:

The delicious singing of the mother, or of the young wife at work, or of
    the girl sewing or washing,
Each singing what belongs to him or her and to none else,
The day what belongs to the day—at night the party of young fellows,
    robust, friendly,
Singing with open mouths their strong melodious songs [I, 13–14].

The women of the men sing at their labor, too, as the poet, figuratively reversing time, places in order first a mother, then a wife, and
finally a girl. These songs of one's own ("what belongs to him or
her") are carols of spiritual possession—of the possessed individuality, of possessed life and potentiality for contribution to the onward
stream of life. If the fused image of mother-wife-girl, following as
it does the catalogue of happy craftsmen, suggests the fulfilled emotions of "Children of Adam," the closing image of the poem, an image of night rather than day, with its "party of young fellows" singing "their strong melodious songs," suggests the fulfilled emotions
of "Calamus." America singing emerges as a happy, individualistic,
proudly procreative, and robustly comradely America. It is surprising that in such a brief poem so much of Whitman's total concept
of modern man could be implied. Perhaps its "casual" inclusiveness
is one of the reasons for its popularity.

    "The World Below the Brine," one of the short "Sea-Drift" poems,
presents a catalogue that constructs a brilliant visual image of the
world beneath the sea:

Forests at the bottom of the sea, the branches and leaves,
Sea-lettuce, vast lichens, strange flowers and seeds, the thick tangle, open-
    ings, and pink turf,
Different colors, pale gray and green, purple, white, and gold, the play of
    light through the water,
Dumb swimmers there among the rocks, coral, gluten, grass, rushes, and
    the aliment of the swimmers,

Sluggish existences grazing there suspended, or slowly crawling close to
   the bottom,
The sperm-whale at the surface blowing air and spray, or disporting with
   his flukes,
The leaden-eyed shark, the walrus, the turtle, the hairy sea-leopard, and
   the sting-ray [II, 21].

The images in this passage are calculated to engage all the senses,
conveying a bright awareness of an independent world that goes its
independent way of man. One feels that in this ocean scene he is
near the origins of all life, that this scene is but a re-enactment of one
that has recurred without cease since time began. But the images
are not randomly chosen: from the "vast lichens" and "dumb swimmers" to the sperm-whale "disporting with his flukes" and "leaden-
eyed shark," the emphasis throughout is on the slowed, clumsy tem-
po of this strange, alien life. The general impression created comes
to brilliant focus in one of the central lines: "Sluggish existences
grazing there suspended, or slowly crawling close to the bottom."
   In the last three lines of the poem, Whitman moves abruptly from
the sea scene to other spheres in a "flash" of insight:

Passions there, wars, pursuits, tribes, sight in those ocean-depths, breath-
   ing that thick-breathing air, as so many do,
The change thence to the sight here, and to the subtle air breathed by
   beings like us who walk this sphere,
The change onward from ours to that of beings who walk other spheres
   [II, 21].

As the world of the sea appears sluggish to us, so, to beings we
know not of, our world may likewise appear brutish. The movement
by the poet up out of the sea into the air and even further up into
the rarefied atmosphere may be so swift as to leave us breathless—
or skeptical. But there is no doubt that his flight is soaring and even
provocative as he perceives the miraculous in the commonplace and
on its basis postulates another miracle no less possible because it is
unknown to the senses. The poet is not affirming a belief but con-
jecturing an imaginative possibility. Out of the "dumb real objects"
of the ocean depths, after he has taken his full delight in his "fact
consciousness," the poet indicates swiftly with the full force of his
imagination the path between reality and the soul.
   As "I Hear America Singing" portrays Whitman's affirmation and
optimism and "The World Below the Brine" demonstrates his bril-

liant use of imagery, so "I Sit and Look Out" dramatizes vividly his attitude toward misery and evil, an attitude widely misunderstood. A "By the Roadside" poem, "I Sit and Look Out" uses the brief catalogue for a clear and pointed purpose. In the opening line, the poet establishes his emotional point of view: "I sit and look out upon all the sorrows of the world, and upon all oppression and shame." The first half of the ensuing catalogue illustrates abuse of personal relationships:

I hear secret convulsive sobs from young men at anguish with themselves,
  remorseful after deeds done,
I see in low life the mother misused by her children, dying, neglected,
  gaunt, desperate,
I see the wife misused by her husband, I see the treacherous seducer of
  young women,
I mark the ranklings of jealousy and unrequited love attempted to be hid,
  I see these sights on the earth [II, 34].

One might note in these lines not just the astonishing perception of the devastating effects of evil but, more important, the deterioration and destruction of those very relationships in which, so to speak, the poet had invested his optimism. Where has the "'Calamus" emotion fled when young men sob secretly for "deeds done," where has the image of the ideal procreative relationship of "Children of Adam" gone when mothers are mistreated by their children, wives by their husbands, young women by their boy friends become seducers? The world in which the poet sits and on which he looks out is the world of "I Hear America Singing" turned upside down, its harmonious happiness turned sour.

This poem and others prove that Whitman was not grossly oblivious, as he has so often been accused, of the sin and sorrow of the world. He notes not only the substitution of hate and lust for affection and love in personal relationships, but he also records the great, obliterating enemies of man: "battle, pestilence, tyranny," "famine at sea," and even "slights and degradations cast by arrogant persons upon laborers, the poor, and upon negroes, and the like." These "sorrows of the world" the poet observes, records, and "accepts":

All these—all the meanness and agony without end I sitting look out upon,
See, hear, and am silent [II, 34].

The basic nature of the poem belies the suggestion of indifference in the attitude of the poet. His very terms—"misused," "slights and degradations," "meanness and agony"—are judgments of condemnation. His silence, then, is not the silence of cynical disengagement or of approving assent but rather the silence of philosophical insight. The sorrows, regrettable but inevitable, must await not man's but "Nature's amelioration," the advance of that "mystic evolution" (of "Song of the Universal") to the level at which "Not the night only [is] justified, [but] what we call evil also justified." The poet looks out on the world, sees, hears, and remains silent, not because he sees no evil or fails to understand the evil he sees, but because his vision of the *context* of evil is so comprehensive as to impress upon him, in the face of its current inevitability, its ultimate insignificance in the total "scheme."

III

The same genius that enabled Whitman to assemble the items of a catalogue and discover in the total a significance greater than the sum of all the parts endowed him also with keen poetic insight into the brief vignettes life seems always freely presenting to the perceptive. Some of Whitman's most brilliant short poems are hardly more than vivid descriptive accounts of such vignettes, through every phrase of which flickers forth the flame of suggestive meaning, the whole finally consumed in a flash of brilliant insight. In this technique, as in the catalogues, the operating principle is the poet's attempt, subtly but firmly, "to indicate the path between reality" and the soul. Three poems that illustrate the technique of the "caught" picture or the vignette are "The Dalliance of the Eagles," "Sparkles from the Wheel," and "A Noiseless Patient Spider."

"The Dalliance of the Eagles," curiously reminiscent of "We Two, How Long We Were Fool'd," is found not as we might expect in "Children of Adam" but in "By the Roadside," perhaps related in part to its section by the opening line's account of the poet's walk along the "river road":

Skirting the river road, (my forenoon walk, my rest,)
Skyward in air a sudden muffled sound, the dalliance of the eagles,
The rushing amorous contact high in space together,
The clinching interlocking claws, a living, fierce, gyrating wheel,

Four beating wings, two beaks, a swirling mass tight grappling,
In tumbling turning clustering loops, straight downward falling,
Till o'er the river pois'd, the twain yet one, a moment's lull,
A motionless still balance in the air, then parting, talons loosing,
Upward again on slow, firm pinions slanting, their separate diverse flight,
She hers, he his, pursuing [II, 35].

No "application" is made, no "truth" generalized in the poem; yet the movement is so sure, the details so pointed, as to impress an instinctive insight upon the reader.

At least the poem impressed D. H. Lawrence, for in the midst of one of his novels he recalls so well Whitman's poem that he uses the relationship of the eagles in it to exemplify the ideal relationship of the sexes in love. In *Aaron's Rod*, Aaron puzzles his way through to an understanding of the means of preserving the individuality of self in the engulfing union of love: "One toils, one spins, one strives: just as the lily does. But like her, taking one's own life-way amidst everything, and taking one's own life-way alone. Love too. But there also, taking one's way alone, happily alone in all the wonders of communion, swept up on the winds, but never swept away from one's very self. Two eagles in mid-air, maybe like Whitman's Dalliance of Eagles. Two eagles in mid-air, grappling, whirling, coming to their intensification of love-oneness there in mid-air. In mid-air the love consummation. But all the time each lifted on its own wings: each bearing itself up on its own wings at every moment of the mid-air love consummation. That is the splendid love-way."[4] It is of significant interest that a novelist of Lawrence's major standing could discover in Whitman's ten-line poem, apparently purely descriptive, not only an understanding of man's dilemma but also an insight into the means of extrication. For both Whitman and Lawrence, the supreme problem was discovery of the way to *preserve* the self at the same time that one *merged* the self, the same problem on a personal level as the democratic dilemma of maintaining individual freedom in the midst of universal equality.

The opening line of "The Dalliance of the Eagles" establishes the point of view and injects the only human element in the poem. The remainder of the poem falls into three sections of four lines, three lines, and two lines each. In the first of these, images of violent

4. D. H. Lawrence, *Aaron's Rod* (London: William Heinemann, Ltd., 1922), p. 163.

movement dominate, reaching a peak of agitation in the brilliant phrase, "a living, fierce, gyrating wheel." The immediately following line ("Four beating wings, two beaks, a swirling mass tight grappling") narrows from "four" to "two," focusing finally on "swirling mass," suggesting successful union of the individualistic eagles. The next three lines of the poem dramatize the union, characterized by graceful movement ("turning clustering loops, straight downward falling") leading to complete quiet ("motionless still balance"). But this union has not been achieved by sacrifice of individuality; in the midst of the harmonious activity the poet emphasizes the paradoxical conjunction of the separate, "the twain yet one." And in the final two lines of the poem, the two eagles disengage, their selfhood or individuality unimpaired—on the contrary, actually deepened in significance—by the experience of merging: on "slow-firm pinions" they make their "separate diverse flight." Here in the simplicity of the primitive world lies the answer to the seemingly impossible challenge to reconcile the contrary impulses toward selfhood and toward submergence of self in relationship with others.

Vying with "The Dalliance of the Eagles" in brilliance of single image is a poem similar in technique, "Sparkles from the Wheel" (in "Autumn Rivulets"). As in "Dalliance," the poet places himself in the poem as a spectator, viewing a vivid scene, a vignette, which seems to grant an insight into the meaning of some obscure corner of life. In this poem the poet is on a city street, but he has withdrawn from the "city's ceaseless crowd" and has joined a group of children gathered together to watch:

By the curb toward the edge of the flagging,
A knife-grinder works at his wheel sharpening a great knife,
Bending over he carefully holds it to the stone, by foot and knee,
With measur'd tread he turns rapidly, as he presses with light but firm hand,
Forth issue then in copious golden jets,
Sparkles from the wheel [II, 164].

Unlike the technique in "The Dalliance of the Eagles," which allowed the description to convey its own significance, the technique in "Sparkles from the Wheel" includes the dramatization of the impressions made by the scene on the poet:

The scene and all its belongings, how they seize and affect me,
The sad sharp-chinn'd old man with worn clothes and broad shoulder-band
   of leather,

Myself effusing and fluid, a phantom curiously floating, now here absorb'd
    and arrested,
The group, (an unminded point set in a vast surrounding,)
The attentive, quiet children, the loud, proud, restive base of the streets,
The low hoarse purr of the whirling stone, the light-press'd blade,
Diffusing, dropping, sideways-darting, in tiny showers of gold,
Sparkles from the wheel [II, 164–65].

Why does the scene "seize and affect" the poet? The answer is
not simple to discover in the complex lines devoted to the poet's reaction. But, to begin with, there appears to be an identification of
the poet and the "sad sharp-chinn'd old man" at his wheel. After describing him the poet exclaims, "Myself effusing and fluid, a phantom curiously floating, now here absorb'd and arrested." His usual
role is reversed; he is normally the man whose emitted sparks (perhaps his poetry) collect a circle of onlookers: now he joins with the
young children to watch the old man. The knife grinder's sharpening of the "great knife" becomes symbolic of the creative act: his
"measur'd tread" and light pressure on the blade send forth the
"copious golden jets." Those who witness the creative act as the au-
dience are described as an island of silence in a sea of noise: the
"unminded point" in the "vast surrounding" is the group of withdrawn, watching children ignored by the surrounding "loud, proud"
streets. It is, however, the creative act itself that partakes of the
miraculous. The drab old man, his whirling stone, and "light-press'd
blade" result in the "tiny showers of gold" that diffuse, drop, and
dart sideways. These "by-products," such as the "faint clews and
indirections" of Leaves of Grass, turn out to be, cryptic as they are,
the main focus of attention. These "golden jets" represent the cosmic
consequences of the "insignificant" act. Perhaps to Whitman they
represent the "suggestiveness" of poetry of the kind he always tried
to write. In this simple scene the poet discovers obscurely symbolized his own intricate function and contribution as an artist.

"A Noiseless Patient Spider" (from "Whispers of Heavenly
Death"), like "The Dalliance of the Eagles" and "Sparkles from the
Wheel," has as its central device the single image vividly dramatized:

A noiseless patient spider
I mark'd where on a little promontory it stood isolated,
Mark'd how to explore the vacant vast surrounding,
It launch'd forth filament, filament, filament, out of itself,
Ever unreeling them, ever tirelessly speeding them [II, 229–30].

In this poem, however, instead of letting the description stand by itself (as in "Dalliance") or dramatizing a complex effect upon the poet (as in "Sparkles"), Whitman makes a direct symbolic application:

> And you O my soul where you stand,
> Surrounded, detached, in measureless oceans of space,
> Ceaselessly musing, venturing, throwing, seeking the spheres
>   to connect them,
> Till the bridge you will need be form'd, till the ductile anchor hold,
> Till the gossamer thread you fling catch somewhere,
>   O my soul [II, 230].

As the spider is discovered in a "vacant vast surrounding," so the poet's soul is surrounded by "measureless oceans of space"; as the spider ceaselessly throws forth its filaments, so the soul ventures tirelessly to connect "the spheres." "A Noiseless Patient Spider" is a brilliant affirmation of the need for spiritual love, just as "The Dalliance of the Eagles" affirms the love of the sexes, the one a summation of the "Calamus" sentiment, the other a summation of "Children of Adam."

Curiously enough, a manuscript version of "A Noiseless Patient Spider" confirms its status as a "Calamus" poem. This version, apparently written some time during the Civil War experience, opens:

> The Soul, reaching, throwing out for love,
> As the spider, from some little promontory, throwing out filament after filament, tirelessly out of itself, that one at least may catch and form a link, a bridge, a connection
> O I saw one passing alone, saying hardly a word—yet full of love I detected him, by certain signs
> O eyes wishfully turning! O silent eyes![5]

This version permits an interesting observation on the growth of one of Whitman's brilliant short lyrics. In the "original," the spider image was embodied in a single line, the second, and was not referred to again. In rereading this early effort, the poet apparently was astute enough to perceive the crucial value of this image, to pluck it out and reconstruct his entire poem around it. Whitman's revision demonstrates again the supreme value he placed on the concrete, the physical, the "fact" as the beginning point of poetry. In "A Noiseless

5. Emory Holloway (ed.), *The Uncollected Poetry and Prose of Walt Whitman* (New York: Doubleday, Page & Co., 1921), II, 93.

Patient Spider" he demonstrates in a very complex and subtle sense the path between reality, his soul, and the reader's soul and reveals his yearning for the "gossamer" connection.

IV

Whitman's departure from conventional poetic forms has led some to believe that he had no ear for the music of poetry. He had, of course, a very keen ear. And it is this very combination of freedom from convention with attention to subtle formal properties ("The profit of rhyme is that it drops seeds of a sweeter and more luxuriant rhyme") that gives Whitman's poetry its distinctive quality. The freedom from the usual poetic restrictions conveys the sense of wild abandonment; the subtle attention to rhythm and sound modifies this sense with the suggestion of almost magical control. The total impression, then, is one of primitive ritual—of rites of abandonment instinct with form.

This aspect of Whitman, so important to the total effect of his poetry, is elusive, almost impossible to isolate for analysis. But there are "faint clews and indirections." One of the most revealing is a passage in "Starting from Paumanok" that shows Whitman's acute awareness of the intrinsic value of the sounds of syllables:

The red aborigines,
Leaving natural breaths, sounds of rain and winds, calls as of birds and
    animals in the woods, syllabled to us for names,
Okonee, Koosa, Ottawa, Monongahela, Sauk, Natchez, Chattahoochee,
    Kaqueta, Oronoco,
Wabash, Miami, Saginaw, Chippewa, Oshkosh, Walla-Walla,
Leaving such to the States they melt, they depart, charging the water and
    the land with names [I, 30].

In the Indian names the poet perceives echoes of the primal world, the world of vegetation and animals, the world in its native glory before the advent of man. The Indian words are the sounds of nature, "syllabled" and providing the states with names. The poet who fashioned two complete lines of poetry out of melodious Indian place names is not unaware of the music inhering in language and the combinations of words.

A short "Autumn Rivulets" poem, "Unfolded Out of the Folds," may best illustrate the incantatory quality of much of Whitman's poetry. "Unfolded Out of the Folds" is a tour de force in the poetic chant. Every line but the last two begins with the ritualistic key word "unfolded," many of them repeating the word or its basic root. The word as it is repeated and associated with the fundamental and basic events of man's life (birth, growth) acquires magical properties. The poet appears the primitive priest, weaving a magic spell about the figure of woman and her miraculous role in the preservation of the tribe:

Unfolded out of the folds of the woman man comes unfolded, and is always to come unfolded,
Unfolded only out of the superbest woman of the earth is to come the superbest man of the earth,
Unfolded out of the friendliest woman is to come the friendliest man [II, 166].

The role of woman is crucial, as it is she in her life-giving and life-shaping position who determines the very nature of man in all its aspects:

Unfolded only out of the inimitable poems of woman can come the poems of man, (only thence have my poems come;)
Unfolded out of the strong and arrogant woman I love, only thence can appear the strong and arrogant man I love,
Unfolded by brawny embraces from the well-muscled woman I love, only thence come the brawny embraces of the man [II, 166].

The tone throughout the poem, created in part by the hypnotic repetition of "unfolded," conveys the impression that a command is being given, a spell woven, that will place the forces of nature under control and bring about the desired results. But more than mere sound, the repeated "unfolded" bears a multiplicity of meaning, from "unfolded out of the folds" of birth to "unfolded by brawny embraces" of love; in either case the man is extricated from the "folds" of the woman. The word is extended further in meaning in the line, "Unfolded out of the folds of the woman's brain come all the folds of the man's brain, duly obedient." The poet is obviously intent on unfolding in his key word all the possible applicable meaning. Departing slightly from his ritualistic formula, the poet concludes:

A man is a great thing upon the earth and through eternity, but every jot of the greatness of man is unfolded out of woman;
First the man is shaped in the woman, he can then be shaped in himself [II, 166].

The idea is one which Whitman stated in "I Sing the Body Electric" of "Children of Adam" ("Be not ashamed women, your privilege encloses the rest, and is the exit of the rest"), but the incantatory language in which the idea is embodied is unique to this poem. Frequently the central poetic device in Whitman's short lyrics is musical in nature—unconventional music, perhaps, but no less musical for that. Some of the poems draw their entire sustenance from such a "device"; remove the device, and the poems have no reason for existence. Without the word "unfolded," "Unfolded Out of the Folds" would be deprived of its cause for being. The incantation permitted by the repetition of this single word constitutes the lifeblood of the poem. Quite frequently Whitman's short lyrics employ some form of primitive, bardic chant. Some of his best brief poems are brilliant incantations that hypnotically weave a mystic magic spell.

V

When we begin to examine Whitman's poems of a length greater than the brief lyrics we have analyzed, we discover, of course, less dependence on a single, dominant poetic device, greater reliance on more intricate and subtle combinations of various techniques and tones. Among the notable Whitman poems of intermediate length are "Eidólons" of the "Inscriptions" cluster and "Pioneers! O Pioneers!" of "Birds of Passage," these two poems utilizing a similar stanzaic form quite unusual in the whole of *Leaves of Grass*. As these poems are eloquent statements of Whitman's faith, "Eidólons" of his faith in the world of spirit, "Pioneers! O Pioneers!" of his faith in the continuous unfolding of mystic evolution, so two other brilliant performances, of intermediate length but more conventionally Whitmanian—"As I Ebb'd with the Ocean of Life" and "Prayer of Columbus"—are statements of doubt and defeat, soul-searching, and final affirmation. As Whitman's poems become longer, they become more specifically and more complexly dramatic, with the poet projecting himself as protagonist or, as in "Prayer of Columbus," actually assuming the role of an imagined or created character.

Let us pass over these poems, however, to select an example for close examination that is one of the brilliant neglected poems of

Leaves of Grass, the "Drum-Taps" poem, "Vigil Strange I Kept on the Field One Night." All the techniques or qualities we have discussed are found in this effectively dramatic poem—the cryptic or the suggestive, the vividly imaged, the sharply outlined vignette, the mesmeric chant—these and other elements combine and fuse to make "Vigil Strange I Kept on the Field One Night" one of the really great poems in the language. The poem is a dramatic monologue, the speaker a soldier in battle, the "listener" the soldier's dead comrade. As the army advances, the soldier's comrade falls from his side:

Vigil strange I kept on the field one night;
When you my son and my comrade dropt at my side that day,
One look I but gave which your dear eyes return'd with a look I shall
    never forget,
One touch of your hand to mine O boy, reach'd up as you lay on the
    ground,
Then onward I sped in the battle, the even-contested battle [II, 67–68].

The single look and the single touch suggest the depth of the "Calamus" feeling that binds the two soldiers in comradeship. But more than these, the opening lines of the poem establish a rhythm (an intricate but flowing combination of iambs and anapests) and sweeping line-length (with carefully placed caesura) that reinforce the pervading tone of overpowering emotion held manfully in restraint.

After the soldier has been dismissed from the advancing line, he returns to search for his comrade:

Till later in the night reliev'd to the place at last again I made my way,
Found you in death so cold dear comrade, found your body son of re-
    sponding kisses, (never again on earth responding,)
Bared your face in the starlight, curious the scene, cool blew the moderate
    night-wind,
Long there and then in vigil I stood, dimly, around me the battle-field
    spreading,
Vigil wondrous and vigil sweet there in the fragrant silent night,
But not a tear fell, not even a long-drawn sigh, long, long I gazed [II, 68].

Just as the look and touch in the opening lines characterized symbolically the depth of the relationship of soldier and comrade, so, when the soldier returns to his dead friend and gazes upon his body, he remembers most vividly his physical existence and presence—"son of responding kisses." But there in the dark of the night, a transfiguring process is already beginning, suggested by the starlight illuminating the face of the dead comrade, the cool "moderate night-wind," and the mystically charged "fragrant silent night." The physical world seems in retreat ("dimly around me the battle-field spreading"), the spiritual world ever more subtly present. The cryptic element introduced in the title (the *strange* vigil) is reintroduced as the poem's central "meaning"; there is some transfiguring presence in this vigil for the dead that makes unnecessary the usual tears and sighs.

The word "vigil" becomes the ritual word of the poem, to be repeated ceaselessly in new contexts, its mystic meaning comprehensively explored until it is so charged with magic significance that its mere chanted repetition weaves the mystic spell:

Then on the earth partially reclining sat by your side leaning my chin in my hands,
Passing sweet hours, immortal and mystic hours with you dearest comrade—not a tear, not a word,
Vigil of silence, love and death, vigil for you my son and my soldier,
As onward silently stars aloft, eastward new ones upward stole,
Vigil final for you brave boy, (I could not save you, swift was your death,
I faithfully loved you and cared for you living, I think we shall surely meet again,) [II, 68].

In these lines the dominant device is the ritualistic chant in which the poet attempts to convey some of the significance of the complex emotion he feels on the death of his comrade—an acute sense of terrible loss gradually transfigured in the "vigil" into reconciliation to a spiritual bond. These "immortal and mystic hours" are a "vigil of silence, love and death." In the silence the sorrowing soldier achieves insight—a recurring theme in *Leaves of Grass*—into the fulfilment of spiritual love in death, an insight affirmed when the soldier says, "I think we shall surely meet again." The hours of the vigil are "sweet" because they are the first fulfilment in this new mystic relationship between soldier and comrade.

The vigil over, the night passed and the day appearing on the horizon, the soldier performs the ritualistic act of burial:

Till at latest lingering of the night, indeed just as the dawn appear'd,
My comrade I wrapt in his blanket, envelop'd well his form,
Folded the blanket well, tucking it carefully over head and carefully under feet,
And there and then and bathed by the rising sun, my son in his grave, in his rude-dug grave I deposited,

Ending my vigil strange with that, vigil of night and battle-field dim,
Vigil for boy of responding kisses, (never again on earth responding,)
Vigil for comrade swiftly slain, vigil I never forget, how as day brightened,
I rose from the chill ground and folded my soldier well in his blanket,
And buried him where he fell [II, 68–69].

In this brilliant passage all the elements seem to be working in perfect harmony to achieve a finely balanced emotional effect. Details of the setting are blended with the situation for maximum symbolic meaning, such as in the vivid phrase (with its emotionally charged pun) "bathed by the rising sun, my son in his grave." An indelible picture is sketched. The act of wrapping the dead soldier in his blanket is the final act of farewell in the ritual of mourning and becomes, as the passage progresses and the act is repeated in memory, a symbolic act of spiritual preservation. The dominant effect, as in the closing lines of "When Lilacs Last in the Dooryard Bloom'd," is one of deeply felt emotion controlled by understanding restraint. The incantatory language, with its occasional repetition of phrases and details, seems to revolve in restless exploration about the situation and its deeply felt emotion, transfiguring and transcending as it moves.

Critical neglect of Whitman's short poems has unfortunately led many to assume that his brief lyrics are not worth serious attention. In reality his poetic genius is evident in a large number of his short poems. They are, no doubt, overshadowed by the longer poems, which are more ambitious and richer in complexity of detail and structure. The characteristic devices Whitman created or discovered for the embodiment of his poetic ideas and dramas may be more subtly and more effectively interrelated and fused in the longer poems, but in isolation these techniques serve very well for the achievement of specific, circumscribed poetic purposes. These devices serve particularly well for the creation of brief lyrics, which not only must stand alone but also must be integrated into a totality that has a unity and structure created by individuality of style as well as of point of view. The foregoing treatment is not a selection of the best short poems in *Leaves of Grass* but rather a selection of excellent lyrics that are representative of particular techniques. There must be a long period of critical revaluation before one can speak with any degree of certainty about the best. That period, well along for the long poems, has yet to begin for the short.

Part Two

*Panorama: The Structure of
"Leaves of Grass"*

Introduction

In an undated manuscript note, Walt Whitman once wrote: "My poems when complete should be a *unity,* in the same sense that the earth is, or that the human body, (senses, soul, head, trunk, feet, blood, viscera, man-root, eyes, hair,) or that a perfect musical composition is" (IX, 3).[1] The poet's great concern near the end of his life for the structure of *Leaves of Grass* as he had shaped it through a lifetime of labor is reflected in one of his exhortations to Horace Traubel: "So far as you may have anything to do with it I place upon you the injunction that whatever may be added to the *Leaves* shall be supplementary, avowed as such, leaving the book complete as I left it, consecutive to the point I left off, marking always an unmistakable, deep down, unobliteratable division line." Wistfully acknowledging his helplessness in the hands of the posterity he addressed so frequently in his poetry, Whitman added, "In the long run the world will do as it pleases with the book. I am determined to have the world know what I was pleased to do" (III, 30).

Whitman's determination has caused the world to know what he was pleased to do: most reprints of *Leaves of Grass* have followed faithfully Whitman's last wishes in the arrangement of the poems by copying what has become commonly known as the "deathbed edition," the last edition supervised by the author and published under the date 1891–92. An author's note in this last lifetime edition left no doubt as to the intensity of Whitman's desire that no one tamper with the order or selection of the poems in future editions of *Leaves of Grass:* "As there are now several editions of L. of G., different texts and dates, I wish to say that I prefer and recommend this

1. Whitman quotations are where possible identified in the text by volume and page number of *The Complete Writings of Walt Whitman,* ed. Richard M. Bucke *et al.* (New York: G. P. Putnam's Sons, 1902).

present one, complete, for future printing, if there should be any; a copy and fac-simile, indeed, of the text of these 438 pages" (I, vi). Such remarks by the poet, together with his revisions and rearrangements made in successive editions of *Leaves of Grass,* have long convinced critics that there is an integrity to the structure of *Leaves of Grass* that should not be violated, but, at the same time, there has been no agreement as to the general or specific nature of that structure.

CHAPTER ELEVEN

Exploration
of a Structure

Two students of Whitman have attempted more or less comprehensive analyses of the structure of *Leaves of Grass*. William Sloane Kennedy's is the first effort to outline in relatively specific terms the major divisions of the book and to suggest the subject matter of these divisions. In preface to his "outline," Kennedy remarks, "The work is a Trilogy, celebrating the Body, Democracy, and Religion,—the mystery of the macrocosm and the nobility of the microcosm—and the keywords to these three groups respectively are Joy, Love, and Faith (Saint Paul's faith, hope, and charity, curious to note)." Kennedy demonstrates the structure of *Leaves of Grass* by assembling the poems in groups:

Poems of Life and the Body.

Song of Myself.
Children of Adam. } *The Physical*

Calamus.
Salut au Monde. } *Comradeship* (based on the sympathetic rather than the cerebral system with Whitman).

Song of the Open Road.
Crossing Brooklyn Ferry.
Our Old Feuillage.
Song of Joy.
Song of the Broadaxe.
Song of the Exposition.
Song of the Redwood Tree.
Song for Occupations, etc.

Sea Poems } Outdoor Life tinged with the Pensive.

Poems of Democracy.
{
The War Poems
    (including the dirge for Lincoln).
By Blue Ontario's Shore.
Return of the Heroes.
Old Ireland.
To a Foiled European Revolutionaire [sic].
To Him that was Crucified.
You Felons.
Laws for Creation.
To a Common Prostitute.
O Star of France, etc.
}

Poems of Religion.
{
Passage to India.
Prayer of Columbus.
To Think of Time.
Whispers of Heavenly Death.
Songs of Parting.
}
Death and Immortality

In defense of this structure, Kennedy reveals the source of most of the clues he utilized in working it out: "Note how nicely the objects which Whitman has said (Preface to 1876 ed., and the *Critic*, Jan. 5, '84, and elsewhere) he had in view in writing his poems fit this classification."[1] Kennedy has relied primarily not on a detailed examination of *Leaves of Grass* but on Whitman's statements about his books. Although the poet's remarks should prove valuable in analysis, they may by no means be accepted as conclusive.

Another detailed analysis of the structure of Whitman's book is Irving C. Story's "The Structural Pattern of *Leaves of Grass*." Basing his analysis on the 1881 edition of *Leaves of Grass*, Story discovers "fifteen groups" of poems, which he arranges as follows:

Inscriptions 24

(Songs of Walt Whitman) 2
Children of Adam 16
Calamus 36

(Chants Democratic) 11
Birds of Passage 7
"A Broadway Pageant"
Sea-Drift 11

By the Roadside 29
Drum-Taps 43
Memories of Pres. Lincoln 4
"By Blue Ontario's Shore"
Autumn Rivulets 38

1. Kennedy, *Reminiscences of Walt Whitman* (London: Alexander Gardner, 1896), pp. 100–102.

The figures indicate the number of poems in each group. The titles in parentheses will be recognized as early titles discarded by Whitman or as titles originally applicable to a group of poems but in the final edition applicable to a single poem. Story thus groups together "Starting from Paumanok" and "Song of Myself" under the title "Songs of Walt Whitman"; the eleven "songs" from "Salut au Monde" through "A Song of the Rolling Earth" as "Chants Democratic"; and the five poems about death and immortality, beginning with "Proud Music of the Storm" through "To Think of Time," as "Passage to India."[2]

No one, I think, could quarrel with these last two groupings, as the relationship of the poems in the "song section" has long been noted and Whitman himself, in his 1876 Preface, has called attention to the unity of the cluster of poems surrounding "Passage to India." But the placing together of "Starting from Paumanok" and "Song of Myself" might well be challenged. Although many of the relationships Story suggests are valid and important, he does not on the whole make out a very good case for his six-part structure. For example, almost no case at all is made for placing "Thou Mother with Thy Equal Brood" and "From Noon to Starry Night" with "Passage to India" and "Whispers of Heavenly Death." Story himself notes that his groupings are deficient, but he discovers the cause not in his analysis but in the structure: "The analysis thus completed does not justify the position of every poem in the *Leaves;* that is not possible. Some poems are too fragmentary or vague; a few major poems seem clearly misplaced." Story concludes that "the 1881 *Leaves* has a logical, though not completely developed or worked out, articulation into groups." One wonders whether it is not an error to call *logical* that structure which seems arbitrarily violated by Whitman in some major instances; and one wonders further whether it might not be an error to search for a *logical* structure at all, particularly in a book of lyric poetry.

2. Irving C. Story, "The Structural Pattern of *Leaves of Grass*," *Pacific University Bulletin*, XXXVIII, No. 4 (January, 1942), 3.

Perhaps the solution to the dilemma is to find a *metaphorical* struc-ture—a structure resembling some object other than a book of poems. Almost every critic who has ever talked about Whitman has at some point or other lapsed into metaphor to convey his meaning. And, although an analogy does not prove the presence of an element, such a comparison aids in understanding the thing if it really exists. Perhaps the most obvious metaphor applicable to Whitman's master-piece is that introduced in the title. As critics have frequently pointed out, Whitman was consciously punning in his use of the word "leaves." *Leaves of Grass* as a title refers simultaneously to the leaves of Whitman's book of poems and to spears of summer grass and by such double reference establishes in the mind of the reader a vividly imaged link between the two. Furthermore, Whitman's varied use of his title, *Leaves of Grass,* through the several editions of his book, demonstrates that he thought of each of his poems as an individual blade of grass. In editions of his work preceding the deathbed edition, Whitman frequently used the title within the volume to refer to various collections of poems. In the 1876 edition, for example, Whitman used "Leaves of Grass" as a title for some seven clusters of poems, and in one instance the "cluster" consisted of a single poem.[3] Whitman's use of his title in this fashion, together with his persistent use of *Leaves of Grass* as the title for his total work from the very beginning, suggests that the relationships among the poems are comparable to those that exist among spears and clusters and varieties of grass. These relationships are many: the poems, like grass, have "grown" organically; like grass, they exclude none, accept all; like grass, these poems simultaneously celebrate individuality and "en-masse"; like grass, the poems are themselves evidence of an ever recurring life and immortality; and as some varieties of grass, like calamus, have special and subtly distinct characteristics, so do some elements of Whitman's poetic vision. Although this list of relationships may be extended considerably, these are enough to show that Whitman's dominant metaphor pre-sents a case, if not for structure, at least for unity or harmony, a basic component of structure.

But if the leaf-of-grass metaphor suggests an organic or external, spiritual and natural, rather than human, origin of the poetry, an-

3. Whitman, *Leaves of Grass* (Camden, N.J.: Author's Edition, 1876).

other metaphor, introduced in the title of the opening section of *Leaves of Grass*, suggests a man-made structure. "Inscriptions" connotes an entrance to an edifice on which is engraved an identification, statement of purpose, or dedication. And for one who scans the whole of the Table of Contents of *Leaves of Grass*, there is a reinforcement of such connotation from the titles of the final sections, the "Annexes." Inscriptions and annexes come at the entrances and exits of buildings, but, of course, there must be something in between, and that something, if it is standing, is a structure. But if *Leaves of Grass* is an edifice, it is a composite of a private dwelling, a public building, and a religious sanctuary. One might even point out, in the first part of the book, the "eating and sleeping rooms" as well as the bathroom and the bedroom, in the middle part the public monument or tomb, and in the latter part the chapel for private prayer. But, after all, Whitman did say, "I will go to the bank by the wood and become undisguised and naked" (I, 34);[4] and one must admit that it seems strange and unnatural to attempt to confine *Leaves of Grass* to a man-made structure, no matter how elegant or plain.

One metaphor that has been repeatedly applied to *Leaves of Grass* has occasionally been taken literally. Whitman once wrote, "The Great Construction of the New Bible. Not to be diverted from the principal object—the main life work—the three hundred and sixty-five.—It ought to be ready in 1859" (IX, 6). Every biography of Whitman not written by one of his intimate acquaintances has noted that the "hot little prophet[s]"[5] frequently worshiped Whitman as a democratic deity and *Leaves of Grass* as his bible. Indeed, the following statement appears in the biographical-critical sketch in the first volume of the 1902 *Complete Writings*: "*Leaves of Grass* offers a species of Bible to our modern democracy. What the Vedas were to Brahmanism, the law and the Prophets to Judaism, the Avesta to Zoroastrianism, the Pauline writings to Christianity, *Leaves of Grass* will be to the future of American civilization" (I, 1).[6] Since Whit-

4. Whitman quotations are where possible identified in the text by volume and page number of *The Complete Writings of Walt Whitman,* ed. Richard M. Bucke *et al.* (New York: G. P. Putnam's Sons, 1902).
5. Bliss Perry, *Walt Whitman* (Boston: Houghton Mifflin Co., 1906), p. 286.
6. This sketch was written by Whitman's literary executors, Richard Maurice Bucke, Thomas B. Harned, and Horace L. Traubel.

man himself thought, at least on occasion, of his masterpiece as a bible and since his intimate associates encouraged him in this belief, it is of course possible that the poet deliberately imitated the structure of that Bible familiar to all. Casual perusal of *Leaves of Grass* reveals that there is no two-part division similar to the Old and New Testaments. But there are enough similarities of other kinds that one is tempted to find the secret of the structure of *Leaves of Grass* in the Bible. Perhaps one can separate the sections of *Leaves of Grass* into historical books and prophetic books. Perhaps one can find the poetry of the Psalms and the drama of Job. Certainly there are biblical images in Whitman's masterpiece—as, for example, that introduced in the title of "Children of Adam" and that found in the Christ-identification passages of "Song of Myself." But to say that the structure of *Leaves of Grass* is patterned after that of the Bible is, really, to say that *Leaves of Grass* has very little orderly sequence. The Bible, after all, is not noted for its organization. Although the comparison may be provocative and even illuminating, it does not lead far in a genuine understanding of the structure of *Leaves of Grass.*

When Whitman wrote, "My poems when complete should be a *unity,* in the same sense that . . . a perfect musical composition is" (IX, 3), he was anticipating the most frequent analogy used in the many discussions of *Leaves of Grass.* Almost every Whitman critic has used the music metaphor to explain the poet's technique in individual poems and in sections of poems, and some have suggested that the whole book is held together very much as is a symphony or other musical composition—by the introduction of and subsequent return to and variations on a number of specific, well-defined, and recognizable themes. W. S. Kennedy began his analysis of the structure of *Leaves of Grass* with the descriptive terms, "a musical symphony or Drama of Creation." A recent book, *Walt Whitman and Opera,*[7] explores the relationship of *Leaves of Grass* to another important musical form and one to which Whitman frequently expressed his indebtedness. The recitative and aria of opera influenced Whitman's concept of form in poetry and go far toward explaining the structure of a number of his important poems. But although the

7. Robert D. Faner, *Walt Whitman and Opera* (Philadelphia: University of Pennsylvania Press, 1951).

music metaphor sheds a good deal of light on *Leaves of Grass,* it must, finally, be abandoned as inadequate to the task of conveying the whole secret of the book's structure. Saying that a poem's structure is like that of a musical composition is far different from saying precisely *what* a poem's structure is. No one has been able to apply with consistency and coherence the musical analogy in a comprehensive analysis of the structure of *Leaves of Grass.*

If some aspects of the structure of Whitman's book remind one on occasion of a man-built structure, a house or building, other aspects, paradoxically enough, remind one of the great outdoors and a journey. From "On Journeys through the States" and "The Ship Starting" in "Inscriptions," through "Song of the Open Road," and concluding with the prose piece with which Whitman closed his book, "A Backward Glance o'er Travel'd Roads," the image of the journey appears again and again in *Leaves of Grass.* One cannot read the concluding sections of "Starting from Paumanok" without feeling that he is being invited on a half-mystical journey—the journey of the book he is beginning:

> O Camerado close! O you and me at last, and us two only.
> O a word to clear one's path ahead endlessly! [I, 32].

And standing at the end of the book, "A Backward Glance o'er Travel'd Roads" conveys in its very title the nature of the experience just concluded. Whitman says: "So here I sit gossiping in the early candle-light of old age—I and my book—casting backward glances over our travel'd road. After completing, as it were, the journey—(a varied jaunt of years, with many halts and gaps of intervals—or some lengthen'd ship-voyage, wherein more than once the last hour had apparently arrived, and we seem'd certainly going down—yet reaching port in a sufficient way through all discomfitures at last) . . ." (III, 41). Although the journey motif running through *Leaves of Grass* is strong,[8] it is difficult to assert just how the successive images of travel, both by land and by water, constitute a structure. If it may be said that the trip is an exploration and that the destination is unknown, then it may be asserted that the apparent disorder in *Leaves of Grass* is justifiable. This metaphor, instead of

---

8. See Gay Wilson Allen, "Walt Whitman's Long Journey Motif," *Journal of English and Germanic Philology,* XXXVIII (January, 1939), 76–95.

unlocking the secret of the book's structure, provides a rationalization for its lack of structure.

In that same manuscript note in which he compared his work to "a perfect musical composition" Whitman also said: "My poems when complete should be a *unity,* in the same sense that the human body, (senses, soul, head, trunk, feet, blood, viscera, man-root, eyes, hair,) . . . is" (IX, 3). This human metaphor recurred often in Whitman's writing about his book. In attempting to distinguish *Leaves of Grass* from the books of poetry of previous eras, he said, "but never before have we had *man in the open air,* his attitude adjusted to the sun by day and the stars by night" (IX, 29). Whitman even suggested that *Leaves of Grass* might better be judged as a man than as a book: "Indeed, the qualities which characterize *Leaves of Grass* are not the qualities of a fine book or poem or any work of art but the qualities of a living and full-blooded man, amativeness, pride, adhesiveness, curiosity, yearning for immortality, joyousness and sometimes of uncertainty. You do not read it, it is someone that you see in action, in war, or on a ship, or climbing the mountains, or racing along and shouting aloud in pure exultation" (IX, 22). Whitman said again and again that the individual in *Leaves of Grass* was to serve as a type portrait, as a democratic composite. Though one might be able to point to sections of *Leaves of Grass* and say, "This part represents the senses, this the soul, this the eyesight," one quickly realizes that this kind of identification could not proceed far without real difficulty or absurdity. It is, perhaps, helpful to think of *Leaves of Grass* as a man, but, as with all the other metaphors examined, the human analogy cannot assist close and detailed analysis of structure.

Grass, house, Bible, music, journey, man—perhaps *Leaves of Grass* is a composite of these several metaphors. Or perhaps each of them in turn influenced the structure of *Leaves of Grass* so that it is proper to say, although none is fully applicable or suitable, together they illuminate and reveal, contradictory as some apparently are. Indeed, some of these metaphors are justifications for the absence of structure rather than keys to an existent structure. In any event, a description of their shortcomings should not be construed as an attack on their usefulness in getting at the structure of *Leaves of Grass.* As with all metaphors, these that are frequently applied to Whitman's book have limitations. Metaphors reveal and illuminate but do not discover or prove. The *thing* revealed by metaphor should be somehow discoverable or provable in its own terms. The structure of *Leaves of Grass*, if it exists, may be analyzed, and, in the process of analysis, metaphorical terms must be abandoned for literary or poetic. For, after all, *Leaves of Grass* is not really a cluster of summer grass or a musical composition or an ocean voyage or even a man—but it *is* a volume of poetry. And as such it contains a number of themes whose complex development, interrelation, and ultimate synthesis constitute its structure. As a means of discovering that structure, let us turn, first, to an examination of the evolution of the book's major thematic patterns.

CHAPTER TWELVE

Evolution
of a Structure

It would indeed be strange if *Leaves of Grass*, the work of a lifetime, did not reflect the vicissitudes and accidents of that life. Although study of an author's life is not necessary for understanding a poem, knowledge of biography will frequently set the critic in the right direction for fruitful discovery. Whitman's life divides naturally into three distinct segments, and separating these segments are events that affected him profoundly. The first, dividing the opening and middle periods of his life, is the Civil War, a national crisis in which Whitman became personally entangled. Throughout his wartime letters to his mother there is a sense of urgency that conveys an impression of the depth of Whitman's personal involvement. He writes, for example, of his arrival in Washington, "As to me, I know I put in about three days of the greatest suffering I ever experienced in my life. I wrote to Jeff how I had my pocket picked in a jam and hurry, changing cars, at Philadelphia—so that I landed here without a dime. The next two days I spent hunting through the hospitals, walking day and night, unable to ride, trying to get information—trying to get access to big people, etc." (VII, 128–29).[1] Such letters as these are convincing evidence that the Civil War and Whitman's intimate experiences in caring for the wounded in it affected him and his poetry profoundly. The other event, which marks the closing of the middle and beginning of the final segments of his life, is not a national but a personal crisis. In a letter (1873) to Anne Gilchrist the poet's intimate association with death emerges: "Since I last wrote clouds have darkened over me, &

1. Whitman quotations are where possible identified in the text by volume and page number of *The Complete Writings of Walt Whitman,* ed. Richard M. Bucke *et al.* (New York: G. P. Putnam's Sons, 1902).

still remain. On the night of 23d of January last I was paralyzed, left side, & have remained so since. February 19th I lost a dear sister, who died in St. Louis, leaving two young daughters. May 23d my inexpressibly beloved mother died in Camden. I was just able to get from Washington to her dying bed, & sit there. I thought I was bearing it all stoutly but I find it affecting the progress of my recovery since & now."[2] Certainly this terrible series of blows and particularly the paralysis that incapacitated a man whose great pride had been his health constituted a spiritual crisis that affected both his work and his life. This crisis precipitated his removal from Washington to Camden, closing conclusively an era in his life circumscribed by a place that was the exhilarating scene of great suffering and great courage.

The two years 1861 and 1873, crisis years for the nation and the poet, divide Whitman's life into three separate parts. These three periods have their own distinct literary activity: the first three editions of *Leaves of Grass* (1855, 1856, 1860) appeared in the first; the next two editions (1867, 1871–72) appeared in the second; and some four editions (1876, 1881, 1889, 1891–92) appeared in the last. The significant point, however, is that these three periods mark distinctive steps in the growth of *Leaves of Grass*. The 1860 edition represented the culmination of the first flush of poetic activity, a considerably bigger, more varied, and more complexly organized book than the 1855 edition, which contained only twelve untitled poems, and certainly less rushed than the 1856 edition, which was probably hurried through the press in order to publish as well as answer Emerson's enthusiastic letter praising the 1855 volume. There is abundant evidence that Whitman considered the 1860 edition as final and did not plan extensive revisions. A second burst of creative activity was brought about by the Civil War and culminated in the publication of *Drum-Taps* in 1865. It was not until the edition of 1871–72 that *Drum-Taps*, having appeared merely as an annex in the 1867 edition, was integrated into the structure of *Leaves of Grass*. There is, again, abundant evidence that Whitman considered the 1871–72 version of *Leaves of Grass* final and complete and regarded the cluster of poems accumulating around "Pas-

2. Emory Holloway (ed.), *Walt Whitman: Complete Poetry and Selected Prose and Letters* (London: Nonesuch Press, 1938), p. 1012.

sage to India" (published as an annex to the 1871–72 edition) as the material for a new volume of poetry. Even in the 1876 edition the "Passage to India" group was published in the second volume, *Two Rivulets,* and was not integrated into the structure of the master work until the 1881 edition, the volume in which Whitman finally arrived at a form that was to remain essentially unchanged through succeeding editions. (The three periods of heightened creative activity correspond to the three biographical segments of Whitman's life, and this activity in each case culminates in major revision of form or structure, at the time considered final, of *Leaves of Grass* in the editions of 1860, 1871–72, and 1881.)

It should be no surprise that the structure of the final editions of *Leaves of Grass* should reflect these three stages of growth, for the successive stages, (encompassing distinctively new subject matter and somewhat new perspectives on life (and death),) resulted in clusters of poems that tended to have their own unity. Whitman's impulse to publish the "Drum-Taps" cluster and the "Passage to India" cluster as separate volumes and his hesitancy in integrating these clusters into the master volume suggest that he himself was quite aware that they had a unity of their own that would be retained even after inclusion within the framework of *Leaves of Grass.* Whitman's meditations on these individual groups as they were published as separate volumes or annexes are of major interest; for in his comments Whitman reveals a good deal about his own thinking on problems of unity and structure in his work. In a letter to William Douglas O'Connor, dated January 6, 1865, Whitman compares in some detail the new book he has readied for the press with his former work. It is, to say the least, astonishing to find the following judgment: "It [*Drum-Taps*] is in my opinion superior to *Leaves of Grass*—certainly more perfect as a work of art, being adjusted in all its proportions, & its passion having the indispensable merit that though to the ordinary reader let loose with wildest abandon, the true artist can see it is yet under control."[3] It should be surprising to some to find Whitman genuinely concerned about "proportions" and keenly aware of a possible difference in the illusion created by a poem and the reality of its creation, but the important point is that

3. *Ibid.,* pp. 949–50.

Whitman looked upon *Leaves of Grass* (the 1860 edition) as a meas-
urable achievement of his past, an achievement possibly to be sur-
passed in present or future poetic creativity.

In this same letter, Whitman proceeds to point out the unifying
theme of *Drum-Taps:* "But I am perhaps mainly satisfied with
Drum-Taps because it delivers my ambition of the task that has
haunted me, namely, to express in a poem (& in the way I like,
which is not at all by directly stating it) the pending action of this
Time & Land we swim in, with all their large conflicting fluctua-
tions of despair & hope, the shiftings, masses, & the whirl & deafening din, (yet over all, as by invisible hand, a definite purport &
idea)—with the unprecedented anguish of wounded & suffering, the
beautiful young men, in wholesale death and agony, everything
sometimes as if blood color, & dripping blood." It is surely significant
that Whitman feels for the first time that he has accomplished his
"ambition" of expressing "this *Time & Land we swim in,*" especially
in view of his stated aims in his 1855 Preface and the considerable
achievement of the 1860 edition of *Leaves of Grass.* Whitman defines the distinctive features of *Drum-Taps:* "The book is therefore
unprecedently [*sic*] sad, (as these days are, are they not?)—but it also
has the blast of the trumpet, & the drum pounds & whirrs in it, & then
an undertone of sweetest comradeship & human love, threading its
steady thread inside the chaos, & heard at every lull & interstice
thereof—truly, also it has clear notes of faith & triumph." Throughout this passage Whitman conceives the distinctive themes in *Drum-
Taps* in vivid images of sound.

In contrast with the themes of *Drum-Taps* are those of the 1860
volume: "*Drum-Taps* has none of the perturbations of *Leaves of
Grass.* I am satisfied with *Leaves of Grass,* (by far the most of it) as
expressing what was intended, namely, to express by sharp-cut self
assertion, One's Self & also, or may be still more, to map out, to
throw together for American use, a gigantic embryo or skeleton of
Personality,—fit for the West, for native models. . . ." Although
Whitman intended to revise the 1860 edition of *Leaves of Grass,* he
had no intention at this time of incorporating *Drum-Taps* in its
structure. The image of "a gigantic embryo or skeleton of Personality" encompassing the 1860 edition of *Leaves of Grass,* like the
"*Time & Land we swim in*" applied to *Drum-Taps,* is not only

sharply vivid but useful in an analysis of the structure of the death-bed edition of Whitman's masterpiece. By these phrases Whitman not only asserts thematic differences in his 1860 and 1865 volumes but suggests relationships that exist, perhaps vaguely, within a larger framework not yet fully recognized or discovered. There seems to be an unconscious, or at least unformulated, realization that there are not only differences but there are "connections" that make it proper, within a larger scheme, for poems delineating the "gigantic embryo" to precede poems engaged with "this *Time & Land*." Whitman eventually found his way to the conclusion that such an order of themes was appropriate within the bounds of an expanded concept of the scope of his master work; for *Drum-Taps* was integrated into *Leaves of Grass* in the 1871–72 edition.

The Preface that appeared in the 1872 pamphlet publication of "As a Strong Bird on Pinions Free" (which became "Thou Mother with Thy Equal Brood" in the final editions of *Leaves of Grass*) is extremely important in revealing Whitman's ideas at the time, not only about *Leaves of Grass*, but also about a projected companion volume of new, or mostly new, poems. There is an air of finality concerning the then current edition of *Leaves of Grass* in the very opening sentence of the Preface: "The impetus and ideas urging me, for some years past, to an utterance, or attempt at utterance, of New World songs, and an epic of Democracy, having already had their publish'd expression, as well as I can expect to give it, in *Leaves of Grass*, the present and any future pieces from me are really but the surplusage forming after that volume, or the wake eddying behind it" (V, 185). Whitman considered the "finished" *Leaves*, in 1871–72 consisting essentially of the 1860 edition with the "Drum-Taps" poems structurally integrated (poems portraying the "skeleton of Personality" together with poems dramatizing this "Time & Land"), as a unified volume constituting an "epic of Democracy." The note of futility felt in such words as "surplusage" and eddying "wake" in the opening of this Preface is, curiously, emphasized in a later passage, which comes after fairly long discussions of the importance of "religion" and of the "colossal drama" of America as themes in his work and which outlines, with excessive qualifications, the general nature of the projected new volume: "*Leaves of Grass*, already publish'd, is, in its intentions, the song of a great composite *democratic individual,* male or female. And following on and amplifying the same purpose, I suppose I have in my mind to run through the chants of this volume (if ever completed), the thread-voice, more or less audible, of an aggregated, inseparable, unprecedented, vast, composite, electric *democratic nationality*" (V, 192). Probably no public statement of artistic intentions was ever made so hesitantly and guardedly. Even immediately after this passage, the qualification is reiterated: "Purposing, then, to still fill out, from time to time through years to come, the following volume (unless prevented. . . ." Perhaps the hesitation derives from a sense of impending personal catastrophe (Whitman's paralytic stroke occurred in February of 1873, though he had suffered spells of dizziness for more than a year before this date), but there is surely a note of weariness with the theme also. The distinction between "democratic individual" and "democratic nationality" is obscure, and Whitman makes no attempt to explain. And it should be recalled that this Preface introduces a work that was produced on request to be read at an appearance at Dartmouth College and is, as the occasion perhaps demanded, patriotic and nationalistic. Significantly the Preface trails whimsically off into a description of the nature ("open air," "fresh scent of grass," "forenoon breeze") surrounding Whitman as he writes.

As an annex to the 1871–72 edition there had appeared a 120-page pamphlet entitled *Passage to India* that included not only the title poem and a number of new poems but a large number of older poems evidently left over after the process of integrating "Drum-Taps." The poems of this annex, together with eighteen new poems and a number of prose pieces, constitute the second volume of the 1876 two-volume centennial edition of *Leaves of Grass.* This second volume, entitled *Two Rivulets,* contains a Preface highly revealing of Whitman's rapidly changing plans, plans that varied considerably from those sketched in the 1872 Preface. Curiously, the most interesting statements in this Preface appear in two long footnotes. Whitman again reveals his concept of the nature of the *Leaves of Grass* volume, which in 1876 (as in 1871–72) consisted essentially of the 1860 edition combined with "Drum Taps": "In that former and main volume, composed in the flush of my health and strength, from the age of 30 to 50 years, I dwelt on birth and life, clothing my ideas in pictures, days, transactions of my time, to give them positive place, identity . . . my enclosing purport being to express, above all artificial regulation and aid, the eternal bodily composite, cumulative, natural character of one's self" (V, 197). The most significant phrase is, perhaps, "enclosing purport." What Whitman formerly referred to as the "gigantic embryo or skeleton Personality" has become "birth and life"; what he called the *"Time & Land we swim in"* has become "transactions of my time . . . positive place"; and the two are encompassed within the "enclosing purport" of expressing the composite, yet unique, "character of one's self." It is thus that Whitman conceives the unity of the second major version of *Leaves of Grass.*

A long footnote to the phrase ending with "one's self" explains in detail the nature of this important unifying theme: "Namely, a character, making most of common and normal elements, to the superstructure of which not only the precious accumulations of the learning and experiences of the Old World . . . shall still faithfully contribute, but which at its foundations and carried up thence, and receiving its impetus from the democratic spirit . . . shall again directly be vitalized by the perennial influences of Nature at first hand . . ." (V, 197). Realizing that these characteristics of this New World "self" are predominantly physical or materialistic, Whitman hastens to add: "Not but what the brawn of *Leaves of Grass* is, I hope, thoroughly spiritualized everywhere, for final estimate, but, from the very subjects, the direct effect is a sense of the life, as it should be, of flesh and blood, and physical urge, and animalism." In this same footnote, Whitman comments on the unity underlying the diverse themes: "While there are other themes, and plenty of abstract thoughts and poems in the volume—while I have put in it passing and rapid but actual glimpses of the great struggle between the nation and the slave-power . . . [yet] to make a type-portrait for living, active, worldly, healthy personality, objective as well as subjective, joyful and potent, and modern and free, distinctively for the use of the United States, male and female, through the long future—has been, I say, my general object" (V, 198).

Throughout this entire footnote, Whitman seems to be groping about for the proper language in which to embody his concept of the unifying element in *Leaves of Grass.* At one point he says parenthetically: "Probably, indeed, the whole of these varied songs, and all my writings, both volumes, only ring changes in some sort, on the ejaculation, How vast, how eligible, how joyful, how real, is a human being, himself or herself" (V, 198). In these remarks Whitman extends his efforts to encompass the "enclosing clue" of *all* his work ("both volumes"), a foreshadowing of the time when the poems included in *Two Rivulets* in 1876 will find their way into a re-expanded *Leaves of Grass*, an inclusion that will not be an arbitrary act but the result of a coherently evolved concept of the central theme of "one's self" (the textual comment that precipitated the speculation here footnoted).

But before advancing to the final structural stage of *Leaves of Grass*, we should find it valuable to examine Whitman's comments in this 1876 Preface concerning his plans and intentions for the poems in the *Two Rivulets* volume. In defense of the unity of his new volume, he says: "And e'en for flush and proof of our America —for reminder, just as much, or more, in moods of towering pride and joy, I keep my special chants of death and immortality to stamp the coloring-finish of all, present and past. For terminus and temperer to all, they were originally written; and that shall be their office at the last" (V, 193–94). The words defining the unifying theme, "chants of death and immortality," plunge Whitman into a footnote comparable in length to the one discussed above and similarly enlightening as to his plans: "I meant, while in a sort continuing the theme of my first chants, to shift the slides, and exhibit the problem and paradox of the same ardent and fully appointed personality entering the sphere of the resistless gravitation of spiritual law, and with cheerful face estimating death, not at all as the cessation, but as somehow what I feel it must be, the entrance upon by far the greatest part of existence, and something that life is at least as much for, as it is for itself" (V, 194). Whitman points out that this original plan for a full volume has been abandoned because such a task is beyond his "powers." In these comments we glimpse Whitman's mental processes after the abandonment of one plan and before the complete evolution of a new.

Throughout this rambling footnote Whitman is groping toward a justification for inclusion of these "Passage to India" poems (in the *Two Rivulets* volume) within *Leaves of Grass* as an integral part of its structure. These poems, he says, are the "terminus and temperer" of his earlier poetry. In Whitman's view, they are linked with *Leaves of Grass* because they represent the "same ardent and fully appointed personality" (the "one's self" or "type-portrait") entering what Whitman calls "the sphere of the resistless gravitation of spiritual law," a sphere in which "perpetuity and conservation" are affirmed. Whitman says: "I end my books with thoughts, or radiations from thoughts, on death, immortality, and a free entrance into the spiritual world. . . . In them I also seek to set the key-stone to my democracy's enduring arch" (V, 194–95). Whitman conceives these poems as not only related to *Leaves of Grass* but as expressing a point of view "necessitated" by the earlier poems. Indeed, these "Passage to India" poems have already become in Whitman's concept not only a part but a necessary and inevitable part of his life's work. They not only continue where *Leaves of Grass* left off, but they also qualify and explain much that preceded: "As in some ancient legend-play, to close the plot and the hero's career, there is a farewell gathering on ship's deck and on shore, a loosing of hawsers and ties, a spreading of sails to the wind—a starting out on unknown seas, to fetch up no one knows whither—to return no more—and the curtain falls, and there is the end of it—so I have reserv'd that poem ["Passage to India"], with its cluster, to finish and explain much that, without them, would not be explain'd, and to take leave, and escape for good, from all that has preceded them" (V, 193). But though these poems belong rightfully and even necessarily at the end of *Leaves of Grass,* Whitman explains parenthetically that they have been anticipated by certain themes which have existence, though perhaps latent, in the earlier volume: "Then probably *Passage to India,* and its clusters, are but freer vent and fuller expression to what, from the first, and so on throughout, more or less lurks in my writings, underneath every page, every line, everywhere" (V, 193). So it is that Whitman sees the interlocking relationships between the "Passage to India" poems and *Leaves of Grass,* and so it is that he is shortly to become engaged in reworking the structure of his masterpiece to give it the shape we know today as *Leaves of Grass.*

Whitman designed a structure for the 1881 edition of *Leaves of Grass* that was to remain essentially unchanged in subsequent editions. In this third and final stage in the evolution of *Leaves of Grass*, the main task of the poet was to integrate the "Passage to India" poems. As the 1876 Preface indicated, Whitman realized that such an integration could be achieved without doing violence to the basic concepts underlying his book and without destroying the natural unity of the "Passage to India" cluster. Whitman's invaluable comments on his book as he had finally ordered and arranged it do not appear, however, until 1888, in the Preface to *November Boughs*, "A Backward Glance o'er Travel'd Roads." Whitman was so satisfied with this prose piece that he placed it at the end of the final lifetime editions of *Leaves of Grass*, and there it remains as a permanent part of the last version of the book.

In "A Backward Glance o'er Travel'd Roads" Whitman reveals his final concept of the basic nature of the book he has written. He is, in the first place, acutely conscious of the evolutionary growth of the book: "Results of seven or eight stages and struggles extending through nearly thirty years, (as I nigh my three-score-and-ten I live largely on memory,) I look upon *Leaves of Grass*, now finish'd to the end of its opportunities and powers, as my definitive *carte de visite* to the coming generations of the New World, if I may assume to say so" (III, 42). In the early pages of this relatively long prose work Whitman outlines the central impluse out of which his poetry first took its origin: "This [desire] was a feeling or ambition to articulate and faithfully express in literary or poetic form, and uncompromisingly, my own physical, emotional, moral, intellectual, and aesthetic Personality, in the midst of, and tallying, the momentous spirit and facts of its immediate days, and of current America— and to exploit that Personality, identified with place and date, in a far more candid and comprehensive sense than any hitherto poem or book" (III, 44). This theme of the prototype of the New World personality dominated Whitman's concept of his work from his earliest comments (for example, the "gigantic embryo or skeleton of Personality" of 1865) to his last. At each stage of the development of *Leaves of Grass*, this fundamental concept has been somehow adjusted or modified or expanded in order to make room for a new and usually "necessary" aspect. Whitman suggests in "A Backward Glance" that this basic theme is the element that gives his book unity: "Perhaps this [the articulation and exploitation of 'Per-

sonality identified with place and date'] is in brief, or suggests, all
I have sought to do" (III, 44). Whitman explains more precisely his
meaning: "Given the nineteenth century, with the United States,
and what they furnish as area and points of view, *Leaves of Grass*
is, or seeks to be, simply a faithful and doubtless self-will'd record.
In the midst of all, it gives one man's—the author's—identity, ardors,
observations, faiths, and thoughts, color'd hardly at all with any
decided coloring from other faiths or other identities" (III, 44–45).
One can detect in this statement, as in the one preceding, the now
inextricably joined themes that had their origin in the separate
stages of growth of *Leaves of Grass*: the dominant theme of one's self;
the theme of nineteenth-century America (first called the "Time &
Place we swim in" when embodied in the "Drum-Taps" cluster); and
the theme of faith or "faiths" (which was first brought to a focus in the
"Passage to India" cluster).

Throughout "A Backward Glance o'er Travel'd Roads" Whitman
places emphasis on his three dominant themes or on themes that
might be subsumed under one of these three. Near the middle of
this prose piece he points out the importance to his book of the
Civil War: "It is certain . . . that, although I had made a start before,
only from the occurrence of the Secession War, and what it show'd
me as by flashes of lightning, with the emotional depths it sounded
and arous'd . . . that only from the strong flare and provocation of
that War's sights and scenes the final reasons-for-being of an au-
tochthonic and passionate song definitely came forth" (III, 57).
Whitman in retrospect sees that his Civil War experience was central to his poetic development, and he can say, now that the "Drum-
Taps" poems are deeply imbedded in the central position in *Leaves
of Grass*: "Without those three or four years and the experiences
they gave, Leaves of Grass would not now be existing" (III, 58).
Near the end of "A Backward Glance," Whitman turns to the theme
of spirituality, which grew to major importance in the "Passage to
India" poems: "Then still a purpose enclosing all, and over and beneath all. Ever since what might be call'd thought, or the budding
of thought, fairly began in my youthful mind, I had had a desire
to attempt some worthy record of that entire faith and acceptance
('To justify the ways of God to men' is Milton's well-known and
ambitious phrase) which is the foundation of moral America" (III,

63). As in the 1876 Preface, Whitman notes that this theme "lurks" in all his work and is the "enclosing" purpose of his poetry: "Invisible spiritual results, just as real and definite as the visible, eventuate all concrete life and all materialism, through Time" (III, 63).

Once the evolution of *Leaves of Grass* is understood, it should be no surprise to find in the book a basic three-part structure. In its simplest terms the book may be said to be the creation of an individual, yet typical, personality for the New World. This creation or delineation first portrays an expanding awareness of the self and its relation to all else; next shows the impingement of a specific time and a particular place on self; and finally engages the self with the fundamental and all-encompassing "law" of spirituality. With the introductory and farewell poems, there are five major groups, as shown on page 186.

Whitman's own phrases appear as the titles for Groups II, III, and IV, the threefold division of theme. It should be stressed that these three groups are not mutually exclusive. Whitman's own description of the relation of the "Passage to India" poems to the rest of his work is highly revealing as to his method throughout: these poems, Whitman said, "are but freer vent and fuller expression to what . . . more or less lurks in my writings, underneath every page, every line, everywhere" (V, 193). In reality this point could be made of each of his three major thematic groups. All these themes "lurk" beneath every page in the book. But, as Whitman put it, he "shifts the slides" so that primary attention is focused on an individual and distinct theme in each group. Moreover, though there is a definite correlation between the final structure of *Leaves of Grass* and the stages of its evolution as a volume of related poems, all of the poetry composed during one specified period was by no means confined to a single theme. Innumerable critics of *Leaves of Grass* have pointed out that the poems in it are not arranged chronologically, and some of the critics have implied that for this reason the order that does exist is defective. On the contrary, the very fact that Whitman chose not to leave his poems in the order of their writing confirms his assertion that he was throughout his life engaged in the task of developing a structure.

The question that remains, of course, concerns the nature, or perhaps even the validity, of the structure. In my examination of the evolution of the structure, I have attempted to show that Whitman did not merely change, in arbitrary fashion, the character of his work each time he wanted to incorporate in it a new group of poems. The basic character of his work remained constant, but his concept of that character grew in dimension and complexity so that new poems

Leaves of Grass: Prototype personality for the New World

I. Introduction to themes and greetings
Inscriptions
"Starting from Paumanok"

II. Gigantic embryo or skeleton of personality
"Song of Myself"
Children of Adam   } the self and others
Calamus

Songs (Eleven individual poems) } the self and the world (place)

Birds of Passage
"A Broadway Pageant"   } the self and history
Sea-Drift   (time)
By the Roadside

III. This time and land we swim in
Drum-Taps
Memories of President Lincoln } national crisis

"By Blue Ontario's Shore"   } rehabilitation
Autumn Rivulets

IV. The resistless gravitation of spiritual law
"Proud Music of the Storm"
"Passage to India"
"Prayer of Columbus"
"The Sleepers"
"To Think of Time"
Whispers of Heavenly Death

V. Review of themes and farewell
"Thou Mother with Thy Equal Brood"
From Noon to Starry Night
Songs of Parting

Afterthoughts: the Annexes
Sands at Seventy
Good-Bye My Fancy
Old Age Echoes[4]

4. Brief poems such as "Reversals" at the end of "By Blue Ontario's Shore" and "Transpositions" following "The Sleepers" I have regarded as fillers only and not significant parts of the structure of *Leaves of Grass.*

and clusters of poems (written, after all, out of the same spirit and the same perspective on life) became organic parts of his total scheme. Whitman's structure is not a mere grouping of poems in accordance with subject matter. It is, rather, an ordering of the poems and groups of poems in accordance with the shifting focus of the pervading theme. These groups are not separate entities, to be shuffled around at will, but exist in an appropriate order in which there is a complex network of relationships. It is necessary that the "gigantic embryo or skeleton of Personality" be first introduced, defined, and related to the world and time in general before it is plunged into this specific "Time & Land we swim in." And it is inevitable that this prototype personality be given birth, identity, and relationships with a certain century and country before primary attention is focused on his relation to death and immortality. There is not only a "poetic" sense to this order, but, throughout, sight is not lost of the basic poetic intent: the articulation of the prototype of the New World personality.

The proposed structure, although it appears at the conclusion of the survey of the evolution of *Leaves of Grass,* is based not primarily on that evolution at all but on analysis of the existing structure of the deathbed edition. Some of the "subtitles" will become clear in the ensuing analysis. The groupings of poems do not derive their unity entirely from thematic emphasis. There are, frequently, images that dominate and give distinctive character to the groups. The nature of this imagery as it relates to structure will be examined in the following analysis. One last bit of explanation needs, perhaps, to be made: examination of the structural outline will reveal that some of the themes most frequently associated with Whitman do not appear. These themes are actually latent in the structure but do not emerge because of the necessary brevity of the outline. For example, sex is treated in the section called "the self and others"; science and democracy, celebrated by implication throughout the work, are not explicit themes so much as submerged foundations on which the poetry solidly rests.

CHAPTER THIRTEEN

Introduction to
Themes and Greetings

That the opening poems of *Leaves of Grass* are introductory in nature is no startling discovery. Many critics have observed that "Inscriptions," as the title indicates, announces the principal themes of the book. It may surprise some, however, to find "Starting from Paumanok" grouped with "Inscriptions" rather than with "Song of Myself," as, for example, Irving C. Story arranged them. The linking of "Starting from Paumanok" with "Song of Myself" probably springs from a superficial interpretation of the titles: both suggest a strong personal content and perhaps even abundant biographical reference. But those familiar, even casually, with the texts of these two poems know that neither is autobiographical in any true sense of the word, and the personal content of each is really no more than one finds in other lyric poems. Paumanok is Long Island and Whitman's boyhood home, but by the time we get to the fifth and sixth lines of the poem, in which the speaker claims to have been a "miner in California" and to have had a "home in Dakota's woods," we know that Whitman is not writing autobiography but using a few biographical facts to delineate a composite portrait. And the first three lines of "Song of Myself,"

> I celebrate myself, and sing myself,
> And what I assume you shall assume,
> For every atom belonging to me as good belongs to you [I, 33],[1]

reveals that the self is sung not because of the personal but because of the impersonal, or universal, element in self: universal (not "personal" in the sense we attach to the word) truths are discovered

1. Whitman quotations are where possible identified in the text by volume and page number of *The Complete Writings of Walt Whitman,* ed. Richard M. Bucke *et al.* (New York: G. P. Putnam's Sons, 1902).

through the universality that resides in self. Neither autobiography nor the personal draws these divergent poems together. "Starting from Paumanok" functions, with "Inscriptions," as introduction and greeting; "Song of Myself" launches the poetic journey.

Various poems have stood at the opening of *Leaves of Grass* in the succeeding editions. "Song of Myself" in its untitled form opened the first (1855) edition. In the third edition (1860) "Proto-Leaf" (now "Starting from Paumanok") was introduced as the opening poem. The single poem "Inscription" opened the 1867 edition, and this title became "Inscriptions" to head a group of introductory poems in 1871–72. The poems that appear in the final arrangement of this group range in date from 1860 to 1881. This brief history suggests that Whitman felt the need, as his book became more complex in theme and structure, of more and more introductory material. In any event, it is certain that he revised all these poems, particularly "Starting from Paumanok," from the date of their first appearance, apparently intending to make them reflect more faithfully the nature of the book they introduce. Both the "Inscriptions" group and "Starting from Paumanok" serve multiple introductory purposes: they dedicate *Leaves of Grass;* they invoke the appropriate muse; they announce the various major and minor themes; they introduce the images that are to dominate the book; they prepare for and even establish important symbols; they invite intimacy with the reader; and they ask him to join in the experience to come. They accomplish all these purposes and more in Whitman's characteristic manner: in "Inscriptions" Whitman exploits his genius for arranging his short lyrics in "symphonic" order; in "Starting from Paumanok" he demonstrates his ability to sustain a dramatic appeal while at the same time introducing, dropping, and returning to various themes vital to his work.

"One's-Self I Sing," the opening poem of "Inscriptions," sets forth the basic theme that obsessed Whitman from the first poetic impulse resulting in *Leaves of Grass* and grew in complexity as Whitman's poetic vision expanded. The nature of Whitman's theme is suggested in the opening two lines:

> One's-self I sing, a simple separate person,
> Yet utter the word Democratic, the word En-Masse [I, 1].

Whitman was fully conscious of the paradoxical elements in his themes and, indeed, utilized these very elements to create tension and drama in his poetry. The paradox in these lines extends from the beginning to the end of *Leaves of Grass* and constitutes the book's core. "One's-Self I Sing" introduces other themes: "freest action form'd under the laws divine" suggests the relation of one's self to spirituality, and "The Modern Man I Sing" suggests that this simple, separate self is to be related to the current time and place of the author—nineteenth-century America.

But if these other themes are merely hinted at in the opening poem, they are announced fully in other poems of "Inscriptions." Perhaps the theme of "this Time & Place" is best noted in "To Thee Old Cause":

> Thou orb of many orbs!
> Thou seething principle! thou well-kept, latent germ! thou centre!
> Around the idea of thee the war revolving [I, 5].

The "old cause" is democracy, the kind of democracy that maintains the proper balance between selfhood and "en-masse." But Whitman makes a direct identification of democracy with the Civil War. He says, "These recitatives for thee,—my book and the war are one," suggesting the importance, as he had suggested again and again in prose, of the Civil War to his poetic growth. The theme of the "resistless gravitation of spiritual law" receives its fullest treatment in "Eidólons," a poem that, if for no other reason than length, dominates "Inscriptions." "Eidólons" is the first poem the reader meets in *Leaves of Grass* that has a regular stanzaic form, constant line-length, and a poetic refrain. The poem's length, form, and central position in "Inscriptions" cause it to radiate out in all directions, permeating and giving spiritual bias to the poems devoted to other themes. "Eidólons" asserts the spiritual reality of each individual self:

> Of every human life,
> (The units gather'd, posted, not a thought, emotion, deed, left out,)
> The whole or large or small summ'd, added up,
> In its eidólon [I, 6].

The poem also suggests the ultimate spiritual manifestation of the "now and here":

> The present now and here,
> America's busy, teeming, intricate whirl,
> Of aggregate and segregate for only thence releasing,
> To-day's eidólons [I, 7].

And there is throughout the poem the reliance on the ultimate spiritual life or immortality:

> And thee my soul,
> Joys, ceaseless exercises, exaltations,
> Thy yearning amply fed at last, prepared to meet,
> Thy mates, eidólons [I, 8].

This spirituality suffuses all Whitman's major themes and becomes the ultimate or final significance of them all. In "Eidólons" one finds re-enacted on a minor scale the drama of the whole of *Leaves of Grass*.

There are other themes introduced in "Inscriptions," topics that may be subsumed under one of the three major themes. The group of poems also invokes the Muse. But this Muse, "A Phantom . . . / Terrible in beauty, age, and power" (I, 1), is not petitioned in the same reverent tones as those assumed by writers of past epics. Whitman assures the "haughty Shade," in language suggesting his equality with her, that his poetry will fulfil her demands that he adopt the theme of war. He will, he says, sing of war—

> . . . the field the world,
> For life and death, for the body and for the eternal Soul,
> Lo, I too am come, chanting the chant of battles,
> I above all promote brave soldiers [I, 2].

This metaphor of war in this ("As I Ponder'd in Silence") the second poem in "Inscriptions" gives way in the succeeding poem ("In Cabin'd Ships at Sea") to an ocean metaphor—

> The boundless vista and the horizon far and dim are all here,
> And this is ocean's poem [I, 3].

In this way, through metaphor, a number of the book's most important images are introduced and established immediately as of significant symbolic value. Particularly does "In Cabin'd Ships at Sea" suggest the complexity of the ocean as a symbol in the poetry to follow. But sifted in among the poems introducing themes, imagery, and symbols are a number of poems dedicatory in nature: "To Foreign Lands"; "To a Historian"; "To the States"; "To a Certain

Cantatrice"; "Shut Not Your Doors"; "Poets To Come"; and, finally, the last two poems, two lines each, "To You" and "Thou Reader." These are only some of the poems containing dedicatory elements, but they are enough to suggest that Whitman used the dedication form, as he used the invocation to the muse, for his own poetic purpose. For example, he sends his poems to foreign lands to "define America" (I, 4); he tells the historian that he as poet projects the "history of the future" (I, 4); he warns the proud libraries "not to shut their doors" (I, 14); he alerts the poets to come that they must "justify" him (I, 15); and he says finally and intimately to "Thou Reader" at the end of "Inscriptions":

> Thou reader throbbest life and pride and love the same as I,
> Therefore for thee the following chants [I, 15].

These two lines in context carry a curious impact. By collecting a number of brief poems at the end of "Inscriptions" and by passing swiftly from thought to thought and image to image, Whitman achieves an illusion of almost religious fervency that heightens and sharpens the final dedication to the reader.

"Starting from Paumanok" gives the impression in its opening lines ("Starting from fish-shape Paumanok where I was born, / well-begotten, and rais'd by a perfect mother") of autobiography, but, by the time one has reached the middle of the first section, it becomes clear that not a specific but rather a composite portrait of an American—a New World personality—is being drawn, and the last three lines suggest an even more complex artistic intent:

> Having studied the mocking-bird's tones and the flight of the mountain-hawk,
> And heard at dawn the unrivall'd one, the hermit thrush from the swamp-cedars,
> Solitary, singing in the West, I strike up for a New World [I, 16–17].

To the reader of *Leaves of Grass*, these three birds have special significance: the mockingbird as an important character in "Out of the Cradle Endlessly Rocking"; the mountain hawk as a symbol of sexuality in "We Two, How Long We Were Fool'd" in the "Children of Adam" section ("We are two predatory hawks, we soar above and look down" [I, 132]); and the hermit thrush as a symbol of spirituality in "When Lilacs Last in the Dooryard Bloom'd." It becomes clear that Whitman wishes "Starting from Paumanok" to serve (as, for example, on a more limited scale, section 1 of "Out of the Cradle" serves in the poem or as "From Pent-up Aching Rivers" serves in the "Children of Adam" section) to introduce the imagery, metaphors, symbols, and themes of the whole of *Leaves of Grass*. To confirm this purpose of the poem, one might note two of the many revisions Whitman made. "Starting from Paumanok" appeared originally in the 1860 edition of *Leaves of Grass* as "Proto-Leaf" (the very title suggesting a special and unique relation with the *whole* book). The line quoted above containing the hermit thrush—swamp cedars imagery was added in 1867, as was a line in section 18: "See, through Atlantica's depths pulses American Europe reaching, pulses of Europe duly return'd" (I, 31). The one line incorporates imagery important to "When Lilacs Last in the Dooryard Bloom'd," while the other embodies an event (the laying of the transoceanic cable) important to "Passage to India," both significant and major poems written after the 1860 edition. Whitman desired to establish these and other dominant images in his reader's imagination at the outset as a preparation for all the *Leaves* to follow.

In the passage (quoted above) closing section 1 of "Starting from Paumanok," the unusual term "strike up" in "I strike up for a New World" is one of Whitman's happiest choices of language and suggests vigorous and exploratory movement as well as the launching of an epic musical composition. Implied in the phrase is the element that distinguishes *Leaves of Grass* from all the poems that have gone before: it embraces, embodies, somehow incloses, a New World. At the opening of section 2 are catalogued the themes appropriate for this New World:

> Victory, union, faith, identity, time,
> The indissoluble compacts, riches, mystery,
> Eternal progress, the kosmos, and the modern reports [I, 17].

Characteristically, Whitman does not suggest a verb for his substantives. Words such as "victory" and "union" have specific application, yet radiate meaning, a meaning that emerges fully only as the poem progresses. The image of the composite personality of the New World, carefully delineated in the first section, gradually shifts to the image of the personality in a specific time and place—nineteenth-century America—until, in section 3, another major theme is announced:

> Americanos! conquerors! marches humanitarian!
> Foremost! century marches! Libertad! masses!
> For you a programme of chants [I, 18].

And the "programme of chants" for America and democracy, for which Whitman pleads acceptance ("Take my leaves America . . . they are your own offspring . . ." [I, 18]), gradually gives way at the end of section 5 to the theme of spirituality:

> Here spirituality the translatress, the openly-avow'd,
> The ever-tending, the finalé of visible forms,
> The satisfier, after due long-waiting now advancing,
> Yes here comes my mistress the soul [I, 19].

Whitman suggests how the theme of spirituality is complexly related to and even implicit in his other themes:

> I will make the poems of materials, for I think they are to be the most spiritual poems,
> And I will make the poems of my body and of mortality,
> For I think I shall then supply myself with the poems of my soul and immortality [I, 20].

The poet envisions the theme of spirituality as binding his other themes into a unity. By far the greater share of "Starting from Paumanok" is devoted to sketching in broad strokes the theme of spirituality and in celebrating its all-encompassing significance. In section 10, a climax is reached in the pronouncement of the fundamental and interrelated themes of *Leaves of Grass*:

> My comrade!
> For you to share with me two greatnesses, and a third one rising inclusive and more resplendent,
> The greatness of Love and Democracy, and the greatness of Religion [I, 23].

In this passage, which has all the intimacy of a confession, Whitman announces the threefold structure of *Leaves of Grass*. The key concept for the New World personality is love; the significant contribution of America to the world is democracy; and, "rising inclusive and more resplendent," is spirituality or religion. "Starting from Paumanok" has already demonstrated that spirituality transcends and includes the other themes: *Leaves of Grass* is to show further that the theme of religion is pervasive, even when other themes are in focus, and, at the last, becomes itself the center of poetic attention.

If there is some order and balance to the preview of themes in the first part of "Starting from Paumanok," there is also careful preparation for the rise in intimate appeal to the reader, which reaches an ecstatic climax at the end of the poem. The direct address begins in section 8, when the poet asks, "What are you doing young man?" This startling question, which suggests the opening of a "private" and intimate conversation between the poet and reader, becomes more probing and insistent in section 9:

> What do you seek so pensive and silent?
> What do you need camerado?
> Dear son do you think it is love? [I, 22].

But even greater than love, the reader discovers in section 10, is religion:

> Know you, solely to drop in the earth the germs of a greater religion,
> The following chants each for its kind I sing [I, 23].

Following these lines, the poet's appeal to the reader becomes impersonal, and the reader seems to merge with the mass. At the end of section 13, Whitman exclaims to all: "Whoever you are, how superb and how divine is your body, or any part of it!" (I, 27). At the opening of section 14, he again asserts: "Whoever you are, to you endless announcements!" (I, 27). By the end of section 14, however, the poet, in a state approaching emotional frenzy, has regained his intimate and direct tone:

> Coming among the new ones myself to be their companion and equal,
>   coming personally to you now,
> Enjoining you to acts, characters, spectacles, with me [I, 29].

The "coming personally to you now" seems to have an immediately applicable meaning, for section 15 opens, "With me with firm holding, yet haste, haste on" (I, 29). The dramatic assumption of personal and actual relationship between the reader and poet has, surely, great emotional impact. And the direct plea to "haste on" with the poet is compelling. It is by conveying directly and intimately this terrible sense of immediacy and urgency that Whitman lends major significance to his rapid, almost staccato, review of themes and symbols. In section 18, the reader is directed to see:

> See, pastures and forests in my poems—see, animals wild and tame—see,
>   beyond the Kaw, countless herds of buffalo feeding on short curly grass,
> See, in my poems, cities, solid, vast, inland, with paved streets, with iron
>   and stone edifices, ceaseless vehicles, and commerce [I, 31].

The reader is invited to journey through *Leaves of Grass* in intimate association with the poet. But the dramatic fiction of direct touch and urgent movement is maintained to the last, and the ecstatic and exclamatory close, in section 19, is in keeping with and grows naturally out of the complex preparation begun in section 8:

> O camerado close! O you and me at last, and us two only.
> O a word to clear one's path ahead endlessly!
> O something ecstatic and undemonstrable! O music wild! [I, 32].

Such extreme fervency, like the unreasoned and intensely emotional fervency of the religious revival meeting (the appeal by the revivalist for the sinner to "join" and be "saved"), succeeds, surely, in arousing a response in the most skeptical reader. And the poem closes, "O to haste firm holding—to haste, haste on with me," an invitation of such urgency as to plunge the reader into the remainder (and true "body") of *Leaves of Grass* and specifically into "Song of Myself," which follows immediately.

CHAPTER FOURTEEN

Gigantic Embryo
or Skeleton of Personality

The purport of the first part proper of *Leaves of Grass* is well suggested by Whitman's phrase from a letter of 1865 when he thought the 1860 edition was to stand essentially unchanged: "to express by sharp-cut self assertion, One's Self & also, or may be still more, to map out, to throw together for American use, a gigantic embryo or skeleton of Personality,—fit for the West, for native models."[1] Such a statement of intent makes clear, in spite of the seemingly abundant personal reference in the first part of *Leaves of Grass*, that the poems beginning with "Song of Myself" are in reality basically impersonal. Whitman's intention is apparently the delineation of an archetypal personality for the New World, the West. His word "embryo" suggests that he is attempting to portray only the rudimentary beginnings of such a personality; "skeleton" suggests that he is granting the reader the task of conceiving the necessary flesh and life.

Analysis of this section of *Leaves of Grass* indicates the grouping of poems shown on page 197. A brief examination of the relationship of these three parts will be followed by a comprehensive analysis of the unifying elements in each.

In the first, Whitman sets forth the basic nature of his archetypal New World personality, showing him as he is in his "self," in his relation to women, and in his relation to men. Thus, the personality is first given identity and discovers the true (and great) significance

1. Emory Holloway (ed.), *Walt Whitman: Complete Poetry and Selected Prose and Letters* (London: Nonesuch Press, 1938), pp. 949–50.

of self; he next discovers physical love; and, finally, spiritual love. Following this initial sketch of the self in relation to others, the song section of *Leaves of Grass* fills in more of the outline of this archetypal personality by relating the self to the world, that is, to space, to place, and to objects. In these songs there is a recurring exploration of the nature of reality. And finally, after the self has been given birth, related to humanity, and related to the world, it is, in the third group of poems, related to history, or time. Another way

A. Modern man: the self and others
  "Song of Myself"   (self)
  Children of Adam   (self and opposite sex [physical love])
  Calamus   (self and same sex [spiritual love])

B. The rolling earth: the self and the world
  "Salut au Monde"   introduction (birth)
  "Song of the Open Road"
  "Crossing Brooklyn Ferry"   } launching the journey
  "Song of the Answerer"
  "Our Old Feuillage"   } occasions for song
  "A Song of Joys"
  "Song of the Broad-Axe"
  "Song of the Exposition"   } some specific instances
  "Song of the Redwood Tree"   (the nature of things)
  "A Song for Occupations"
  "A Song of the Rolling Earth"   conclusion (continuation)
    ("Youth, Day, Old Age and Night")

C. Mystic evolution: the self and history
  Birds of Passage
  "A Broadway Pageant"
  Sea-Drift
  By the Roadside

of viewing these three groups of poems is to note that the first establishes the identity of the personality in human relationships, the second asserts the identity in space, and the third in time. Throughout, focus is maintained on the human even in settings in which the non-human seems overwhelming.

I. *Modern Man: The Self and Others*

The image established at the outset of "Song of Myself" and dominating the poem is human. When the poet says, "I celebrate myself, and sing myself" (I, 33),[2] there begins to form in the reader's mind (aided, in all Whitman's editions of the poem, by the "vaga-bond" photograph) a visual image of the speaker, and when he says, "I loafe and invite my soul" (I, 33), the image sharpens:

> My tongue, every atom of my blood, form'd from this soil, this air,
> Born here of parents born here from parents the same, and
>   their parents the same,
> I, now thirty-seven years old in perfect health begin,
> Hoping to cease not till death [I, 33].

All these small, yet significantly human, details create an unmistak-ably real personality within the poem. The lineage, the age, the health, the hope—all these intimate facts help to establish a close relationship with the reader. The speaker is not only human but familiarly and closely human. But soon all these personal details are offset by a multitude of impersonal facts. For example:

> I am of old and young, of the foolish as much as the wise,
> Regardless of others, ever regardful of others,
> Maternal as well as paternal, a child as well as a man [I, 52–53].

A tension is established in the poem, a balance between the person-al and the impersonal, individuality and "en-masse," the single leaf of grass and its cluster. As a result the dominant image that gradu-ally emerges is that of a sharply clear and vivid, but composite and multiple, personality. And at times the image assumes superhuman proportions:

> My ties and ballasts leave me, my elbows rest in sea-gaps,
> I skirt sierras, my palms cover continents,
> I am afoot with my vision [I, 73].

In this passage Whitman seems to comply literally with his stated intention of delineating a "gigantic embryo or skeleton of Person-ality." In lines such as these the human image emerges on a scale commensurate with the poet's claims for the New World personality.

If "Song of Myself" establishes the significance of the self, a sig-nificance summed up in such a phrase as "I am an acme of things accomplish'd, and I an encloser of things to be" (I, 980), "Chil-dren of Adam" begins the delineation of that created and newly

2. Whitman quotations are where possible identified in the text by volume and page number of *The Complete Writings of Walt Whitman*, ed. Richard M. Bucke *et al.* (New York: G. P. Putnam's Sons, 1902).

f in a human context. Whitman implies the transcend-
e of the human in contrast with all that is non-human.
at dominates "Children of Adam," like that of "Song of
e human being, here the Adamic man, obsessed with
eliria," with the wonders of the sexuality of his nature,
with the awesome position of woman in the human destiny. The second poem in this cluster, "From Pent-up Aching Rivers," is a rhap-
sodic intermingling of all the images of the poems to follow bound
together by a statement of poetic intent:

> From pent-up aching rivers,
> From that of myself without which I were nothing,
> From what I am determin'd to make illustrious, even if I stand
>   sole among men,
> From my own voice resonant, singing the phallus,
> Singing the song of procreation [I, 110–11].

But if the dominant image is Adamic man, as the poems progress
the figure of woman as Eve looms large in significance. In "I Sing
the Body Electric," the longest poem of the section, woman is celebrated as inclosing all:

> The female contains all qualities and tempers them,
> She is in her place and moves with perfect balance,
> She is all things duly veil'd, she is both passive and active,
> She is to conceive daughters as well as sons, and sons as well
>   as daughters [I, 118].

As "Song of Myself" explores the self's sacred relation to self, "Children of Adam" establishes the mystical and divine relation of man
to woman through "defiant" and exhilarated celebration of "you act
divine and you children prepared for, / And you stalwart loins"
(I, 113).

"Calamus" completes the poet's exploration of human relationships by examining those that exist on a rare spiritual level. "In
Paths Untrodden," like "From Pent-up Aching Rivers" in "Children
of Adam," is the program poem of the cluster, setting forth in unmistakable terms the poetic intent and presenting simultaneously
the primary images:

> Clear to me now standards not yet publish'd, clear to me that my soul,
> That the soul of the man I speak for rejoices in comrades,
> Here by myself away from the clank of the world,
> Tallying and talk'd to here by tongues aromatic,

No longer abash'd, (for in this secluded spot I can respond as I would not
  dare elsewhere,)
Strong upon me the life that does not exhibit itself, yet contains all the
  rest,
Resolv'd to sing no songs to-day but those of manly attachment [I, 137].

These songs of "manly attachment," as well as the songs of procreation in "Children of Adam," have been the subject of a great many
controversies. Whatever the inadvertent revelations may be in these
sections, the poetic (and structural) intentions are surely innocent
enough. There are two dominant images in "Calamus": the human
and the natural, comrades and clusters of calamus, the latter serving
as symbols of the former. As "Children of Adam" asserted the divinity of the procreative relationship of man and woman, "Calamus"
asserts the divinity of the spiritual relationship of man and man. In
one poem the poet distinguishes specifically between the two kinds
of love and relationships:

> Fast-anchor'd eternal O love! O woman I love!
> O bride! O wife! more resistless than I can tell, the thought
>   of you!
> Then separate, as disembodied or another born,
> Ethereal, the last athletic reality, my consolation,
> I ascend, I float in the regions of your love O man,
> O sharer of my roving life [II, 160].

If at times the "Calamus" emotion seems highly personal and intensely passionate, at other times it appears as a strong social or
democratic force. In the emotion the poet discovers the basic impulse necessary to the two conflicting elements in his ideal state, individuality and equality, or "one's-self" and "en-masse."

The human context for the self created in "Song of Myself" is
completed in "Calamus." In all three of these important opening
sections of *Leaves of Grass* attention is steadily focused on the human. From these sections emerges the picture of the "skeleton" personality, a personality whose relation to self and others is revolutionary, contemptuous of outmoded and hypocritical conventions,
and suitable to serve as the prototype for the New World.

II. *The Rolling Earth: The Self and the World*

"Full of Life Now," the last poem in "Calamus," represents the
poet, his "perturbations" past, dramatizing his own physical annihi-

lation ("When you read these, I that was visible am become invisible" [I, 162]) and assuring the reader: "Be it as if I were with you. (Be not too certain but I am now with you.)" (I, 162). This assertion of spiritual affinity between the poet and his reader receives startling imaginative confirmation in the opening line of the first of the eleven "songs," in which the reader is represented as speaking:

> O take my hand Walt Whitman!
> Such gliding wonders! such sights and sounds!
> Such join'd unended links, each hook'd to the next,
> Each answering all, each sharing the earth with all [I, 163].

In "Salut au Monde" attention is detached from human relationships and focused on the relation of the individual to the "gliding wonders," the "sights and sounds" of the earth. The song section, which treats several facets of this relation of the self to the world, may be best understood as an organized unit of *Leaves of Grass* in the following grouping of the poems:

The Self's Engagement with the World

"Salut au Monde"	greeting and inventory
"Song of the Open Road" "Crossing Brooklyn Ferry"	} the mystical journey
"Song of the Answerer" "Our Old Feuillage"	} the poet and his material (the world)
"A Song of Joys" "Song of the Broad-Axe" "Song of the Exposition" "Song of the Redwood Tree" "A Song for Occupations"	} bouquets of divine leaves
"A Song of the Rolling Earth"	the continuing earth

These clusters and their titles will become clear in the ensuing analysis.

Before justification is devised for dividing the poems into groups, a case needs to be made for their unity. As in other sections of *Leaves of Grass*, there is a key image which, introduced in strategic positions, draws all the songs together. The image is present in the titles of the first and the last of the poems and plays a significant role in each. The first ("Salut au Monde"), in which the world is greeted as though by a newborn and saucy infant, introduces the world's globe specifically in answer to the question, "What do you see Walt Whitman?"

I see a great round wonder rolling through space,
I see diminute farms, hamlets, ruins, graveyards, jails, factories, palaces,
  hovels, huts of barbarians, tents of nomads upon the surface,
I see the shaded part on one side where the sleepers are sleeping, and the
  sunlit part on the other side,
I see the curious rapid change of the light and shade [I, 165].

The inventory of this "great round wonder rolling through space" continues through several sections of "Salut au Monde," but the image of the moving globe remains dominant. Similarly, in the final poem of the song section, "A Song of the Rolling Earth," the continuing globe is the dominant image, though it is several times clothed in metaphor. In several instances it is a "divine ship" sailing the "divine sea," and in one place Whitman attempts an extended conceit:

Of the interminable sisters,
Of the ceaseless cotillions of sisters,
Of the centripetal and centrifugal sisters, the elder and younger
  sisters,
The beautiful sister we know dances on with the rest [I, 270].

Whether the earth is conceived as a "divine ship" sailing or a "sister" dancing, there is implied an unceasing movement onward. This image, dominant in both the first and the last poems in this group, appropriately focuses attention on man's position in the universe, his relation to the infinite objective world (or worlds) about him. Sailing or dancing, the world seems to have its appointed place in the universe, and man his appointed place in the world.

The above grouping of the song-section poems suggests their relationships with one another and each poem's contribution to the function of the section as a whole. "Salut au Monde" serves as the introduction and is, appropriately, a greeting to the world and also a gigantic catalogue of its multiple and varied contents. At the end the poet himself merges with the great manifestations of the world's nature:

You vapors, I think I have risen with you, moved away to
  distant continents, and fallen down there, for reasons,
I think I have blown with you you winds;
You waters I have finger'd every shore with you,
I have run through what any river or strait of the globe
  has run through [I, 175].

The poet suggests the ideal harmony that should exist between man and his world. The "for reasons" (in the first line above) implies the existence of some all-encompassing plan in tireless and endless operation behind all phenomena of the universe. After the greeting of "Salut au Monde," two poems filled with the imagery of dynamic movement appear: "Song of the Open Road" and "Crossing Brooklyn Ferry." The first suggests the launching of a journey by land, the second a voyage by sea. In both instances, the trip is symbolic: the exploration of the newly greeted earth, either on land or on water, is to result not in material but spiritual discoveries. As the "long brown path" leads on about the world endlessly, so the cyclic ferry never ceases (at least in the poetic imagination) to cross and recross the ever flowing water. In both these poems suggesting the constant and never ending onward rush of life, the reader assumes a leading role. In "Song of the Open Road" the poet pleads directly with the reader:

> Camerado, I give you my hand!
> I give you my love more precious than money,
> I give you myself before preaching or law;
> Will you give me yourself? will you come travel with me?
> Shall we stick by each other as long as we live? [I, 190].

This interchange of selves, the poet's and the reader's, is continued in "Crossing Brooklyn Ferry":

> What is more subtle than this which ties me to the woman or man that looks in my face?
> Which fuses me into you now, and pours my meaning into you? [I, 197].

These two "travel" poems "fuse" in an intimate relationship the poet and the reader at the beginning of their joint exploration of this strange world and its puzzling objects and materials.

The next two poems, "Song of the Answerer" and "Our Old Feuillage," in contrast with the preceding pair, are almost entirely devoid of images of movement. Instead, both are, if not static, at least reflective in nature, suggesting pauses in the mystic tour of the world for intensive contemplation. "Song of the Answerer" begins:

> Now list to my morning's romanza, I tell the signs of the Answerer,
> To the cities and farms I sing as they spread in the sunshine before me [I, 200].

The poem is a *morning* "romanza" because it comes at the beginning of that journey launched in "Song of the Open Road." "Song of the

Answerer" tells the signs by which the genuine poet will be known. Such knowledge will prove of value in the exploration that lies ahead. "Our Old Feuillage" attempts to catalogue the abundant materials that lie at hand for the New World Answerer:

Always our old feuillage!
Always Florida's green peninsula—always the priceless delta of Louisiana—
always the cotton-fields of Alabama and Texas,
Always California's golden hills and hollows, and the silver mountains of
New Mexico—always soft-breath'd Cuba [I, 206].

This use of the title metaphor of *Leaves of Grass* not only exploits the abundant complexity of the symbolic meaning by now present but also extends the metaphor and creates new meaning: "Singing the song of These, my ever-united lands—my body no more inevitably united, part to part, and made out of a thousand diverse contributions one identity, any more than my lands are inevitably united and made ONE IDENTITY" (I, 212). Primarily a "listing" of some of those "thousand diverse contributions" to the "ONE IDENTITY" of the New World, "Our Old Feuillage" concludes:

Nativities, climates, the grass of the great pastoral Plains,
Cities, labors, death, animals, products, war, good and evil—these me,
These affording, in all their particulars, the old feuillage to me and to
America, how can I do less than pass the clew of the union of them,
to afford the like to you?
Whoever you are! how can I but offer you divine leaves, that you also be
eligible as I am?
How can I but as here chanting, invite you for yourself to collect bouquets
of the incomparable feuillage of these states? [I, 212].

In these closing lines of "Our Old Feuillage" on the appropriate and even inevitable materials of the genuine Answerer are indications of the significance of the next five following poems: "A Song of Joys," "Song of the Broad-Axe," "Song of the Exposition," "Song of the Redwood Tree," and "A Song for Occupations." These five songs are the "divine leaves" or the "bouquets of the incomparable feuillage of these states" projected in "Our Old Feuillage." They "pass the clew of the union" of the endless diversity of the "particulars" of the New World promised in the preceding poem. "A Song of Joys" is such a "bouquet" or "union" of "particulars," certainly, in its drawing together and placing in juxtaposition diverse and even paradoxical sources of pleasure. It opens:

> O to make the most jubilant song!
> Full of music—full of manhood, womanhood, infancy!
> Full of common employments—full of grain and trees [I, 213].

There appears to be no systematic canvassing of the joys of life but rather an ecstatic progression from one joy to another—the engineer's, the horseman's, the fireman's, the mother's, the fisherman's, the soldier's, the whaleman's, the orator's, the farmer's. The element which unifies all these (and which is of particular significance to this entire segment of *Leaves of Grass*) is stated thus:

> O the joy of a manly self-hood!
> To be servile to none, to defer to none, not to any tyrant known
> or unknown,
> To walk with erect carriage, a step springy and elastic [I, 220].

All the assorted and sundry persons catalogued in their joy are in reality experiencing not the joy of a particular calling but rather the joy of "self-hood." It is for such joy that the poet ends his poems exuberantly and vividly:

> O to have life henceforth a poem of new joys!
> To dance, clap hands, exult, shout, skip, leap, roll on, float on!
> [I, 222].

Whereas "A Song of Joys" gathers together diverse particulars and discovers their common element, "Song of the Broad-Axe" begins with a single identity, the ax itself, and discovers it to be the symbol of a multiplicity of scattered and paradoxical elements: the same ax is used by the European headsmen to deprive men of their lives as is used by the pioneers to clear the wilderness and create a New World. By the end of the poem, the ax has become a symbol all-embracing and universal in its application: "Shapes bracing the earth and braced with the whole earth" (I, 237). "Song of the Exposition" discovers a transcendent significance in the diverse trades and arts exhibited at the great display of industry: "This, this and these [the halls housing the exhibits], America, shall be *your* pyramids and obelisks" (I, 244). Again the poet demonstrates the unity latent in a superficial variety. He concludes, addressing the Union: "Think not our chant, our show, merely for products gross or lucre—it is for thee, the soul in thee, electric, spiritual!" (I, 250). "Song of the Redwood Tree," like "Song of the Broad-Axe," begins with a single unit that represents a multiplicity of diverse particulars.

Something of the complexity of the symbolic significance of the redwood tree is suggested by the dedication of itself to, among other elements,

> You unseen moral essence of all the vast materials of America, (age upon age working in death the same as life,)
> You that, sometimes known, oftener unknown, really shape and mould the New World, adjusting it to Time and Space,
> You hidden national will lying in your abysms, conceal'd but ever alert [I, 254].

Although the tree calls to mind the whole pageant of the conquering of the wilderness and the movement of the frontier across the continent, it is singular in its dedication to the "unseen moral essence" that pervades all "the vast materials of America." In "A Song for Occupations," Whitman confirms what he suggested in "A Song of Joys": that the diversity of callings, occupations, and activity is as nothing compared to the unity of selfhood felt by all peoples:

> You workwomen and workmen of these states having your own divine and strong life,
> And all else giving place to men and women like you [I, 266].

Whitman finds the "eternal meanings" in the "labor of engines and trades and the labor of fields" (I, 257), meanings that reiterate the central significance of the selfhood of the individual man.

"A Song of the Rolling Earth," as the counterpart to "Salut au Monde," serves as the conclusion to the song section. But instead of serving as a farewell (as "Salut au Monde" served as a greeting), "A Song of the Rolling Earth" asserts the existence of a continuing and endless relationship between humanity and the world. The title itself suggests such continuation, and the imagery in the poem connotes no finality. For example:

> Tumbling on steadily, nothing dreading,
> Sunshine, storm, cold, heat, forever withstanding,
>   passing, carrying,
> The soul's realization and determination still inheriting,
> The fluid vacuum around and ahead still entering and
>   dividing [I, 271–72].

This dominant picture of the onrushing "ball" of earth does not permit the conception of an end or conclusion. But the poem, standing as it does as a conclusion, attempts to formulate the enigmatic significance of the onrushing globe:

I swear there is no greatness or power that does not emulate those of the
earth,
There can be no theory of any account unless it corroborates the theory
of the earth [I, 273].

At the last, the poet finds words inadequate to the task of getting at
the essential meaning of the relation of the self and the world: "My
tongue is ineffectual on its pivots" (I, 274).

This sketch of the interrelationships of the poems in the song section has so far not revealed one of the cohesive elements of major
importance, a theme that threads its way through all these poems.
This theme is introduced in the opening poem, "Salut au Monde" in
a series of questions:

> What widens within you Walt Whitman?
> What waves and sails exuding?
> What climes what persons and cities are here? [I, 163].

In the reply, the poet indicates that the "within you" is not a figur-
ative phrase:

Within me latitude widens, longitude lengthens,
Asia, Africa, Europe, are to the east—America is provided for in the west,
Banding the bulge of the earth winds the hot equator [I, 163–64].

The idea implicit is that the only existence the objective world has
is its existence within mankind. Throughout the remainder of "'Salut
au Monde," the extensive use of "I hear" and "I see" suggests the
entire dependence of the so-called objective world on the frail and
indwelling senses of the human being. In "Crossing Brooklyn Ferry,"
the "dumb, beautiful ministers" (I, 198), the external objects and
things, serve the primary intent of the poem of removing the barriers that separate man from man because these objects and things
have their common source of existence *within* all humanity. The external world (space) cannot separate man from his fellow man if
that external world is in reality the creation (and common or *shared*
creation) of the senses of all mankind.

This theme is central to the comprehensive intent of the poems in
the song section, the intent of relating the self to the world. By this
theme Whitman is again placing primary significance on the human
rather than the non-human by making the former the only source
for the latter. The theme reaches a climax in "A Song for Occupations," when the poet asserts:

List close my scholars dear,
Doctrines, politics and civilization exurge from you,
Sculpture and monuments and any thing inscribed anywhere are tallied
    in you,
The gist of histories and statistics as far back as the records reach is in you
    this hour, and myths and tales the same,
If you were not breathing and walking here, where would they all be?
The most renown'd poems would be ashes, orations and plays would be
    vacuums [I, 262].

As a result of the central importance of the human being, on whom
all the external world depends for its very "life," all that is non-human, no matter how sacred or valuable, must take a position secondary to the human. Whitman says, "When the psalm sings instead of
the singer, / When the script preaches instead of the preacher . . .
/ I intend to reach them my hand, and make as much of them as I
do of men and women like you" (I, 255–67). In the concluding
poem of the song section, "A Song of the Rolling Earth," Whitman
again asserts the importance of his idealism to his establishment of
the relation between self and the earth:

I swear the earth shall surely be complete to him or her who shall be
    complete,
The earth remains jagged and broken only to him or her who remains
    jagged and broken [I, 273].

As the earth is but the projection of the senses of an individual, so
that earth reflects the internal condition of the individual. Selfhood
remains supreme in an external world of the self's own creation.

III. *Mystic Evolution: The Self and History*

As the song section of *Leaves of Grass* serves to relate the archetypal New World personality to space, so the next succeeding group
of poems serves to relate him to time. Both these sections portray
the prototype self as triumphant over both space and time—triumphant in the sense of retaining significance and identity in the face
of those elements that tend to destroy individuality. As the principal
image in the song section was the rolling earth, so the key concept
in this group of poems is mystic evolution. The first poem in "Birds
of Passage," "Song of the Universal," opens with a statement by the
Muse:

> Come said the Muse,
> Sing me a song no poet yet has chanted,
> Sing me the universal [I, 276].

These lines indicate that there is a significant shift in thematic focus in *Leaves of Grass* beginning with "Birds of Passage." The theme prepared for and outlined in the remainder of the poem dominates (and clarifies) all the succeeding poems up to "Drum-Taps": "Birds of Passage," "A Broadway Pageant," "Sea-Drift," and "By the Roadside." These titles evoke a remarkable succession of images. In each instance there is the suggestion of movement that recalls the journey imagery of earlier sections of *Leaves of Grass*. Setting aside the apparent intruder—the only individual poem, "A Broadway Pageant"—for the moment, we may note in the titles of the three remaining groups an interesting variation in the medium of the movement from air to water to land. Moreover, there is a progression from the non-human to the human (birds—fish—men) and from swift flight to slow drift to static quiet. This latter progression is of particular significance in suggesting the slowing down, deliberately by the poet, of the passage of time. In these successive sections, the poet is primarily concerned with setting a number of incidents and events in proper perspective in time—in mystic evolution. As the poet works his way toward the poems treating the major event of his time—the Civil War, the event in which he is to become personally and emotionally engaged—the swift flight of time slows to imperceptible movement. In effect, these images embody the paradoxical truth—the amelioration of all-embracing mystic evolution but, at the same time, the certain impingement of the immediate happenings of one's age on one's consciousness. One might imagine a circular canvas on which are painted sharply detailed pictures of life's virtues and evils. If the circular canvas is still or turns only slowly, the onlooker is locked in fascination with the details; but if the canvas spins rapidly, the details of the pictures disappear and the colors merge into a harmonious and universal blend. Man's relation with time depends on his perspective. Normally, however, he is viewing the quiet canvas in all the glory—and horror—of its vivid details.

"Song of the Universal" sets forth the theme on which the successive poems work variations. In brief, "Song of the Universal" asserts that good and evil may be reconciled in that the latter disap-

pears in eternity: evil exists only in time; "only the good is universal" (I, 277). Whitman seizes upon a number of striking images to
convince imaginatively of the truth of his theme. For example, the
seed:

> Amid measureless grossness and the slag,
> Enclosed and safe within its central heart,
> Nestles the seed perfection [I, 276].

This image reverses the usual concept that a thing badly corrupt is
corrupt to the very core; Whitman discovers, rather, that the very
core is "the seed perfection." In one of his images Whitman suggests
a possible significance of the title of this group of poems ("Birds of
Passage"):

> Over the mountain-growths disease and sorrow,
> An uncaught bird is ever hovering, hovering,
> High in the purer, happier air [I, 277].

The bird, like the seed perfection, is that element of eternity in the
event encaged in time, that element of universal good always present in temporary and passing evil. It is possible that the "Birds" in
"Birds of Passage" are meant to be instances of the "uncaught bird"
of "Song of the Universal"; the poems of this group are, perhaps,
meant to discover this element of the eternal in the events of the
passing moment. Seed or bird, this ever present element is the soul,
and

> For it the mystic evolution,
> Not the right only justified, what we call evil also
>   justified [I, 277].

The second poem in "Birds of Passage," the most popular (and
formal) of the entire group, "Pioneers! O Pioneers!" has as its primary symbol the explorer, the discoverer, the pioneer. But the poem
is not, ultimately, about the West, the frontier, or even about America; it is about the significant events (and the people who participate
in or create them) in mystic evolution. As evolution "in spiral routes
by long detours" (I, 277) works its way toward the "ideal," the "universal," so America and America's pioneers (both factual and spiritual) make their significant contribution to the progression. Inasmuch as civilization has in reality moved toward the west, the westward movement may be recognized as a fulfilment or culmination
in mystic evolution. But, in point of fact, all life is "pioneer" in mystic evolution, and none is excluded:

Life's involv'd and varied pageants,
All the forms and shows, all the workmen at their work,
All the seamen and the landsmen, all the masters with their slaves,
Pioneers! O pioneers!

All the hapless silent lovers,
All the prisoners in the prisons, all the righteous and the wicked,
All the joyous, all the sorrowing, all the living, all the dying,
Pioneers! O pioneers!

Whitman extends his symbol to include all humanity, all mankind. In this concept, each individual, no matter his trade, his moral quality, or his station in life, contributes toward the onward impulse of mystic evolution. But beyond mankind, all the "forms and shows" also contribute; everything is, in the final analysis, of some significance in the great onward push and accumulation of time. In a sense, then, when (perhaps because) time is transformed into eternity or the universal, everyone and everything are ultimately triumphant over time.

"To You," which immediately follows "Pioneers! O Pioneers!" asserts the vital importance and significance of each individual. Whitman suggests that the endless stream of time, instead of annihilating, actually elevates the individual man. "You," then, are not to be "lost" in oblivion but "found" in mystic evolution. There is in each individual that element of the eternal or universal called, in "Song of the Universal," the "seed perfection":

The mockeries are not you,
Underneath them and within them I see you lurk,
I pursue you where none else has pursued you [I, 285–86].

The remaining poems in "Birds of Passage" are variations on the theme of mystic evolution. In "France," a poem celebrating the French Revolution, the "seed perfection" or that element of the eternal in this great historical event is conceived as a newborn baby:

And I do not deny that terrible red birth and baptism,
But remember the little voice that I heard wailing, and wait with
perfect trust, no matter how long [I, 288].

"Myself and Mine," counterpart of "To You," asserts the individuality and independence of the poet, both of which are based on a confident knowledge of the inevitability and inexorability of mystic evolution. Because of such knowledge, the poet can "charge" that there be "no theory or school founded out of" him: "I charge you to leave all free, as I have left all free" (I, 290). "Year of Meteors," subtitled "(1859–60)," is a strange poem cataloguing the seemingly major events of a year, reaching a climax with the appearance of the comet and the meteor procession. But the poem seems to place emphasis on the transience of all things:

Year of comets and meteors transient and strange—lo! even here one equally
    transient and strange!
As I flit through you hastily, soon to fall and be gone, what is this chant,
What am I myself but one of your meteors? [I, 292].

As the poet compares himself and his poem to the swiftly passing meteor, he is suggesting that the temporal significance of himself and his "chant" (and of all events, even of profound impact) is slight compared to their significance in eternity or in the "universal." It is in mystic evolution in its entirety, not in any individual segment of time, that events and persons assume their true meaning. "With Antecedents," the final poem in the "Birds of Passage" section, restates with vigor the importance that mystic evolution lends the individual, the here, and the now:

We stand amid time beginningless and endless, we stand amid evil and
    good,
All swings around us, there is as much darkness as light [I, 293].

The poet asserts that the past and the future "curiously conjoint in the present time" (I, 294):

And that where I am or you are this present day, there is the centre of all
    days, all races,
And there is the meaning to us of all that has ever come of races and days,
    or ever will come [I, 294].

The concept of mystic evolution allows the poet to make the *now* and the *here* the center or focal point (if but temporarily) of the endless flow of time: time past has culminated in the present; time future awaits the present's unfolding. Curiously enough, the optimism that mystic evolution generates is grounded in part in an evolutionary (or poetic) determinism: "I assert that all past days were what they must have been" (I, 294). And again, "today and America could nohow be better than they are" (I, 294).

When, in "Pioneers! O Pioneers!" Whitman included as significant as all else in the unfolding of mystic evolution "life's involv'd and varied pageants, / All the forms and shows," he was in a sense preparing for, or at least indirectly justifying, the appearance of the long "topical" poem, "A Broadway Pageant," immediately after "Birds of Passage." This poem is ostensibly about an event, insignificant in itself, of the day in which two Japanese envoys "ride . . . through Manhattan" (II, 1). The event is similar in nature to those listed in "Year of Meteors." But "A Broadway Pageant" is only superficially "topical." The visit of the Orientals becomes for Whitman a symbol of the arrival of an important stage in mystic evolution: "at last the Orient comes" (II, 2). "The Originatress . . . , the nest of languages, the bequeather of poems, the race of eld" comes to the New World, and in the coming reveals that time no longer focuses on Asia (or even on Europe) but on America:

Were the children straying westward so long? so wide the tramping?
Were the precedent dim ages debouching westward from Paradise so long?
Were the centuries steadily footing it that way, all the while unknown, for
    you, for reasons? [II, 5].

The "centuries steadily footing" is a vivid metaphor for mystic evolution. Time past focuses with steadfast gaze on the young republic of the New World—Libertad. And, as Whitman points out, the visit of the two oriental envoys signifies the completion or culmination of the "westward" movement of civilization; and the beginning of a movement eastward signifies a changing or changed relationship: "They [the centuries]shall now also march obediently eastward for vour sake Libertad" (II, 5).

"Sea-Drift" and "By the Roadside," the two remaining sections in this group of poems, represent different aspects of mystic evolution. The first section is concerned primarily with events in personal crises, the latter with events in social or national crises. In both sections, however, Whitman is fundamentally concerned with probing the significance of the incidents or happenings in the light of mystic evolution and the concept of the "universal." The "Sea-Drift" poems are bound together by the recurring image of the sea, defined symbolically in "Song for All Seas, All Ships" as "a spiritual woven signal for all nations, emblem of man elate above death" (II, 23). The sea in these poems functions, as did the "seed perfection" or the "uncaught bird" in "Song of the Universal," as the symbol of that element of the eternal or universal, latent in the present or in all time, that assures perfection (or happiness) in immortality. It is significant that the first "Sea-Drift" poem begins, "Out of the cradle endlessly rocking" (II, 6). The sea, evoked in this image as an endlessly rocking cradle (suggesting the immortality of mankind in the continuing cycle of death and birth), heads the list of materials that go into the making of the poet's "reminiscence." And it is the sea, "like some old crone rocking the cradle" (II, 13), that gives the "clew" the boy so much desires—the word "death." This "strong and delicious" word, which the outsetting bard is to weave among his songs—coming as it does from the endlessly rocking cradle—signifies rebirth, and therefore a fruitful, not futile, culmination to one's life. In "As I Ebb'd with the Ocean of Life," the poet, in a mood of apparent despair, compares himself and his life to the litter ("tufts of straw, sands, fragments" [II, 16]) of sea-drift:

> We, capricious, brought hither we know not whence, spread
>   out before you,
> You up there walking or sitting,
> Whoever you are, we too lie in drifts at your feet [II, 17].

But, as these final lines of the poem indicate, although one might be possessed by the feeling of the capriciousness of one's fate and life, there is reassurance in the certainty of someone "up there" at whose feet one may lie. There is reassurance in the certainty of the ultimate goal of mystic evolution. All these "Sea-Drift" poems, by intricate use of the sea as a symbol of the eternal, transfigure despair into hope and fear into certainty, for they are all exemplifications of the truth of mystic evolution. In "On the Beach at Night":

> Something there is more immortal even than the stars,
> (Many the burials, many the days and nights, passing away,)
> Something that shall endure longer even than lustrous Jupiter
>   [II, 20].

As "Sea-Drift" deals with the doubts—and assurances—of one's personal life, "By the Roadside" probes the ultimate meaning of public or national life. No individual poem develops the image introduced in the group title. But in addition to the suggestion of static quiet, there are two connotations that have some significance for the poems in the section. In the first place, "By the Roadside" suggests miscellaneousness or casualness, and one cannot help noting that among these brief poems there does not appear a single example of Whitman's major poetic achievement. In fact, these short poems (many of them titled simply "Thought") pass so quickly from subject to subject that they have the character of a miscellany. But this superficial view is dispelled, once one notes the applicability of the other connotation of "By the Roadside": the suggestion that the poet in these poems has, for reasons of his own, assumed the role of passive observer of life's "involv'd and varied pageants." In this image, the road becomes the symbol of the continuing movement of mystic evolution. There is indication of the conscious use of the road as such a symbol in "Thoughts":

(But I see the road continued, and the journey ever continued;)
Of what was once lacking on earth, and in due time has become supplied—
    and of what will yet be supplied,
Because all I see and know I believe to have its main purport in what will
    yet be supplied [II, 32].

Whitman seems to be restating the faith he first expressed in "Song of the Universal," a faith grounded on a firm belief in ultimate justification in mystic evolution. There is explicit statement of such faith in "Roaming in Thought (after Reading Hegel)":

Roaming in thought over the Universe, I saw the little that is Good steadily
    hastening towards immortality,
And the vast all that is call'd Evil I saw hastening to merge itself and
    become lost and dead [II, 35].

The poet discovers in Hegel confirmation of the concept of mystic evolution. In a sense, the poems in "By the Roadside" derive from Whitman's "roaming in thought over the universe."

But in these poems it is only the thought that roams; the poet himself remains by the roadside and watches: "I sit and look out upon all the sorrows of the world, and upon all oppression and shame" (II, 34). Confident in his belief in the ultimate exoneration of what man calls evil, the final disappearance of it in the universal, the poet can "hear secret convulsive sobs from young men at anguish with themselves" or see the "workings of battle, pestilence, tyranny" and remain calm:

All these—all the meanness and agony without end I sitting look out upon,
See, hear, and am silent [II, 34].

This point of view is not callous disregard for the painful but rather a cosmic faith in the divine operation of mystic evolution. In the two opening poems of "By the Roadside," two bloody conflicts are examined and found contributory, even amid apparent havoc, to the ultimate triumph of the good in the evolutionary process. "A Boston Ballad" asserts that time has proved the value of the American Revolutionary War. Though the price was great, the chaotic conflict of the past has given way to an orderly and peaceful present. Whitman addresses the bystander watching the fantastic Boston parade (which includes the exhumed bones and skull of King George): "Stick your hands in your pockets, Jonathan—you are a made man from this day, / You are mighty cute—and here is one of your bargains" (II, 27). "Europe" asserts that the 1848 revolutions, though frustrated by the deaths of the young participants, contributed to the ultimate victory of liberty:

Not a grave of the murder'd for freedom but grows seed for freedom, in its
    turn to bear seed,
Which the winds carry afar and re-sow, and the rains and the snows nourish
    [II, 29].

Whitman reverts to the seed image of "Song of the Universal" to evoke the core of good in these bloody revolutions. As the poet begins "By the Roadside" with poems about the 1776 and 1848 revolutions, so he ends the section with a foreshadowing of the Civil War. "To the States, To Identify the 16th, 17th, or 18th Presidentiad" asks, "Why reclining, interrogating? Why myself and all drowsing?" (II, 39). But the answer, though it encompasses the knowledge of the approaching explosion, expresses the confident faith of the purposeful unfolding, in due course, of mystic evolution:

Then I will sleep awhile yet, for I see that these States sleep, for reasons;
(With gathering murk, with muttering thunder and lambent shoots we all
    duly awake,
South, North, East, West, inland and seaboard, we will surely awake.)
    [II, 39].

The "for reasons" reveals that the poet perceives, even in the chaotic state of affairs in the Union, the "seed perfection" that exists hidden and will endure through the approaching holocaust.

All the poems—"Birds of Passage," "A Broadway Pageant," "Sea-Drift," and "By the Roadside"—in this section of *Leaves of Grass* are concerned with relating the various facets of man, his public,

218 A CRITICAL GUIDE TO "LEAVES OF GRASS"

personal, and political nature and activity, to time and, more specifically, to the concept of time as the endless progression of a divine plan—mystic evolution. These poems discover man to be triumphant over time in eternity as the preceding songs discovered man to be triumphant over space in infinity. With this proper placement of the New World personality in the universe, Whitman draws to a close his delineation of the "gigantic embryo or skeleton of Personality." It now remains for him to bring the embryo to birth, to give flesh to the skeleton. Such a birth, in a specific place at a specific time, has been prepared for at the close of "By the Roadside": a time of great national crisis in nineteenth-century America.

This Time
and Land We Swim In

The poems devoted to engaging the newly created New World personality in a real here and now—nineteenth-century America—constitute the central section of *Leaves of Grass*. There are three clusters and one single long poem that may be grouped:

> *National crisis*
> Drum-Taps
> Memories of President Lincoln
>
> *Rehabilitation and adjustment*
> "By Blue Ontario's Shore"
> Autumn Rivulets

"Drum-Taps" deals directly with the Civil War as a national crisis that reaches a climax in the death of the national leader memorialized in "Memories of President Lincoln." "By Blue Ontario's Shore" and "Autumn Rivulets" are concerned with the nation after the crisis has passed, with the aftermath: the first is a "carol of victory" and a "song of the throes of Democracy" (II, 207);[1] the second is composed of a number of "songs of continued years" (II, 127). All these related poems, however, may be looked upon as "magnifying" a single instance in mystic evolution—an instance as it would appear to an individual directly engaged, physically and emotionally, in the multitude of situations and events composing it. These poems form not only a unit in themselves but logically follow the preceding poems that sketch the New World personality.

"Drum-Taps" constitutes one of the most impressive bodies of

1. Whitman quotations are where possible identified in the text by volume and page number of *The Complete Writings of Walt Whitman,* ed. Richard M. Bucke *et al.* (New York: G. P. Putnam's Sons, 1902).

war poetry in existence. Threading its way through the section and tightening the relationship of the poems is the title sound image, drum taps. The image is introduced in the opening poem:

> First O songs for a prelude,
> Lightly strike on the stretch'd tympanum pride and joy
> in my city [II, 40].

This light, almost delicate, tapping gives way to the more strident alarm-sounding in "Beat! Beat! Drums!":

> Beat! beat! drums!—blow! bugles! blow!
> Through the windows—through doors—burst like a ruthless force,
> Into the solemn church, and scatter the congregation [II, 44].

This penetrating beat is the confident call to arms. As the war progresses and the horrors of war are impressed on the shocked consciousness of the poet, the proud call to arms is abandoned, and in its place appears the slow, sad dirge (in "Dirge for Two Veterans"):

> I hear the great drums pounding,
> And the small drums steady whirring,
> And every blow of the great convulsive drums,
> Strikes me through and through [II, 80].

Near the end of "Drum-Taps," the image is given its final treatment in "Spirit Whose Work Is Done":

> Rousing the land with breath of flame, while you [the spirit] beat and beat the drum,
> Now as the sound of the drum, hollow and harsh to the last, reverberates round me,
> As your ranks, your immortal ranks, return, return from the battles [II, 90].

This "hollow and harsh" sound of the drum is a far cry from the light striking of the "'stretch'd tympanum'" of the opening poem, and the feeling of almost provincial pride in one's city has matured into a pervading conciliatory feeling that embraces the land of the enemy. This important progression in the emotional response to the war embodied in the dominant image provides the chief dramatic development in the poems and makes them an integral unit.

The change in attitude toward the war from one of almost hysterical jubilation to one of revulsion and reflective quiet was, in an earlier version of "Drum-Taps," given pointed significance in a prefatory poem:

Aroused and angry,
I thought to beat the alarum, and urge relentless war;
But soon my fingers fail'd me, my face droop'd, and I resign'd myself,
To sit by the wounded and soothe them, or silently watch the dead
    [III, 196].

This poem, now incorporated in the first part of "The Wound-
Dresser," utilizes the drum-beating image to suggest the change in
emotional response to the war: the poet was at first anxious to "beat
the alarum," but, after the terrible experiences of war, soon his
"fingers fail'd" him, and he found his martial spirit transfigured into
a spirit of comradeship or love. In this transformation the poet serves
as the national prototype, for the nation too observed a similar
change in its feelings. In fact (and perhaps herein lies the remarkable quality of these war poems), "Drum-Taps" had discovered the
universal in the specific: it is in the nature of war to evoke the
extremes of emotion so vividly expressed in "Drum-Taps."

In the opening poems in "Drum-Taps" the concept of war is obviously a romantic elaboration of the mistaken notions engendered
by glamorous military parades:

Forty years had I in my city seen soldiers parading,
Forty years as a pageant, till unawares the lady of this teeming
    and turbulent city,
Sleepless amid her ships, her houses, her incalculable wealth,
With her million children around her, suddenly,
At dead of night, at news from the south,
Incens'd struck with clinch'd hand the pavement [II, 40–41].

This romantic concept of righteous wrath and the arousing to re-
taliation of great, immediate power (which, in reality, did not exist)
rises to a climax in lines which almost seem a parody:

Mannahatta a-march—and it's O to sing it well!
It's O for a manly life in the camp [II, 42].

The illusion of war as the "manly life in the camp," which ap-
proaches the view of war as a sport, pervades all the early poems
through "The Centenarian's Story"—over one-third of the pages of
"Drum-Taps." At this point a series of four short vignettes appears—
"Cavalry Crossing a Ford," "Bivouac on a Mountain Side," "An
Army Corps on the March," and "By the Bivouac's Fitful Flame."
These short poems, among the best in "Drum-Taps," are the first
that seem to grow directly out of the poet's Civil War experience.

As a series, they give characteristic (and unromantic) glimpses of the movement of the army—of masses of men—so that the reader is given the illusion of being gradually drawn to the scene of the great conflict until, in the last of the group, he sits with the poet by the "fitful flame" of the bivouac.

Having been drawn into intimate association with the real war, the reader is almost immediately introduced, in the two succeeding poems, to the terrible consequences of war, at home as well as on the battleground. In these poems the poet dramatizes a personal rather than a national emotion. In "Come Up from the Fields Father" and "Vigil Strange I Kept on the Field One Night," surely the poet was conscious of the ironic contrast of the two "fields," one the scene of quiet peace and abundant fertility ("Where apples ripe in the orchards hang and grapes on the trellis'd vines" [II, 66]), the other the scene of "even-contested battle" and death ("Long there and then in vigil I stood, dimly around me the battlefield spreading" [II, 68]). But the impact on the emotions is the same, no matter the scene and no matter the relationship, whether mother or comrade. In "Come Up from the Fields Father," the mother suffers a secret despair:

In the midnight waking, weeping, longing with one deep longing,
O that she might withdraw unnoticed, silent from life escape and withdraw,
To follow, to seek, to be with her dear dead son [II, 67].

It seems inevitable that the reader will associate the "dear dead son," Pete, with the dead comrade of "Vigil Strange I Kept on the Field One Night." And it seems inevitable, too, that the despair of mother-love under trial will be contrasted with the strange satisfaction of comrade-love: "Passing sweet hours, immortal and mystic hours with you dearest comrade—not a tear, not a word" (II, 68). These "mystic hours" end in a burial ritual that succeeds in evoking the very emotion that, in the speaker, remains suppressed in his almost trancelike attention to small, if not irrelevant, details:

Vigil for comrade swiftly slain, vigil I never forget, how as day brighten'd,
I rose from the chill ground and folded my soldier well in his blanket,
And buried him where he fell [II, 69].

Although placing these two poems side by side suggests comparisons and contrasts the poet intended, it also embarrassingly demonstrates the sentimentality of the first in contrast with the almost perfectly controlled emotion of the second; the confused point of view of the first in contrast with the consistent point of view of the second.

But these two poems, together with the three succeeding ("A March in the Ranks Hard-Prest, and the Road Unknown," "A Sight in Camp in the Daybreak Gray and Dim," and "As Toilsome I Wander'd Virginia's Woods"), constitute, if not the heart of "Drum-Taps," at least the point of greatest emotional intensity. All these poems represent a discovery on the part of a poet who was, only a short time before, so anxious to beat the martial drums. These are poems of the discovery of the real meaning of war—death. "A March in the Ranks Hard-Prest, and the Road Unknown" ironically recalls "Song of the Open Road," in which the journey was reason for great elation, or "By the Roadside," in which the poet remained disengaged. It is ironic, too, that the scene of sickness and death is a "large old church at the crossing roads" (II, 69). This place of the worship of heaven has become transformed into a kind of hell:

Faces, varieties, postures beyond description, most in obscurity, some of them dead,
Surgeons operating, attendants holding lights, the smell of ether, the odor of blood [II, 70].

"A Sight in Camp in the Daybreak Gray and Dim" memorializes three dead soldiers, one an "elderly man," another a "sweet boy," and the third—

. . . a face nor child nor old, very calm, as of beautiful yellow-white ivory;
Young man I think I know you—I think this face is the face of the Christ himself
Dead and divine and brother of all, and here again he lies [II, 71].

"As Toilsome I Wander'd Virginia's Woods" portrays the poet happening upon the grave of a soldier and discovering the "inscription rude": "*Bold, cautious, true, and my loving comrade.*" All these poems, in contrast with the opening poems of "Drum-Taps," represent genuinely and deeply felt emotions, emotions as universal as they are personal. Surely with the vision of Christ in the face of the dead soldier comes the realization that war is not a "manly life in the camp" but a life of human suffering and agony as terrible as it is senseless, as personally tragic for the foe as for the friend.

The remainder of "Drum-Taps" reflects a much deeper understanding of the significance of war than the opening poems, though the virile call to arms is not dropped entirely. In such poems as "Long, Too Long America" and "Give Me the Splendid Silent Sun" the poet expresses a public sentiment favoring vigorous prosecution of the war. But the really memorable and moving poems in this latter half of "Drum-Taps" are those that portray personal tragedy in death, such as "Dirge for Two Veterans," or those that show the terrible psychological effects of war that long outlast the final battles, such as "The Wound-Dresser" and "The Artilleryman's Vision." In the first of these poems the "old man bending" vividly relives his wartime nursing experiences:

> Thus in silence in dreams' projections,
> Returning, resuming, I thread my way through the hospitals,
> The hurt and wounded I pacify with soothing hand [II, 76].

The poet's psychological understanding is even more dramatically revealed in "The Artilleryman's Vision," which portrays the ex-soldier first at uneasy rest amid a scene of quiet and peace:

While my wife at my side lies slumbering, and the wars are over long,
And my head on the pillow rests at home, and the vacant midnight passes,
And through the stillness, through the dark, I hear, just hear, the breath of
    my infant [II, 82–83].

But from this gentle domestic scene the artilleryman is plunged back in time, into the midst of battle:

There in the room as I wake from sleep this vision presses upon me;
The engagement opens there and then in fantasy unreal,
The skirmishers begin, they crawl cautiously ahead, I hear the irregular
    snap! snap! [II, 83].

The "unreal" fantasy takes on the proportions of a nightmare as the artilleryman relives the tense moments of battle. By poems of this kind the poet suggests the complexity of the lasting effects of war and, incidentally, reveals an understanding in advance of his time of the psychological results of participation in battle.

As "Drum-Taps" draws to a close, the note of reconciliation sounds louder and louder, reaching a height in the poem called "Reconciliation." By this time, the robust enthusiasm for war has become transfigured into a relief at the oblivion into which war must pass: "Beautiful that war and all its deeds of carnage must in time be utterly lost" (II, 87). And the cause for the transformation is the realization that in war there must be an enemy, and the enemy must be human:

> For my enemy is dead, a man divine as myself is dead,
> I look where he lies white-faced and still in the coffin—I draw near,
> Bend down and touch lightly with my lips the white face in the coffin [II, 87].

This symbolic act signifies a reconciliation of spirits unnaturally wrought asunder. And, finally, the poet urges that, the war over, the country should turn toward the future (in "Turn O Libertad"):

> Then turn, and be not alarm'd O libertad—turn your undying
>   face,
> To where the future, greater than all the past,
> Is swiftly, surely preparing for you [II, 92].

"To the Leaven'd Soil They Trod," the last poem in "Drum-Taps," portrays a country symbolically reunified by the poet:

> The prairie draws me close, as the father to bosom broad the son,
> The Northern ice and rain that began me nourish me to the end,
> But the hot sun of the South is to fully ripen my songs [II, 93].

The poet envisions his poetry as drawing together the West, North, and South.

But the climax of the national crisis for the poet, the death of Abraham Lincoln, is yet to be assessed and memorialized. The four poems of "Memories of President Lincoln" constitute a sustained elegy. As "Drum-Taps" celebrates man "en-masse," man acting in the mass, in a specific time and place, so "Memories of President Lincoln" celebrates "a simple separate person" who, though he sacrificed none of the qualities he held in common with his countrymen, yet was a distinct and great individual. In the Civil War, Whitman sees achieved in reality the reconciliation of the necessary opposites of the democracy he has dreamed of—equality and individuality— with neither submerged or overwhelmed by the other. The first of the Lincoln poems, "When Lilacs Last in the Dooryard Bloom'd," portrays the outpouring of uncontrolled personal grief gradually brought under control. Through the skilful use of his symbols—the star, the cloud, the lilac bush, and the bird—Whitman re-creates the sweeping drama of Lincoln's death and the national mourning and the impingement of these national events on his own consciousness, without once mentioning the President's name. Through masterful technique the poet has elevated what might have been a topical poem of interest only to its own time to a level of universal interest:

> Nor for you, for one alone,
> Blossoms and branches green to coffins all I bring,
> For fresh as the morning, thus would I chant a song for you
>   O sane and sacred death [II, 96].

Whereas "When Lilacs Last in the Dooryard Bloom'd" is in the nature of a personal expression of grief and reconciliation to death, "O Captain! My Captain!" seems a public expression, in the formal dress appropriate for public grief, of a public sentiment. Although "O Captain! My Captain!" seems to "contain" a great deal of emotion, it generally fails to evoke any, its very formality apparently working against its success. "Hush'd Be the Camps Today" expresses the grief of the soldiers whose commander Lincoln was. The poet advises:

> . . . let us drape our war-worn weapons,
> And each with musing soul retire to celebrate,
> Our dear commander's death [II, 106].

Such private meditation does indeed seem appropriate for soldiers of "heavy hearts." In "This Dust Was Once the Man," Whitman expresses directly, without metaphor or symbol, the relation of Lincoln to the national crisis which has had its extensive treatment in "Drum-Taps": It was Lincoln "under whose cautious hand . . . / Was saved the Union of these States" (II, 106).

"By Blue Ontario's Shore" and "Autumn Rivulets," still concerned with "this Time & Place we swim in," turn their attention from the crisis just concluded and look to the future, both near and distant. "By Blue Ontario's Shore" is, in part, the translated 1855 Preface and is concerned primarily with the nation's destiny. What tended to be a rambling commentary in the early Preface has been given, in the poem, dramatic justification. The device of the "Phantom," America's genius, accosting the poet as he sits musing by the shore and setting his thoughts in motion, allows for the looseness of continuity that is present. It is appropriate that the poet, reflecting on the "warlike days and of peace return'd" (II, 207), should find his thoughts revolving about the country's future. The Phantom, in his first appearance, announces the themes that are to appear as the musings of the contemplative poet:

Chant me a poem, it [the Phantom] said, that comes from the soul of
  America, chant me the carol of victory,
And strike up the marches of Libertad, marches more powerful yet,
And sing me before you go the song of the throes of Democracy [II, 207].

In the national self-examination that follows, we find epigrammatic
statements, such as "Produce great Persons, the rest follows" (II,
108) (this particular statement seems of special significance in explaining the impulse behind the preceding section, "Memories of
President Lincoln"). In section 9, the Phantom is reintroduced:

I listened to the Phantom by Ontario's shore,
I heard the voice arising demanding bards,
By them all native and grand, by them alone can these States be fused
  into the compact organism of a Nation [II, 114].

As seemed inevitable when he wrote of democracy or the Union,
for either their support or advancement Whitman relied primarily
on the development of native bards: "Of all races and eras these
States with veins full of poetical stuff most need poets, and are to
have the greatest, and use them the greatest" (II, 114). At the end
of the poem, after a full description of the attributes of the New
World poet, Whitman recalls to his reader the basic dramatic situation of the poem:

Thus by blue Ontario's shore,
While the winds fann'd me and the waves came trooping toward me,
I thrill'd with the power's pulsations, and the charm of my theme
  was upon me,
Till the tissues that held me parted their ties upon me [II, 125].

Released from the "ties," the poet has a vision in which pass before
him the poets and bards of past ages. As they stride before him, the
poet cries out that he is being mocked, that it was not for bards of
the past that he has sung "so capricious and loud" his "savage song":

Bards for my own land only I invoke,
(For the war, the war is over, the field is clear'd,)
Till they strike up marches henceforth triumphant and onward,
To cheer O Mother your boundless expectant soul.
Bards of the great Idea! bards of the peaceful inventions! (for the war,
  the war is over!) [II, 125–26].

Now that the war is successfully over, Whitman looks forward to
the fulfilment of the nation's promise and envisions the poet's role
in the achievement of that fulfilment as very great indeed.

As "By Blue Ontario's Shore" is the immediate assessment of the
nation's destiny after the war, a glimpse into an uncertain future, so
"Autumn Rivulets" is composed of "songs of continued years." These
two sections of *Leaves of Grass* have in common the water imagery
of their titles, the first a large body of confined water, suggesting
contemplation and time arrested, the other a number of small streams
flowing, suggesting minor activity and the slow passage of time. In
both instances the water suggests contrast with the two preceding
sections dealing with the national crisis: whereas "Drum-Taps" and
"Memories of President Lincoln" were filled with the sterility of war
and death, "By Blue Ontario's Shore" and "Autumn Rivulets" suggest the fertility of peace and fruitful life.

The first poem in "Autumn Rivulets," "As Consequent, etc.," is
the single poem of the cluster that develops the title image. Some
indication of the symbolic meaning of "rivulets" and the variety of
themes of the poems to follow is suggested in the opening stanza:

> As consequent from store of summer rains,
> Or wayward rivulets in autumn flowing,
> Or many a herb-lined brook's reticulations,
> Or subterranean sea-rills making for the sea,
> Songs of continued years I sing [II, 127].

These "rivulets" are from the autumn not of the poet's life (as is
sometimes supposed) but from the autumn of the nation's development. The nation, having just successfully finished a war, a war that
has matured as well as sobered the country, is on the verge of genuine fruition. One might imagine the preceding dry summer as, symbolically, the sterile war filled with death; since the "summer rains"
have been "stored" (unspent), they now pour forth to create the
"rivulets" in autumn, the abundance of life and harvest. But the
"rivulets" also characterize the poems in the cluster: they are,
mostly, brief; they do not move swiftly in any single direction and
are of a variety of kinds. As, in autumn, there are "wayward rivulets," "herb-lined brooks," and "subterranean sea-rills," so the poems
in "Autumn Rivulets" are attempts to characterize the variety, multiplicity, the lack of conformity of life. But although these are poems
of variety and lack apparent unity, there is a unifying element:

> Life's ever-modern rapids first, (soon, soon to blend,
> With the old streams of death.) [II, 127].

It is contemporary life—"life's ever-modern rapids"—life of the *now* in all its complexity and diversity, that the poet attempts to portray. The parenthetical reference to death foreshadows the theme of the poems that follow "Autumn Rivulets." But the unity of these poems is also suggested by an extension in meaning of the title image:

> In you whoe'er you are my book perusing
> In I myself, in all the world, these currents flowing,
> All, all toward the mystic ocean tending [II, 127].

There is a universality in the very diversity of life described in these poems, and this universality ("in all the world, these currents flowing") is the constant theme; and as all currents flow toward the "mystic ocean," so all acts and events, no matter the kind or magnitude, make their contribution in the unfolding of mystic evolution.

The poems in "Autumn Rivulets" may be looked upon as "currents for starting a continent new, overtures sent to the solid out of the liquid" (II, 127), or they may be viewed as tokens of time:

> Or from the sea of Time, collecting vasting all, I bring,
> A windrow-drift of weeds and shells [II, 128].

In "collecting vasting all," the poet indicates that he omits nothing and that he magnifies what he brings. But though the resulting collection may seem a "windrow-drift," still, as tokens of time, the shells, "so curious-convolute," when held to the ear emit "eternity's music faint and far." The "seed perfection" or "uncaught bird" of the universal exists in or hovers over these seemingly trivial individual moments.

The longest poem in "Autumn Rivulets," and that which gives the setting in time for the group, is "The Return of the Heroes." This poem was once prefaced by a prose note: "In all History, antique or modern, the grandest achievement yet for political Humanity—grander even than the triumph of this Union over Secession—was the return, disbanding, and peaceful disintegration from compact military organization, back into agricultural and civil employments, of the vast Armies, the two millions of embattled men of America—a problem reserved for Democracy, our day and land, to promptly solve" (III, 217). In addition to the outline of the theme of the poem, one might note the emphasis placed on "our day and land" as a continuation of the theme that underlies this entire section of *Leaves of Grass*. After praising "fecund America," an America that visits its abundance in beauty and nourishment on the people, Whitman differentiates his present song from those past:

When late I sang sad was my voice,
Sad were the shows around me with deafening noises of hatred and smoke
of war;
In the midst of the conflict, the heroes, I stood,
Or pass'd with slow step through the wounded and dying [II, 130].

But now his song is on

. . . these days of brightness,
On the far-stretching beauteous landscape, the roads and lanes, the high-
piled farm-wagons, and the fruits and barns [II, 131].

The poet's song dramatically portrays the return of the veterans to participate in the creation and consumption of this abundance—America's abundance.

Of the number of interesting and even arresting poems in "Autumn Rivulets," two may be singled out for their direct bearing on the unifying theme and for their emphasis on the relation of "Autumn Rivulets" to the whole of *Leaves of Grass*. "This Compost," visualizing the earth as one huge mixture of decay and fertility, capitalizes on the paradox:

Behold this compost! behold it well!
Perhaps every mite has once form'd part of a sick person—yet behold!
The grass of spring covers the prairies [II, 140–41].

The phenomenon serves the poet as he re-creates the image of the revolving globe (a dominant image in the song section):

It [the earth] grows such sweet things out of such corruptions,
It turns harmless and stainless on its axis, with such endless successions of
diseas'd corpses,
It distills such exquisite winds out of such infused fetor [II, 142].

The image of the continuing earth, not halted but thriving on the putrefaction of life, suggests the disappearance of evil in the "universal," in mystic evolution. The application of this concept, in time, on a specific occasion, is suggested in another poem which embraces the theme in a different series of images, "Wandering at Morn." The dominant image is a bird (cf. the "uncaught bird" of "Song of the Universal"), a thrush, which the poet beholds as he yearns for a "harmonious Union," and whose song of "joy and faith" cheers the poet:

There ponder'd, felt I,
If worms, snakes, loathsome grubs, may to sweet spiritual songs be turn'd,
If vermin so transposed, so used and bless'd may be,
Then may I trust in you, your fortunes, days, my country [II, 175].

The fortunes and days of the poet's postwar country, the proper subject of "Autumn Rivulets," find their significance in their contribution to a greater, unseen universal good, in their contribution to the nation's "future song . . . with joyous trills, / Destin'd to fill the world" (II, 175).

The reader may find himself sympathetic with the attitude of the poet in "I Was Looking a Long While" when he says:

I was looking a long while for Intentions,
For a clew to the history of the past for myself, and for these chants—and now I have found it [II, 162].

The reader, too, has sought the "clew" for a long while, and it is with a good deal of curiosity that he reads on:

It is in the present—it is this earth to-day,
It is in Democracy—(the purport and aim of all the past,)
It is the life of one man or one woman to-day—the average man of to-day,
It is in language, social customs, literatures, arts [II, 162].

This poem virtually constitutes a restatement of the central theme of this section of *Leaves of Grass:* the impingement of "this Time & Land we swim in" on the consciousness of an average New World personality. The diversity of "to-day" justifies the diversity of poems in "Autumn Rivulets." In the final poem of the group, "The Prairie States," Whitman uses again the image he had exploited in "Children of Adam"—the Garden of Eden:

By all the world contributed—freedom's and law's and thrift's society,
The crown and teeming paradise, so far, of time's accumulations,
To justify the past [II, 177].

The prairie states are found to be the "crown" in the present's stage of mystic evolution and therefore a justification of the past in all its "bad" and "good" diversity. As the present justifies the past, so the future will justify the present.

CHAPTER SIXTEEN

The Resistless
Gravitation of Spiritual Law

Beginning with "Proud Music of the Storm,"
the "slides shift" and the focus moves in *Leaves of Grass* from "this
Time & Land" to the domain of spirituality, beyond both time and
land. This theme, not new to the book by any means, but for the
first time of central importance through an entire series of poems,
remains dominant through "Whispers of Heavenly Death":

> "Proud Music of the Storm"
> "Passage to India"
> "Prayer of Columbus"
> "The Sleepers"
> "To Think of Time"
> Whispers of Heavenly Death

All these poems are, as announced in "Proud Music of the Storm,"
poems "bridging the way from Life to Death." As the giant embryo
or skeleton of personality was first created for the New World and
then given growth and flesh in his engagement with specific time
and place, so in these poems he penetrates the secret of spiritual
law and achieves a supreme faith in the confrontation of death. If the
previous poems gave the delineated personality a human existence,
these poems give him a spiritual existence; if the previous poems
related the personality to a moment in time and a place in space,
these poems relate him to eternity and infinity.

In order to understand "Proud Music of the Storm," it is of some
value to recall an image from the first poem in "Autumn Rivulets,"
"As Consequent, etc.":

(Not safe and peaceful only, waves rous'd and ominous too,
Out of the depths the storm's abysmic waves, who knows whence?
Raging over the vast, with many a broken spar and tatter'd sail.)
    [II, 127–28].[1]

1. Whitman quotations are where possible identified in the text by volume and
page number of *The Complete Writings of Walt Whitman,* ed. Richard M. Bucke
et al. (New York: G. P. Putnam's Sons, 1902).

This image was meant to suggest that the "continued years," celebrated in "Autumn Rivulets," had their turbulence and restlessness,
that life, indeed, was inevitably made up of the disruptive as well
as the peaceful. "Proud Music of the Storm" reintroduces this key
image but focuses not on the disruptiveness of the storm but on the
"proud music":

> Proud music of the storm,
> Blast that careers so free, whistling across the prairies,
> Strong hum of forest tree-tops—wind of the mountains,
> Personified dim shapes—you hidden orchestras [II, 178].

The image that was the subject of the last poem in "Autumn Rivulets," "The Prairie States," recurs. Whereas "The Prairie States"
celebrated the creation of a "teeming paradise" in the West, "Proud
Music of the Storm" lists the prairie alongside treetops, mountains,
rivers, and related images to create a composite picture of America,
as it also, by two brief lines, re-creates the Civil War:

> You sounds from distant guns with galloping cavalry,
> Echoes of camps with all the different bugle-calls [II, 178].

The swift passage from image to image in this first section of "Proud
Music of the Storm" recalls the major subjects and dominant themes
of that section of *Leaves of Grass* treated, in the preceding chapter,
as "This Time & Land We Swim In": "Drum-Taps" through "Autumn Rivulets." But the emphasis is on the sound rather than the
sight, and there is the suggestion throughout that some underlying
or unifying significance is about to be discovered:

> Trooping tumultuous, filling the midnight late, bending me powerless,
> Entering my lonesome slumber-chamber, why have you seiz'd me?
> [II, 178].

The answer lies in the first line of section 2: "Come forward O my
soul, and let the rest retire" (II, 178). The interpretation of this
"proud music" is to be by the soul—the music is to reveal the spiritual significance of the material and the actual.

One is apt to pass without notice the basic dramatic situation in
"Proud Music of the Storm": the poet is in a dream state throughout the first five sections, and the varied sounds, dredged from his
subconscious and fused into a great crashing symphony, invade his
consciousness. In section 6 the poet awakens and says to his "silent
curious soul":

> Come, for I have found the clew I sought so long,
> Let us go forth refresh'd amid the day,
> Cheerfully tallying life, walking the world, the real,
> Nourish'd henceforth by our celestial dream [II, 185].

The poet explains to his soul that the sounds he has heard have not really been what they seemed, but, rather,

> ... to a new rhythmus fitted for thee,
> Poems bridging the way from Life to Death, vaguely wafted
>   in night air, uncaught, unwritten,
> Which let us go forth in the bold day and write [II, 185].

"Proud Music of the Storm" marks a new point of departure in *Leaves of Grass;* the poems to follow are "to a new rhythmus fitted." As the poems that went before were, in some sense, about "life," the poems to follow are to bridge the way "from Life to Death." Somehow, the poet says, these poems are to be the poetic transcription of the "uncaught," "unwritten" poems he has heard in the night. These sounds (the "new rhythmus"), come to him in his "celestial dream," are "eternity's music faint and far" (of the "curious-convolute" shells in "Autumn Rivulets") become loud and near.

Whitman customarily introduces a unit of his poetry by a section or poem that fuses the major images or metaphors of the unit: "Inscriptions" and "Starting from Paumanok" for the entire *Leaves of Grass;* "From Pent-up Aching Rivers" for "Children of Adam"; section 1 for "Out of the Cradle Endlessly Rocking." "Proud Music of the Storm," holding a similar relation to the poems that follow, through "Whispers of Heavenly Death," introduces not the dominant images but the experiences out of which the poetic materials, including the images, were forged. "Proud Music of the Storm" embraces the materials which, transfigured through spiritualized interpretation, become the poems that follow. The sounds heard are not really sounds but poems that the poet "catches" and "writes." These sounds are the material from which the spiritual has been derived. "Proud Music of the Storm" has been called a "sound" or musical biography of the poet. In the poem he seems to assume a position similar to that of section 26 of "Song of Myself," in which he announces that he "will do nothing but listen." From the influx of his life, from his total experiences dramatized in sound, he distils the spiritual knowledge of the poems that follow.

"Passage to India" does, indeed, bridge the way "from Life to

Death." It is through contemplation of three great material achievements of *life*—the Suez Canal, the transcontinental railroad, and the
transatlantic cable—that a great discovery about *death* is brought
into focus. After winning his way to an intuitive knowledge of the
attributes of God—"Light of the light, shedding forth universes, thou
center of them" (II, 195)—the poet proceeds to dramatize his feelings about death:

> Swiftly I shrivel at the thought of God,
> At Nature and its wonders, Time and Space and Death,
> But that I, turning, call to thee O soul, thou actual Me,
> And lo, thou gently masterest the orbs,
> Thou matest Time, smilest content at Death,
> And fillest, swellest full the vastnesses of Space [II, 195].

It was the poet's soul that was called forward at the beginning of
"Proud Music of the Storm" (while "the rest" retired) to hear the
symphony of sounds, and it was the poet's "silent curious soul" that
was addressed and told the "clew." And now, in "Passage to India,"
it is the soul, addressed as the "actual me," that is objectified and
made "master" of orbs, "mate" of time, "smiler" at death, and that
fills the "vastnesses of Space." Through a belief in the tyranny of
spirituality the poet finds his way to a faith in death as a fulfilment.
It is, indeed, "passage to more than India" that is won at the end of
the poem; the circling of the globe has resulted in "passage to you,
your shores, ye aged fierce enigmas!" (II, 196).

As "Passage to India" celebrates a series of events of the modern
world, so the following poem, "Prayer of Columbus," selects an
event of the distant past and dramatizes a selected episode to treat
a similar theme. It was Columbus' search for a passage to India that
caused the discovery of America, one of the gigantic steps forward
in man's westward encirclement of the globe. But the Columbus of
"Passage to India" is portrayed at the height of his career; the protagonist of "Prayer of Columbus" is old and near death. Though a
wide gap in time separates the "plots" of these two poems, the
events are more similar than not. Columbus, in his meditations, recalls his accomplishments:

> By me and these the work so far accomplish'd,
> By me earth's elder cloy'd and stifled lands uncloy'd, unloos'd,
> By me the hemispheres rounded and tied, the unknown to the known
>   [II, 199].

Like the canal, the cable, and the railroad, Columbus has spanned space and annihilated distance. He has, in part and singlehandedly, achieved that "rondure" of the globe brought about in its entirety by the engineering feats of the nineteenth century. In a prefatory note to this poem in 1876 Whitman said: "See, the figure of the great Admiral, walking the beach, as a stage, in this sublimest tragedy—for what tragedy, what poem, so piteous and majestic as the real scene?—And hear him uttering—as his mystical and religious soul surely utter'd, the ideas following—perhaps, in their equivalents, the very words" (III, 233). Once again in this series of poems, it is the *soul* brought to the fore. Whitman conceived "Prayer of Columbus" as a soliloquy of the "mystical and religious soul." As in "Passage to India," the protagonist discovers a sustaining knowledge of God:

> That Thou O God my life hast lighted,
> With ray of light, steady, ineffable, vouchsafed of Thee,
> Light rare untellable, lighting the very light,
> Beyond all signs, descriptions, languages [I, 200].

"Light of the light" in "Passage to India," "lighting the very light" in "Prayer of Columbus"—God illuminates life's (and death's) great enigmas. The battered, wrecked old man experiences a vision of promise:

> Shadowy vast shapes smile through the air and sky,
> And on the distant waves sail countless ships,
> And anthems in new tongues I hear saluting me [II, 200].

The poem ends with this image of sound ("anthems in new tongues") recalling the tranfigured or spiritualized music of "Proud Music of the Storm."

"The Sleepers," once called "Night Poem" and then "Sleep-Chasings," is one of Whitman's most remarkable performances. The technique is that of the dream—the unhindered flow of the images of the subconscious. The poem's opening, "I wander all night in my vision" (II, 201), launches the poet on a night journey that brings about his encounter with haters as well as lovers, with the macabre as well as the enchanting—all enwrapped and pervaded by night. Night becomes a symbol of the innate spirituality of all things. Darkness brings to the fore that "seed perfection" which resides hid-

den within. Night, coming from without, fusing with that const
elements within, results in a spiritual peace unknown to day:

I swear they are all beautiful,
Every one that sleeps is beautiful, every thing in the dim light is beautiful,
The wildest and bloodiest is over, and all is peace [II, 209].

Night becomes a miniature (and daily) death, accomplishing on its
small scale and temporarily what death does on a large scale and
permanently. Whereas the poet made intuitive discoveries about
God in the two preceding poems, in "The Sleepers" he acquires insight into the "myth of heaven":

Peace is always beautiful,
The myth of heaven indicates peace and night.

The myth of heaven indicates the soul,
The soul is always beautiful, it appears more or it appears less,
    it comes or it lags behind,
It comes from its embower'd garden and looks pleasantly on
    itself and encloses the world [II, 209].

Knowledge of the "myth of heaven" leads to the assertion that the
"universe is duly in order, everything is in its place" (II, 210), which
in turn allows a confident faith in death:

The sleepers that lived and died wait, the far advanced are to go on in
    their turns, and the far behind are to come on in their turns.
The diverse shall be no less diverse, but they shall flow and unite—they
    unite now [II, 210].

Like the preceding poems (omitting "Transpositions" as a space
filler), "To Think of Time" attempts to bridge the way "from Life to
Death," but in a "direct" assault, without central symbol or metaphor. The title itself suggests the exploration of immortality, and in
the first section of the poem the pertinent questions are raised:

Have you guess'd you yourself would not continue?
Have you dreaded these earth-beetles?
Have you fear'd the future would be nothing to you?

Is to-day nothing? is the beginningless past nothing?
If the future is nothing they are just as surely nothing [II, 213].

The image that pervades the poem is the image of death:

The twitching lips press lightly on the forehead of the dying,
The breath ceases and the pulse of the heart ceases,
The corpse stretches on the bed and the living look upon it,
It is palpable as the living are palpable [II, 214].

Two lines stand out starkly against the paleness of the poem's predominant direct statement. In section 3, "Slow-moving and black lines creep over the whole earth—they never cease—they are the burial lines" (II, 214); and in section 8, "Slow moving and black lines go ceaselessly over the earth" (II, 218). These death lines dramatize the omnipresence and ceaselessness of death; yet the poet, when he imagines himself in this dark procession, is not beset by fears:

> Pleasantly and well-suited I walk,
> Whither I walk I cannot define, but I know it is good,
> The whole universe indicates that it is good,
> The past and the present indicate that it is good [II, 219].

As previously, the poet discovers a supporting faith through insight into the order and harmony in the universe. The faith is so great that it elevates "immortality" to the position of primary goal:

I swear I think there is nothing but immortality!
That the exquisite scheme is for it, and the nebulous float is for it, and the cohering is for it!
And all preparation is for it—and identity is for it—and life and materials are altogether for it! [II, 220].

"Whispers of Heavenly Death," a cluster of some nineteen poems, concludes the New World personality's "resistless gravitation [to] . . . spiritual law." The image of sound introduced in the title and extended in the second poem (which shares the name) recalls the sound image of the introductory poem of this segment of *Leaves of Grass*, "Proud Music of the Storm." The "proud" (and sometimes thundering) music of this opening poem has become, as the poet at the end had indicated it would, transfigured into "whispers." Distillation of the music results in a capturing of the essence that is "soft" and even elusive—and that essence of life is not death, but *heavenly* death, which is, in actuality, the real (or spiritual) life. These "whispers of heavenly death" are "labial gossip of night" (suggesting the significance of the pervading night of "The Sleepers") and "sibilant chorals" originating from that same (but transfigured) nature that made up a major share of the music in "Proud Music of the Storm":

Footsteps gently ascending, mystical breezes wafted soft and low,
Ripples of unseen rivers, tides of a current flowing, forever flowing,
(Or is it the plashing of tears? the measureless waters of human tears?)
    [II, 222].

Here, caught and written, are the "uncaught, unwritten" poems of "Proud Music of the Storm." The "new rhythmus fitted for thee" (of "Proud Music of the Storm") are the "footsteps gently ascending" and the "ripples of unseen rivers," for these rhythms affirm the existence of the spiritual beyond the material world. The rhythm of the "great cloud-masses" mournfully "rolling," "swelling," "mixing," and the rhythm of the appearance and disappearance of the "half-dimm'd sadden'd far-off star"—creative rhythms of a material universe spiritually controlled and oriented—affirm the intuitive perception that death is, paradoxically, birth:

> (Some parturition rather, some solemn immortal birth;
> On the frontiers to eyes impenetrable,
> Some soul is passing over) [II, 222].

"Darest Thou Now O Soul," the first poem in "Whispers of Heavenly Death," is a dramatic monologue in which the poet addresses his soul in an attempt to describe the spiritual experience of death in terms of the senses (which, upon death, will cease to exist):

Till when the ties loosen,
All but the ties eternal, Time and Space,
Nor darkness, gravitation, sense, nor any bounds bounding us.

Then we burst forth, we float,
In Time and Space O soul, prepared for them,
Equal, equipt at last, (O joy! O fruit of all!) them to fulfill O soul [II, 221].

Although the sensation of floating is a result of the senses and the poet, earlier in the poem, asserts that the senses will be annihilated in death ("Nor face with blooming flesh, nor lips, nor eyes, are in that land" [II, 221]), nevertheless the reader may conceive the spiritual equivalent of floating as the state of death. And inasmuch as this state is "fruit of all," it may be looked upon as a parturition or birth.

"Chanting the Square Deific," a poem whose position in "Whispers of Heavenly Death" is frequently challenged, dominates the section through sheer length. Although the poem may seem at first glance misplaced, in the context of Whitman's intention of portraying the "resistless gravitation of spiritual law" or of bridging the gulf between life and death the poem not only belongs but contributes. In effect the poet defines the nature of the "spiritual law" in "Chanting the Square Deific." The poem constitutes an insight into the order of the universe—an insight that may legitimately result in a faith in death as not an end but a beginning. Compared with Jehovah as law (or time), the Consolator as love, and Satan as revolt, Santa Spirita is the all-pervading unifying element:

Beyond the light, lighter than light,
Beyond the flames of hell, joyous, leaping easily above hell,
Beyond Paradise, perfumed solely with mine own perfume,
Including all life on earth, touching, including God, including Saviour and Satan [II, 224].

Santa Spirita is the "general soul" and, in finishing the square, is the "most solid." Whereas in "Passage to India" God is called "light of the light," and in "Prayer of Columbus" is described as "lighting the very light," Santa Spirita is "beyond the light" and "lighter than light." The poet elevates this fourth side of the square to the position of greatest eminence and, though including, is actually independent of ("perfumed solely with mine own perfume") God, Saviour, and Satan. Certain it is that, in any universe pervaded and spiritualized by a Santa Spirita, death can be no less than a birth into the "life of the real identities."

Of the several impressive lyrics that present variations on the basic theme of "Whispers of Heavenly Death," "That Music Always Round Me" is noteworthy not only because it bears on the sound image in the cluster title ("whispers") but also because it recalls the dominant image of "Proud Music of the Storm." When the poet says, "Yet long untaught I did not hear," he seems to be in a situation similar to that at the end of "Proud Music of the Storm," in which he sensed, in the music, poems "vaguely wafted in night air, uncaught, unwritten." But, says the poet in "That Music Always Round Me," "now the chorus I hear and am elated" (II, 228). The poet is now "catching" and writing those "vaguely wafted" poems. The chorus that elates the poet is composed of four elements:

A tenor, strong, ascending with power and health, with glad notes of daybreak I hear,
A soprano at intervals sailing buoyantly over the tops of immense waves,
A transparent base shuddering lusciously under and through the universe,
The triumphant tutti, the funeral wailings with sweet flutes and violins, all these I fill myself with [II, 229].

The "exquisite meanings" which move the poet may be insight, again, into the fourfold nature of the universe; for these four ele-

ments of the chorus correspond to the four sides of the "square
deific": the strong tenor as Jehovah; the buoyant soprano as Consolator; the shuddering "base" as Satan; and the triumphant tutti as
Santa Spirita. The music is translated, as promised, into spiritual
terms, into poems "bridging the way from Life to Death."

The last three poems of "Whispers of Heavenly Death," all brief,
demonstrate the poet's versatility in presenting his theme. In "The
Last Invocation," the poet shows some concern for the precise nature of the final moments of life and asks that he "be wafted" tenderly "from the walls of the powerful fortress'd house" (II, 233). In
this poem the poet stresses, after his many poems celebrating death,
his love of life:

> Tenderly—be not impatient,
> (Strong is your hold O mortal flesh,
> Strong is your hold O love.) [II, 233].

In the next poem, the poet presents one of his characteristic "pictures" with allegorical meaning:

> As I watch'd the ploughman ploughing,
> Or the sower sowing in the fields, or the harvester harvesting,
> I saw there too, O life and death, your analogies;
> (Life, life is the tillage, and Death is the harvest according.)
> [II, 234].

And in the last poem of the section, the poet reverts to that paradoxical relationship of life and death he has exploited before (particularly in "Of Him I Love Day and Night") and in which the two
are reversed:

> Pensive and faltering,
> The words the Dead I write,
> For living are the Dead,
> (Haply the only living, only real,
> And I the apparition, I the spectre.) [II, 234].

The poet has already asserted that the "life of the real identities"
lies with the Santa Spirita. Like many mystics, he comes to the realization that the real reality is the spiritual—and that what we call
the real world is illusion. With the final statement of this realization,
the poet brings to a close his treatment of the "spiritual law." In
these poems bridging the way from life to death, the impingement

of the laws of the spirit (which underlie the order and harmony in the universe) on the consciousness of the New World personality results in the confidence and optimism of a faith that looks forward not to death but to birth, not to a lesser but a greater joy in selfhood, not to annihilation but to a fruition before unknown.

CHAPTER SEVENTEEN

Review of
Themes and Farewell

The remainder of *Leaves of Grass* proper (excluding the three annexes) is devoted to a review of themes, glimpses at the future, and a farewell to the reader. One long poem and two clusters constitute this final section of the book:

> "Thou Mother with Thy Equal Brood"
> From Noon to Starry Night
> Songs of Parting

The first of these, the single long poem, counterpart in a sense of the introduction's "Starting from Paumanok," but more closely related to such poems as "A Broadway Pageant" and "By Blue Ontario's Shore," is a final treatment of the theme of nationality or America's destiny. "From Noon to Starry Night" and "Songs of Parting," counterpart of "Inscriptions" at the beginning of the book, weave together a number of the poet's major themes and bid the reader a fond goodbye.

"Thou Mother with Thy Equal Brood" states, in the opening section, the poet's motive:

> A special song before I go I'd sing o'er all the rest,
> For thee, the future [II, 235].[1]

This reference is the first in *Leaves of Grass* to the imminence of the poet's departure and clearly indicates that "Thou Mother" is a farewell treatment of the theme of nationality ("I'd sow a seed for thee of endless Nationality" [II, 235]). The poet returns to the device, characteristic of the epic, used in the opening poems of *Leaves of Grass,* of announcing the theme he "sings":

1. Whitman quotations are where possible identified in the text by volume and page number of *The Complete Writings of Walt Whitman,* ed. Richard M. Bucke *et al.* (New York: G. P. Putnam's Sons, 1902).

Belief I sing, and preparation;
As Life and Nature are not great with reference to the present only,
But greater still from what is yet to come,
Out of that formula for thee I sing [II, 235].

This "formula" turns out to be advice for the future and prophecy of things to come:

Brain of the New World, what a task is thine,
To formulate the Modern—out of the peerless grandeur of the modern,
Out of thyself, comprising science, to recast poems, churches,
    art [II, 236–37].

Emphasis on the modern is carefully balanced by the suggestion of the importance of the past in a conventional image strikingly used:

Sail, sail thy best, ship of Democracy,
Of value is thy freight, 'tis not the Present only,
The Past is also stored in thee [II, 237].

America's destiny is not the destiny of one country merely, but of the human race in its progression in mystic evolution ("Time's spirals rounding" [II, 241]).

At one point the poet pauses for an aside to indicate as precisely as he can the nature of his vision:

But I do not undertake to define thee, hardly to comprehend thee,
I but thee name, thee prophesy, as now,
I merely thee ejaculate! [II, 239].

Though America of the future cannot be defined or comprehended, it can be envisioned emotionally—"ejaculated." And, though the promise of America is great and is destined for fulfilment, there is to be also abundant evil. Some of the most vivid imagery in "Thou Mother with Thy Equal Brood" is devoted to prospective corruption:

In many a smiling mask death shall approach beguiling thee, thou in disease shalt swelter,
The livid cancer spread its hideous claws, clinging upon thy breasts, seeking to strike thee deep within,
Consumption of the worst, moral consumption, shall rouge thy face with hectic [II, 241].

But in spite of these failures and defects, America will find fulfilment in the future. The "New, indeed new Spiritual World" cannot be held in the present:

> For such unparallel'd flight as thine, such brood as thine,
> The Future only holds thee and can hold thee [II, 242].

Finally, at the end of the poem, the poet returns to his title image of the strong mother bird who, "on pinions free," cleaves the "amplest spaces heavenward." The "brood" may be either the states or the people, or perhaps both.

"From Noon to Starry Night" constitutes the poet's final farewell to his major themes. A review of such scope is suggested by the symbolism of the title, exploited in the first and final poems. The "noon" represents the poet's point of fullest fruition, the "starry night" his old age and imminent departure. The first poem in the cluster, "Thou Orb Aloft Full-Dazzling," is an invocation to the sun, addressed as "thou hot October noon!" (II, 243). The sun is an October sun because, after a long preparation (the summer), there followed the first fruitful harvest of poetry. The poet sees in the sun attributes characteristic of himself:

> As for thy throes, thy perturbations, sudden breaks and shafts of flame
>   gigantic,
> I understand them, I know those flames, those perturbations well [II, 243].

The sun, with its "fructifying heat and light" (II, 244), is asked to "strike through these chants" (II, 244). The poet identifies not only himself but also his poetry with the sun. Finally, the poet equates his life with the afternoon of a day and suggests his own decline with the slow descent of the sun:

> Nor only launch thy subtle dazzle and thy strength for these,
> Prepare the later afternoon of me myself—prepare my lengthening shadows,
> Prepare my starry nights [II, 244].

The image of the "starry nights" suggests a talent dispersed and in the dispersal grown weak (like the annexes of *Leaves of Grass*), just as the brilliant sun suggests a concentrated talent that, even though waning, gathers to a focus (like the whole body of *Leaves of Grass*). There is, too, in the "starry nights" the dominant connotation of imminent death.

"A Clear Midnight," the last poem in "From Noon to Starry Night," extends the title image and, together with the opening poem, incloses the cluster in a frame that bestows unity. The "clear midnight" is, for the poet, the approaching hour of death, the hour for the soul's "free flight into the wordless" (II, 270). At this point the poet must depart from books and art, for the "day [is] erased," the "lesson done":

> Thee [the soul] fully forth emerging, silent, gazing, pondering
>   the themes thou lovest best,
> Night, sleep, death and the stars [II, 220].

In a sense, all of "From Noon to Starry Night" has been a "pondering" of the poet's major themes, and now the poet's soul emerges to ponder (wordlessly) those themes best loved ("Night, sleep, death and the stars"), themes most intimately connected with the poet's final years.

"Faces," the second poem in "From Noon to Starry Night," stresses the democratic theme in the poet's philosophy:

Sauntering the pavement thus, or crossing the ceaseless ferry, faces and
  faces and faces,
I see them and complain not, and am content with all [II, 245].

But there is implicit throughout the poem a faith in an ultimate justification. The poet asks, "Do you suppose I could be content with all if I thought them their own finale?" Even the "most smear'd and slobbering idiot" at the asylum has his spark of divinity:

I knew of the agents that emptied and broke my brother,
The same wait to clear the rubbish from the fallen tenement,
And I shall look again in a score or two of ages,
And I shall meet the real landlord perfect and unharm'd, every inch as
  good as myself [II, 246–47].

This faith is a faith in a divine plan, in the "seed perfection" existent even in the lowliest or meanest of creatures, to come to fruition in the progression of mystic evolution. The poem concludes with the full portrait of a mother, wearing her Quaker cap, sitting in the "armchair under the shaded porch of the farmhouse" (II, 248). The poet comments:

> The melodious character of the earth,
> The finish beyond which philosophy cannot go and
>   does not wish to go,
> The justified mother of men [II, 249].

Whitman evokes the feeling that a life of simplicity as implied by the picture of the mother is a fulfilled life that is right and in harmony with the world and the universe.

"The Mystic Trumpeter" bears out the view of "From Noon to Starry Night" as a "poetic" biography, as a recapitulation of the major themes of the poet from his greatest height of poetic power to his decline and loss (or starry night).[2] The dominant metaphor in "The Mystic Trumpeter," an image of sound, is similar to that of "Proud Music of the Storm." But, instead of presenting the uninterpreted music as in "Proud Music of the Storm," Whitman presents in "The Mystic Trumpeter" the "translation":

> That now ecstatic ghost, close to me bending, thy cornet
>   echoing, pealing,
> Gives out to no one's ears but mine, but freely gives to mine,
> That I may thee translate [II, 249].

The trumpeter to whom the poet, at night, listens as though possessed is, perhaps, the spirit of poetry, the muse, grown "wild" and "strange" because the poet has reached that point, possibly old age, at which there is a decline in the poetic power. The trumpeter's tunes are "capricious," controlled by neither their source nor the poet. But, as the poet, soothed by a "holy calm" and transported to the "walks of Paradise," translates the "chaotically surging" music from the calm perspective of "heaven's lake" on which he floats and basks, the meanings become clear and orderly. In section 4 of the poem appear the "old pageants" of the "feudal world":

> Ladies and cavaliers long dead, barons are in their castle halls, the troubadours are singing,
> Arm'd knights go forth to redress wrongs, some in quest of the holy Graal [II, 250].

These several images fuse to conjure up the feudal world the reader recognizes as embodied in poetry of the past. Such pageantry is precisely what our poet has rejected as the theme of his poetry. Beginning with section 5, the remainder of "The Mystic Trumpeter" is an analysis of the major themes of *Leaves of Grass*.

Section 5 announces the theme of love:

> Blow again trumpeter! and for thy theme,
> Take now the enclosing theme of all, the solvent and the setting,
> Love, that is pulse of all, the sustenance and the pang,
> The heart of man and woman all for love,
> No other theme but love—knitting, enclosing, all diffusing love [II, 250].

2. See W. L. Werner, "Whitman's The Mystic Trumpeter as Autobiography," *American Literature*, VII (January, 1936), 458.

One recognizes immediately the applicability of this theme of love to the whole first section of *Leaves of Grass,* dealt with in this study as "Gigantic Embryo or Skeleton of Personality." Perhaps no other word sums up so well the characteristics of the New World personality delineated in the first part of *Leaves of Grass.* Sections 6 and 7 of "The Mystic Trumpeter" review the theme to which the second section of *Leaves of Grass* (here called "This Time and Land We Swim In") is devoted. The poet calls on the trumpeter to "conjure war's alarums":

Swift to thy spell a shuddering hum like distant thunder rolls,
Lo, where the arm'd men hasten—lo, mid the clouds of dust the glint of bayonets,
I see the grime-faced cannoneers, I mark the rosy flash amid the smoke,
    I hear the cracking of the guns [II, 251].

The rolling thunder is reminiscent of "Drum-Taps," as are the brief vignettes of war. In section 7 the trumpeter sends "sullen notes" and "darkness" through the poet:

Utter defeat upon me weighs—all lost—the foe victorious,
(Yet 'mid the ruins Pride colossal stands unshaken to the last,
Endurance, resolution to the last.) [II, 252].

This attitude recalls that expressed in several other poems, especially "By Blue Ontario's Shore," where the poet envisions democracy, though surrounded by "treacherous lip-smiles everywhere," the "destin'd conqueror" (II, 107). Section 8 of "The Mystic Trumpeter," the closing section, is devoted to the theme of *Leaves of Grass* which is the focus of those poems assembled in this study under the title, "The Resistless Gravitation of Spiritual Law":

Now trumpeter for thy close,
Vouchsafe a higher strain than any yet,
Sing to my soul, renew its languishing faith and hope [II, 252].

As love was the "enclosing theme" and "solvent," so faith and hope are the "culminating" themes. The songs from "Proud Music of the Storm" through 'Whispers of Heavenly Death" are "hymns to the universal God from universal man" (II, 252). "The Mystic Trumpeter" is *Leaves of Grass* in miniature and confirms the three-part thematic structure of the book.

The remaining poems in "From Noon to Starry Night" treat various themes and other elements in Whitman's poetry. "To a Locomo-

tive in Winter" is an indirect comment on the nature of the art in
Leaves of Grass. As the poet has delineated the New World type in
his poetry, so he sees the locomotive as a "type of the modern" (II,
253). And the poet addresses the "fierce-throated beauty":

Roll through my chant with all thy lawless music, thy swinging lamps
  at night,
Thy madly-whistled laughter, echoing, rumbling like an earthquake, rous-
  ing all,
Law of thyself complete, thine own track firmly holding [II, 254],

The poet's *Leaves of Grass,* like the locomotive, is a law to itself
complete and holds to its "own track," or so the poet likes to think.
And, certainly, such a view is consistent with his theories of organic
form. "O Magnet-South" and "Mannahatta" are final treatments of
two locales that have played important roles in *Leaves of Grass.*
"By Broad Potomac's Shore" portrays a nostalgic return to the
scenes of younger days ("again old heart so gay, again to you, your
sense, the full flush spring returning" [II, 264]). "Old War-Dreams"
returns to the "Drum-Taps" theme by presenting the nightmarish
quality of the experience as it is relived in dreams:

Of the look at first of the mortally wounded, (of that indescribable look,)
Of the dead on their backs with arms extended wide, I dream, I dream, I
  dream [II, 266].

"As I Walk These Broad Majestic Days," the last poem (except for
the brief "A Clear Midnight") in "From Noon to Starry Night," asserts that the poet, although he too "announces" and celebrates
"solid things" ("Science, ships, politics, cities, factories, are not for
nothing" [II, 269]), finds none else more real than his "realities":

Libertad and the divine average, freedom to every slave on the face of
  the earth,
The rapt promises and luminé of seers, the spiritual world, these centuries-
  lasting songs,
And our visions, the visions of poets, the most solid announcements of any
  [II, 269].

With this emphasis on freedom, equality, and spirituality, the poet
closes his review of the major themes of *Leaves of Grass.*

There remains, however, the final leave-taking. As a number of
the poems in "Inscriptions" invited the reader to join the poet on a
journey or voyage, the poems of "Songs of Parting" indicate that the

time for separation has come, that the poet must take his leave of the reader. These poems focus on death, its varied aspects, its personal meaning for both the poet and the reader. In the opening poem, "As the Time Draws Nigh," the poet contemplates his approaching departure: "Perhaps soon some day or night while I am singing my voice will suddenly cease" (II, 271). In what seems like a moment of despair, the poet questions: "O book, O chants! must all then amount to but this?" (II, 271). But faith rushes in to fill the barely felt vacuum:

Must we barely arrive at this beginning of us?—and yet it is enough, O soul; O soul, we have positively appear'd—that is enough [II, 271].

The paradoxical beginning that arrives at the end is exploited throughout "Songs of Parting." But the significant point is that the poet finds faith in the belief that appearance is "enough."

Thoughts of death naturally turn to thoughts of the future. Threading their way through "Songs of Parting" are three variations on the basic theme: prophecy of things to come, contemplation of the death of others; and contemplation of the poet's own death. "Years of the Modern," like "Thou Mother with Thy Equal Brood," envisions the future fulfilment of America:

Years of the modern! years of the unperform'd!
Your horizon rises, I see it parting away for more august dramas,
I see not America only, not only Liberty's nation but other nations preparing [II, 271].

But as the poet's insight penetrates the future, he sees beyond the fulfilment ("The perform'd America and Europe grow dim, retiring in shadow behind me" [II, 273]) to a period dim and shadowy, perhaps the ultimate spiritual or ideal realm toward which all things tend: "The unperform'd, more gigantic than ever, advance, advance upon me" (II, 273). The poem "Thoughts," like "Years of the Modern," suggests that the present (or future) glory of America is but one phase in the upward-spiraling mystic evolution: "these [triumphs and glories] of mine and of the States will in their turn be convuls'd, and serve other parturitions and transitions" (II, 276). The contemplation of the death of others is the subject of a number of poems, some of them reminiscent of "Drum-Taps." "Ashes of Soldiers" is a chant of the poet's "silent soul in the name of all dead soldiers" (II, 274). "Pensive on Her Dead Gazing" and "Camps of Green" stand side by side, the first a cry from the "Mother of all" to the earth to "lose not an atom" of the "torn bodies" of the battle-field (II, 282), the second an extended analogy between the camps of war and the camps of death (suggesting that the dead are a "mystic army" resting on their journey [II, 283]). Two poems in "Songs of Parting," "As at Thy Portals Also Death" and "The Sobbing of the Bells," memorialize the death of the poet's mother and the death of Garfield, respectively. A number of poems focus on the poet's own death. "Song at Sunset" recalls the dominant imagery of the preceding cluster of poems, "From Noon to Starry Night":

> Splendor of ended day floating and filling me,
> Hour prophetic, hour resuming the past [II, 278].

The poet asserts his resolution to inflate his throat and sing, "till the last ray gleams" (II, 278), the "divine average," "vistas of death," and "unmitigated adoration" of the sun (or of life). In "My Legacy" the poet, like anyone anticipating death, wills his possessions: "I bind together and bequeath ['certain remembrances' and 'little souvenirs'] in this bundle of songs" (II, 281). Like "My Legacy," "As They Draw to a Close" refers to the poet's songs and is an attempt to explain "what underlies" them. His aim, in part, has been "To put rapport the mountains and rocks and streams. . . . With you O soul" (II, 285)—a reconciliation of the physical with the spiritual world.

But as the title of this final cluster suggests, the dominant motif is the leave-taking of the poet from the reader. The physical, intellectual, and spiritual journey the poet and reader have shared in *Leaves of Grass* must draw to a close, and the poet must take his separate way. In "Joy, Shipmate, Joy!" the poet indicates that at the end of the journey awaits the voyage (of death): "Our life is closed, our life begins" (II, 285). "Now Finale to the Shore" suggests that the voyages of the past, in which the poet has "adventur'd o'er the seas, / Cautiously cruising, studying the charts" (II, 286), have all ended by a return: "Duly again to port and hawser's tie returning" (II, 286). But there now approaches, in accordance with the poet's "cherish'd secret wish," the final, ceaseless voyage:

> Embrace thy friends, leave all in order,
> To port and hawser's tie no more returning,
>   Depart upon thy endless cruise old Sailor [II, 286].

In "So Long," the concluding poem in "Songs of Parting," the poet embraces his friends in the final farewell. The poem is a combination of prophecy and intimacy. The poet asserts that he and his poetry will have their "due fruition" when "America does what was promis'd" (II, 287). He then proceeds to "announce," in the tone of the obsessed seer, the fulfilment of all his themes, from "liberty and equality," to union and adhesiveness, and many more. But the measure becomes faster and the tone more persistently intimate as the poem progresses, until there is a renewal of that evangelistic fervor of direct appeal noted at the end of "Starting from Paumanok":

> My songs cease, I abandon them,
> From behind the screen where I hid I advance personally solely to you.
> Camerado, this is no book,
>   Who touches this touches a man [II, 289].

The poet creates the illusion of his own physical presence and establishes an almost embarrassing intimacy with the reader. As the time draws nigh, the poet seems on the verge of a mystical experience: "An unknown sphere more real than I dream'd, more direct, darts awakening rays about me, So long!" (II, 290). The poet then departs "from materials" and becomes "as one disembodied, triumphant, dead" (II, 290). And so ends the long mystic journey of exploration and discovery—*Leaves of Grass*.

Afterthoughts: The Annexes

Although "Songs of Parting" concludes the main body of *Leaves of Grass*, there are three "Annexes": "Sands at Seventy," "Good-Bye My Fancy," and "Old Age Echoes." These clusters of poems do not form a part of the book's basic structure, but Whitman clearly wished them preserved. The fact that Whitman did not incorporate these poems in the body of *Leaves of Grass* suggests that he believed them deficient; the fact that he included them in the volume suggests that he attached to them some merit. Most of the poems in these three annexes show a declining poetic power, and the poet demonstrates his realization of the decline not only in a series of the poems but also in the titles of the annexes. "Sands at Seventy"

suggests the imminence of death (the sands of the hourglass count-
ing out the final minutes) as well as the aridity or even sterility of
old age. "Good-Bye My Fancy," title not only of a cluster but also
of an important poem, suggests in its literal meaning a departure of
an important poetic faculty. "Old Age Echoes" suggests poems that
are not even the genuine article but mere "echoes," weak imitations.
In a preface to the second of these annexes, Whitman poses the
question most pertinent of all to the poems: "Had I not better with-
hold (in this old age and paralysis of me) such little tags and
fringe-dots (maybe specks, stains,) as follow a long dusty journey,
and witness it afterward?" (III, 3). The answer, of course, is present
in the publication of these annexes, though the poet protests, "certainly I have nothing fresh to write" (III, 2).

Not the least virtue of these poems is their frankness. The poet
does not attempt to hide his fears about his own garrulity:

As I sit writing here, sick and grown old,
Not my least burden is that dullness of the years, querilities,
Ungracious glooms, aches, lethargy, constipation, whimpering *ennui,*
May filter in my daily songs [II, 295].

Most readers will readily agree that a number of these elements in-
advertently creep into some of these poems. But there is also present
in many some of the old genius for creation of brilliant image. For
example, "With Husky-Haughty Lips, O Sea!" contains imagery in-
spired with the same life as of old:

By lengthen'd swell, and spasm, and panting breath,
And rhythmic rasping of thy sands and waves,
And serpent hiss, and savage peals of laughter,
And undertones of distant lion roar [II, 304].

By the use of such vivid imagery the poet succeeds in bringing the
sea to violent life to tell its "tale of cosmic elemental passion" (II,
304).

Naturally, throughout these annexes one finds echoes of the basic
themes of *Leaves of Grass.* In one curious poem entitled "L. of G.'s
Purport," the poet says that his purpose has not been to "pick out
evils from their formidable masses (even to expose them)" but to
"add, fuse, complete," to "span vast realms of space and time" (III,
24). After suggesting his major themes, the poet presents a miniature biography:

> Begun in ripen'd youth and steadily pursued,
> Wandering, peering, dallying with all—war, peace, day and
>   night absorbing.
> Never even for one brief hour abandoning my task
> I end it here in sickness, poverty, and old age [III, 25].

If "L. of G.'s Purport" seems to trail off in the querulousness that even the poet feared, "Unseen Buds" seems a fresh statement of the dominant theme of "Birds of Passage":

> Unseen buds, infinite, hidden well,
> Under the snow and ice, under the darkness, in every
>   square or cubic inch,
> Germinal, exquisite, in delicate lace, microscopic, un-
>   born [III, 26].

Like the "seed perfection" or the "uncaught bird," the unseen buds urge "slowly, surely forward" the unfolding of mystic evolution. "Good-Bye My Fancy!" exploits further the conceit of death as birth in the realization by the poet that, instead of bidding his "fancy" adieu at death, he and it remain one:

> May-be it is you [fancy] the mortal knob really undoing, turning
>   —so now finally,
> Good-bye—and hail! my Fancy [III, 27].

The very fact that these annexes appear as annexes, that these poems were not distributed among the various sections of *Leaves of Grass*, indicates something of Whitman's strong feeling for the integrity of the form of his masterpiece. When the poet said to Horace Traubel, "In the long run the world will do as it pleases with the book. I am determined to have the world know what I was pleased to do" (III, 30), he was affirming his faith in the inviolability of the form he had achieved, even though he could not, or would not, crystallize his intuitive feeling for the form into a precise analysis and defense of its parts. It has, however, frequently been overlooked that Whitman intended "A Backward Glance o'er Travel'd Roads" as an integral part of *Leaves of Grass*. In the author's prefatory note to the 1891–92 edition (the deathbed edition), after recommending to posterity that future printings ("if there should be any") be a "copy and fac-simile" of that final edition, Whitman asserted that the "adjusting interval" required of "form'd and launch'd . . . books" had passed for *Leaves of Grass* and indicated that his "concluding words," formulated only after the passing of this period, were presented at the end of his volume in "A Backward Glance o'er Travel'd Roads" (I, vi). In an introductory sentence in this essay, Whitman suggests the complexity of the structure of his book: "These lines ['A Backward Glance'] . . . will probably blend the weft of first purposes and speculations, with the warp of that experience afterwards, always bringing strange developments." Although the warp intersects the weft, there is, as the poet says, a "blend"; the interlocking relationship of weft and warp implies, appropriately, the intricate structure of *Leaves of Grass*.

CHAPTER EIGHTEEN

America's Epic

Did Whitman write the epic for modern America? There have been many who contend that *Leaves of Grass* is merely a collection of lyric poetry, some good, some bad, all of it of a peculiarly personal nature that disqualifies its attitudes and philosophy generally. There have been others who have defended Whitman's book as the embodiment of the American reality and ideal, as a superb fulfilment of all the genuine requirements of the national epic.[1]

What did Whitman believe? The answer may be found in a number of prose works, beginning with the 1855 Preface. It is clear in this early work that Whitman desired *Leaves of Grass* to bear a unique relationship with America: "Here [in America] at last is something in the doings of man that corresponds with the broadcast doings of the day and night. . . . It awaits the gigantic and generous treatment worthy of it."[2] It is generally recognized that the entire Preface is a veiled account of Whitman's concept of his own role as poet. Certainly he includes himself in the category when he asserts: "The poets of the kosmos advance through all interpositions and coverings and turmoils and stratagems to first principles."[3] Although Whitman does not use the term, it is clear throughout the 1855 Preface that he believes his book to have the basic nature and general scope of the traditional national epic.

In *Democratic Vistas*, in the same indirect manner, Whitman again reveals his concept of the nature of his poetry: "Never was anything more wanted than, to-day, and here in the States, the poet

1. See Fern Nuhn, "Leaves of Grass Viewed as an Epic," *Arizona Quarterly,* VII (Winter, 1951), 324–38.

2. Facsimile of 1855 text of *Leaves of Grass* (New York: Columbia University Press, 1939), p. iii.

3. *Ibid.,* p. ix.

of the modern is wanted, or the great literatus of the modern. At all times, perhaps, the central point in any nation, and that whence it is itself really sway'd the most and whence it sways others, is its national literature, especially its archetypal poems" (V, 54–55).[4] Whitman was by this time (1871) acutely aware that America had not accepted his book as he had planned and hoped. There can be little doubt that he conceived *Leaves of Grass* as an "archetypal" poem produced and offered to America at its "central point"—a book "sway'd" by the nation and written to sway others. Such a work as Whitman calls for in *Democratic Vistas* is surely the epic of America. And, basically, it is his own work which he desires to be recognized as such.

In "A Backward Glance o'er Travel'd Roads" (1888), summing up the contribution of his own work, Whitman again emphasizes the need of the nation for a commensurate poetry. But no longer is he evasive; his claim is direct: "As America fully and fairly construed is the legitimate result and evolutionary outcome of the past, so I would dare to claim for my verse." The Old World, as the poet points out, "has had the poems of myths, fictions, feudalism, conquest, caste, dynastic wars, and splendid exceptional characters," but the "New World needs the poems of realities and science and of the democratic average and basic equality." And, instead of the "splendid exceptional characters" of the Old World epics, the New World epic will portray simply—man: "In the centre of all, and object of all, stands the Human Being, towards whose heroic and spiritual evolution poems and everything directly or indirectly tend, Old World or New" (V, 54).

Should there be any doubts about the ambition of Whitman to write America's epic, the opening pages of *Leaves of Grass* should dispel them. In "Inscriptions" and "Starting from Paumanok" there are innumerable indications of the epic nature of the work. In the very opening poem, Whitman uses the construction, "I Sing," characteristic of the epic in introducing themes—"One's-Self I Sing," "The Female equally with the Male I sing," "The Modern Man I sing." In this first poem, too, the Muse is mentioned—"Not physiog-

4. Whitman quotations are where possible identified in the text by volume and page number of *The Complete Writings of Walt Whitman,* ed. Richard M. Bucke *et al.* (New York: G. P. Putnam's Sons, 1902).

nomy alone nor brain alone is worthy for the Muse, I say the Form complete is worthier far"; but it is not until the second poem, "As I Ponder'd in Silence," that the Muse is invoked, addressed, and re-assured. As the poet considers his work, he is visited by the Old World Muse:

> A Phantom arose before me with distrustful aspect,
> Terrible in beauty, age, and power,
> The genius of poets of old lands [I, 1].

This Muse is skeptical, for all past epics countenanced by the "haughty shade" have had as their subject the "theme of War, the fortune of battles, / The making of perfect soldiers." The poet wel-comes the challenge and assures the Muse that he, too, sings of "war, and a longer and greater one than any." In the poet's war, the field is the world, the battle "For life and death, for the Body and for the eternal Soul." The central point of this key "Inscriptions" poem is that the poet's book qualifies as an epic, even under the Old World definition, if sufficient liberality is allowed in interpreting the terms.

There are other instances in *Leaves of Grass* in which Whitman calls attention to the epic nature of his book. In "Starting from Paumanok" he outlines his plan for encompassing in his poetry the entire nation—"Solitary, singing in the West, I strike up for a New World." The poems of *Leaves of Grass* are to constitute "a pro-gramme of chants" for "Americanos." The poet advises:

Take my leaves America, take them South and take them North,
Make welcome for them everywhere, for they are your own offspring [I, 18].

Whitman's insistence on an intimate and unique relation between his book and his country appears no more frequently than his ap-peal to the Muse. In "Song of the Exposition," the form is epic if the tone is comic:

> Come Muse migrate from Greece and Ionia,
> Cross out please those immensely overpaid accounts [I, 238].

If in this poem the Muse loses some of her dignity as the poet instals her amid the drainpipes, artificial fertilizers, and the kitchen ware, in "By Blue Ontario's Shore" the Muse is transfigured into a "Phan-tom gigantic superb, with stern visage," who commands the poet:

Chant me the poem, it said, *that comes from the soul of America, chant
me the carol of victory,*
And strike up the marches of Libertad, marches more powerful yet,
And sing me before you go the song of the throes of Democracy [II, 107].

It is characteristic of Whitman that he would reverse the Old World
epic practice by which the poet called upon the Muse for help and
would place the Muse in the position of pleading with the poet to
continue his writing so that vital themes would not go unsung.

It is clear from both external and internal evidence that Whitman
thought of his work in epic terms. The extent to which he fulfilled
his epic ambitions, however, may be measured only in terms of his
final achievement. The answer that achievement provides is impressive.

For the hero of his epic, Whitman created the archetypal personality for the New World (the modern man of "One's-Self I Sing"),
a man both individual and of the mass. This hero, unlike the hero
of past epics, discovers his heroic qualities not in superman characteristics but in the *selfhood* common to every man. Every man in
America, according to Whitman, is potentially an epic hero, if he
is sufficiently aware of the potentiality of his selfhood, if he celebrates his vital procreative role, and if he is capable of depth of
feeling in spiritually complex attachments. In doing and being all
these things, the New World epic hero sings the song of himself,
acknowledges the parentage of Adam, and finds spiritual fulfilment
in "Calamus" comradeship. He accepts, moreover, his New World
place in space and position in time. He relishes his home on the
rolling earth, and he finds that his appointed position in the unfolding of mystic evolution places him where all time past converges
and all time future originates.

Having created his epic hero by broad, free strokes in the first
part of *Leaves of Grass,* Whitman next engages him in the usual
trial of strength in a great and crucial war on which the national
destiny depends. As Whitman's modern man of the New World represents above all a reconciliation of the paradoxically opposed ideals
of democracy—individuality and equality (separateness and "en-
masse")—so his epic hero paradoxically exemplifies both traits in war.
"Drum-Taps" demonstrates the triumph of the American epic hero
"en-masse." No individual is singled out from the rest for heroic

deeds, but, throughout, the emphasis is on the ranks, the large mass of men welded together in comradeship and a common national purpose. The poet at one point asserts that America has too long "learn'd from joys and prosperity only":

But now, ah now, to learn from crises of anguish, advancing, grappling with direst fate and recoiling not,
And now to conceive and show to the world what your children en-masse really are,
(For who except myself has yet conceiv'd what your children en-masse really are?) [II, 77].

But, as the Civil War proved the heroic quality on an epic scale of America's "children en-masse," the same national crisis also demonstrated democracy's ability to produce individuality of epic proportions. "Drum-Taps" gives way to "Memories of President Lincoln" and that magnificent threnody, "When Lilacs Last in the Dooryard Bloom'd." But the traits of this epic hero are not different from but similar to the traits of the soldiers "en-masse." He is the "powerful western fallen star"; he is the captain of the ship whose loss is universally mourned; he is the "dear commander" of the soldiers; but he is above all the "departing comrade" who possessed an infinite capacity for love.

In the latter part of Leaves of Grass, the mythological background of the epic hero of the New World is completed as he is related to the "resistless gravitation of spiritual law." The entire section of the book from "Proud Music of the Storm" through "Whispers of Heavenly Death" not only presents the New World hero with "religious" convictions and impresses him with the reality of the spiritual world but also provides him with his immortality. Even the gods (like the heroes) in this New World epic are conceived in democratic terms. At the climactic point in "Passage to India" the poet exclaims:

Surrounded, copest, frontest God, yieldest, the aim attain'd,
As fill'd with friendship, love complete, the Elder Brother found,
The Younger melts in fondness in his arms [II, 196].

God is the "final" comrade, the perfect embodiment of those ideal traits earlier invested in the New World epic hero. The relationship to God is not the relationship of a subject to his superior but the relationship of the ideal brotherhood, the perfectly fulfilled comradeship.

In a very complicated way, Whitman's epic embodies at the same time that it creates America's image of itself—the American dream, the American vision, as it reached its climactic elaboration during the nineteenth century. If in retrospect Whitman's faith in science and democracy seems naïve, we must remember that our perspective is a bit jaded. And Whitman's faith was the American faith, his naïveté the American naïveté. In insisting on being the poet of science and democracy and, above all, of "religion," Whitman was not clinging to personal attitudes but was rather defining the nineteenth century's view of the universe and itself and reflecting it in his epic, as the epic poets of the past—Homer, Vergil, Dante, and Milton—reflected their own times in order to become epic spokesmen for their ages. Whitman embraced the modern "myth" of science, democracy, religion, and much more. The question of the "truth" of these nineteenth-century beliefs and attitudes is as irrelevant as the question of the "truth" of Homer's gods or Milton's devils. The relevant fact is that these views were held by an entire culture and the people lived and acted in the simple faith that their beliefs were true.

Leaves of Grass has just claim as America's epic. No attempt before it (and there were many) succeeded in becoming more than awkward imitations of the epics of the past. No book after it can ever again achieve its unique point of view. Coming shortly after the birth of the nation, embodying the country's first terrible trial by fire, prophesying the greatness to be thrust upon these states, *Leaves of Grass* possesses a position of intimate relationship with America that no other work can now ever assume. For better or worse, *Leaves of Grass* is America's, a reflection of her character and of her soul and of her achievements and her aspirations. If *Leaves of Grass* transfigures what it reflects, that is because its poet wanted to dwell not on the reality but on the ideal. If *Leaves of Grass* has its shortcomings and defects, so, surely, does the culture it attempted to embody. But after all the reservations are stated and the qualifications noted, we must confess that the book does measure up. If Whitman's vision exceeded his achievement, the scope of his achievement was still sufficient to win him just claim to the title of America's epic poet.

Index

Index

265

PHOENIX BOOKS
in Art, Music, Poetry, and Drama

PHOENIX POETS

PHOENIX BOOKS
Literature and Language